W9-CZT-057

THE STEIN BOOK

ILLUSTRATED CATALOG
CURRENT PRICES
COLLECTOR'S INFORMATION

BY
GARY KIRSNER
&
JIM GRUHL

FEATURING THE STROH BREWERY CO. COLLECTION

GLENTIQUES, LTD., GLENFORD, NEW YORK

Library of Congress Cataloging in Publication Data

Kirsner, Gary, 1945 -
The stein book.
Bibliography: p.311
Includes index.
1. Steins—Germany—Catalogs.
2. Steins—Germany—Collectors
and collecting. I. Gruhl, Jim. II. Title.
NK8647 .K5 1984 730'.0943'075 84-82432
ISBN 0-9614130-0-X

Printed in the United States of America
Published by Glentiques, Ltd.
Box 337
Glenford, N.Y. 12433
Telephone (914) 657-6261

CONTENTS

Cover Photo: Mettlach stein 2455, 6.8L; Glass stein, amber, 2.0L; Regimental stein, 63 Fld. Artl., 1908-1910; Character stein, Uncle Sam, .5L.

One of the earliest drawings of a stein, a flagon type, in the foreground of this 1501 woodcut by Sebastian Brant depicting the feast of Aeneas and Dido.

Preface

During the writing, and right after the release, of *The Mettlach Book* the same question was repeatedly asked. "Why would you want to tell everybody about the steins that a few advanced collectors, museums, and dealers know are worth three or four times the price for which they can often be purchased?" It has been suggested that publishing this kind of *inside information* would be bad for the stein dealers' businesses. Again, with this book that question has come up, and the answer is the same as before. When a hobby begins to slip under the control of those who have *inside information* it breeds mistrust, suspicion, and disappointment among the majority of collectors. The publication of "real" prices in *The Mettlach Book* has proved that the resultant trust, openness, and enthusiasm are great for the hobby as well as for dealers.

The praise for *The Mettlach Book* has been unexpectedly generous, such as, "THE key reference." But the praise was always followed with "NOW, there is a tremendous need for such a book about steins in *general.*" So this book was put together to answer that request. It is hoped that with the extensive use of pictures and supplementary information this book will contribute to the growing and thriving of all areas of stein collecting. This book attempts to answer the most common questions about steins:

- how and why did they originate?
- what do the different types look like?
- which ones are most valuable?
- how old are various types?
- what effect does condition have on what collectors will pay?

Unfortunately, where *The Mettlach Book* could be thorough, *The Stein Book* has had to be selective. The breadth of the topic has forced the making of some really tough decisions about what to include. Nevertheless, it is hoped that even stein experts will find exciting pictures and new important information about their individual specialties.

Before acknowledging the tremendous assistance that has been graciously contributed by many stein experts, some personal information is reluctantly given. Gary Kirsner studied economics and accounting at New York University and Miami University of Ohio. A business in general antiques, begun in the early 1970's, was soon focused almost exclusively on steins. That business soon grew into the leader in the purchase and sale of quality steins. Gary also enjoys restoring old German sports cars. With his wife, Karen, and two daughters, Beth and Britt, he lives in a renovated, quaint old farm building in Glenford, upstate New York.

Jim Gruhl received a doctorate from M.I.T. and researches energy and environmental problems. His interest in steins goes back to a boyhood spent in Milwaukee and relatives in the beer industry. Jim has been collecting steins for more than 20 years, and researching steins for about 10 years. He lives next to a canyon near Tucson, Arizona with his wife, Nancy, and children, Amanda and Steven.

Both families have offered important support to tasks involved in assembling this book. There are also a number other people who deserve *specific* thanks for their help, information, hospitality, and because they are some of the fine people who make being part of the stein community such a pleasant experience: Mel Alpren, Andre Ammelounx, Lawrence Beckendorf, John Boller, Sam Brainard, Bill Burkle, Dave Cantwell, Gene Carvalho, Earl & Vera Christy, Jack Cooper, Dave Cunningham, Colette DeFlon, Joe & Mary Durban, Mark Durban, Ron Fox, Bill Gavin, Bernie Gould, Jim Hansen, John Harrell, Art Heckler, Joseph Hersh, Terry Hill, Bob Lenker, Harold Long, Frank Love, Dick Lovell, Gunter Merk, Irving Miller, Harvey Murphy, Gene McClung, Les Paul,

Bill Pollard, Berk Tarcen, Fredlein Schroeder, Robert Wilson, Jim Widener, and those who wish to remain anonymous. In this group also belongs Lotti Lopez who also deserves *special* thanks for help at several stages in this project.

Because of the success of *The Mettlach Book* there are many similar expectations for this book. Hopefully it too will:

- show the whole range of steins to collectors, so they will not need to use "trial and error" in order to discover what they like best,
- release steins from collectors who have just been holding onto odd pieces because they didn't know their value,
- build a stronger demand for steins at every level, and
- help collectors build up a lifetime of pricing experience that will improve their confidence and knowledge.

And again with this book, the hope is that people will see stein collecting to be more than just a hobby. It is investment, beauty, excitement, and history, and it tells us something very wonderful about the previous generations and about ourselves.

Gary Kirsner
Jim Gruhl

1. Stein History

Stein is a shortened form of *Steinzeugkrug* which is the German word for "stoneware jug or tankard." By common usage, however, *stein* has come to mean any beer container with a hinged lid and a handle, regardless of the material or size. Technically, more appropriate than the word *stein* would be *tankard,* and these two words are used interchangeably in this book. Be warned, however, that some people reserve the word *tankard* for the all-pewter or all-silver varieties of steins. One final definition: *mug* is universally used as the name for those vessels with handles but which would never have had a lid. So much for the semantics; those with a deeper interest in definitions should refer to the Glossary.

1.1 Earliest Steins, 1525 - 1700

From about 1340 to 1380 the bubonic plague, or Black Death, killed more than 25 million Europeans! As horrible as this historic event must have been, it resulted in *tremendous* progress for civilization. And of interest here, it is also responsible for the *origin* of the beer stein.

Recall from the earlier discussion that the distinction between the *mug* and the *stein* is the *hinged lid.* This lid was originally conceived entirely as a sanitary measure. During the summers of the late 1400's, hoards of little flies frequently invaded Central Europe. By the early 1500's several principalities in what is now Germany had passed laws requiring that *all* food and beverage containers must be *covered* to protect consumers against these dirty insects. The common mug also had to be covered and this was accomplished with the addition of the hinged lid with thumblift. This ingenious invention soon covered all German beverage containers while still allowing them to be used with one hand.

This "covered container," as well as several other *public health laws,* were enthusiastically passed and vigilantly enforced as a result of public fears about a return of the Black Death. In the period from Roman times to the 1300's, for a number of reasons, sanitation had continually declined. During the years of the Black Death it became obvious to all, with 95% dead in filthy areas and only 10% dead in clean surroundings, that the bubonic plague was somehow related to unsanitary conditions.

The "covered container" law was only one of a whole series of sanitary regulations that were passed in Germany after the plague: pigpens couldn't be adjacent to streets, old or diseased meat had to be labelled as such, and beer could be brewed only from hops, cereals, yeast, and water.

The original value of the lidded stein was to keep the flies out of the foam.

Such strictly enforced regulations concerning the quality and transport of beer in many of the German provinces resulted in a tremendous improvement in the taste of beer and this also had an impact on stein making. Many records show that average beer consumption moved up to about two liters per day in many places. Beerhouses, City Hall cellars, and taverns began to abound in the 1500's. Everyone in Germany needed a personal drinking vessel of which to be proud! There is an old saying, "the German will place great value on that which brings him his food or drink."

Local brews in many other parts of Europe were still being made with rotten bread, cabbages, eggs, and anything else at hand. Soon the Bremen, Hamburg, and other clean, pure Northern German beers became famous and were exported throughout Northern Europe, even as far as the East Indies and Jerusalem. Such beers raised a new need for relatively inexpensive, but durable, large containers; the search for adequate materials was on.

Activities at a brewery in the early 1600's.

As for individual beer vessels, up to the 1400's the well-to-do Germans had pewter beakers; a few of the wealthiest had silver vessels. These metal containers and those of glass, remained too expensive for general use or for large containers. Some wooden beakers were being used, but other than wood, porous earthenware was by far the most common material for beer beakers, mugs, and the larger containers. However, both the wood and the earthenware broke easily, which may have been a blessing because they soaked up beer, giving off a smell that got worse with each subsequent use.

Scientific experimentation was begun to try to improve the earthernware. All such scientific inquiry would previously have been squelched by the all-powerful church, long at odds with science, but during the Black Death the Church lost much power. It happened that the churches had either claimed prayer would end the plague or they had announced that Revelation had begun - in both cases they lost some of their hold on the public, and more pragmatic scientific views began to prevail. The subsequent rise of science and its marriage with art has been credited with starting the Renaissance.

The obvious experiments to perform with respect to earthenware, were to raise the firing temperature, 500°C (900°F), past the usual level. Higher temperatures, however, could not be achieved merely by throwing more wood into the furnace, they required new furnace designs. A new design was invented that produced temperatures up to 1200°C (2200°F). It had a furnace on the lower floor, then above it, through some slats, was the ceramic firing chamber entirely enclosed in brick except for small flues. At these extreme temperatures not only was all the moisture driven out of the clay as in earthenware, but the clay *vitrified,* or partially melted, into a solid stone-like material, hence *stoneware.*

Stoneware required days of firing and many dozen cords of wood, but the product proved to be far superior to earthenware. It is relatively difficult to chip or crack, and is not porous and so makes a much more sanitary container.

The expense of stoneware steins, especially after the "covered beverage container" laws requiring pewter lids, made steins worthy of some fine decorative ceramic art. Renaissance artists supplied many designs for applied and carved stein decorations. A clear salt glaze was invented about 1400; a blue glaze from cobalt oxide was also known at that time; a chocolate salt glaze was invented in the 1600's; a manganese oxide purple glaze was invented in about 1650.

Tankards soon became festooned with shields, historical, allegorical, and biblical scenes. Beer drinking had now also become a pleasure for the eyes! And the landless day laborers, the masses, who had survived the Black Death were in a position to command relatively higher wages for their services. They could afford a few modest luxuries, and the personal tankard had become a most important status and display piece for these Germans.

Once again consider the historical situation. The guild system was well in place in the 1500's and the guilds held powerful positions on the city councils. Although no records of it exist, the Pewter Guild was no doubt an important sponsor of the "covered container" laws that founded the beer stein. The Potters' Guilds are known to have continually pushed up the minimum standards on the quality of both the decorations and the stoneware, thus making steins increasingly more attractive.

The Black Death by depleting the population had created a surplus of food, especially grains. Much of this surplus grain made its way into local beers, making a fine pure beverage really worthy of celebration. Eventually surplus grains were able to make their way in large quantity to the breweries in the North (there were only a few cloister brewers in the South at that time). In the 1500's Hamburg had 600 breweries, producing 25 million liters of beer, and directly or indirectly employing half of the population of that city.

Originally, a few glass bottles were made in Delft, for shipping some of that Northern beer. But soon the fine clay of the Cologne area was used to make large stoneware jugs, the shipping industry was respawned, and the beer export business and the stein making business were booming and producing some extremely wealthy merchants.

History, however, did not let such wealth go uncontested, and the resultant 30 Years' War had changed much by its end in the 1640's. It was a war fought with fire. Virtually all of the Northern breweries were destroyed and most of the Southern vineyards as well. A few Southern breweries in Cloisters had survived and more or less by default Bavaria then became Central Europe's *beerland.* Beer soon replaced cider and wine as the beverage of choice throughout Germany.

An expanded new market for beer steins had been developed, and the stoneware from the area of Koln and Koblenz responded. Pewter, silver and glass luxury steins were also available, but the Chinese connection for the luxurious Ming porcelain mugs had been disrupted by rebellions in China in the middle 1600's. No one in Europe knew how to make porcelain, but several German potters were quick to jump in with a porcelain substitute -*faience.*

Faience is earthenware with a porcelain-like white glaze made from tin oxide. German faience was not as durable as the Chinese porcelain, but it was far cheaper and had two aesthetic advantages. First, the motifs on German faience were the popular late-Renaissance and early-Baroque designs, not the foreign looking Chinese figures. And second, the cobalt oxide of China was contaminated with purple manganese oxide, and the Persian cobalt oxide that the Chinese artists sparingly mixed in, would often diffuse badly. The German purer cobalt oxide supplies were bright blue and allowed for crisp lines. So even when the Chinese porcelain supply was reestablished, German faience had gained a firm hold on the stein market.

1.2 Transition Period, 1700 - 1850

Throughout the 1700's, the Pewter Guilds kept their tight hold on the "covered container" laws. It seems certain that this is responsible for keeping the lidded design of the stein from fading away. For there has always been a tendency to go to beakers and a master stein, or to find some other way of getting around the expense of the individually hinged lids. By the end of the 1800's, when the "covered container" laws were apparently no longer in force, over 300 years of conditioning had caused Germans to view a stein as incomplete without the lid. Thus, lids, and steins, were here to stay.

Many of those trends that were in place just before 1700 continued even stronger thereafter. For example, by 1750 there were over 4000 breweries in Bavaria. And the art and production of stoneware and faience steins increased strongly, all the way into the late 1700's.

European porcelain was invented in 1709, but did not begin to make a big impact on stein making until the 1720's. Several porcelain factories were started in the 1700's, but their products were very expensive. Only the wealthiest Germans were drinking their beer from porcelain or glass vessels.

The quality and taste of beer, the "flowing bread," continued to improve. Besides taste and fellowship, beer was considered to be important for the constitution, with qualities including strength, health, and relaxation. From the earliest times right up to the 1800's, many considered beer to be the most effective medicine known, the *drink from the gods.*

Although glass beer beakers were used in Roman times, glassmaking during the Middle Ages was suppressed by the Church as being *heathenish.* The art of making and enameling glass was not relearned by the Germans until the late 1500's. These early enameled items were mainly beakers and pokals.

Some of the typical shapes of early steins, and their most common names and period when they were *most* popular.

Some typical shapes of later steins, as well as a few of the covered containers that are closest to the *stein* shape.

A few engraved glass steins began to be used in the 1700's. However, partly because of their fragility, and partly because of their original rarity due to costliness, not many of these early glass tankards still exist. The color of their glass was almost always clear, which required some special efforts because the usual *Waldglas* of the time was made partly with wood ashes and had a definite greenish tinge. This clarity would seem to support the theory that an important feature of the early glass stein was to show off the rare clarity and color of the costliest beers brought from some distance.

Toward the end of the Baroque period, about 1800, pewter and silver tankards were still uncommon in Germany. However, the English, and to some extent the Scandinavians, had by now adopted the "finished" look of a lidded mug. And except for a few ceramic factories, they were exclusively making pewter and silver steins.

The Scandinavians had also perfected a way of making a nice all-wooden tankard complete with wooden hinge. The few German wooden steins from this period generally have pewter mountings and pewter overlaid designs, and even these were no longer being made by 1800.

Horn drinking vessels, so popular in Roman times, did not adapt well to the "covered container" law and became rare. Ivory steins were made only for the exceptionally wealthy.

In the 1600's it was rather easy to determine from where steins had come, every small region had considerable pride in their typical forms. The Bohemian, Austrian, and other Southern tankards were wide and sturdy; the Northerners preferred sleek and tall drinking vessels. The Western steins were blue-decorated gray stoneware; the Eastern steins were brown glazed stoneware.

During the 1700's, however, *shape* became less important. The faience steins predominantly assumed a pleasing cylindrical shape about twice as high as wide. The stoneware, glass, porcelain, pewter, and other steins soon followed suite. Regional differences of importance were reduced to differences in materials and motifs.

Soon after 1800 another transition was begun that was as significant and unpredictable as that which brought on the Renaissance! The Napoleonic and other wars and rebellions of the time so diminished the aristocrats' wealth and power that the newly monied Middle Class became the most important marketplace for steins and other artistic products. This Middle Class cast off the Baroque extravagences, preferring instead a sturdy, functional, *folk art*. In Germany this was known as the *Biedermeier* period.

Also around 1800 secularization had resulted in many monastery closings, but there were enough private breweries to assure that cloudless beer, without dregs, would still be available to the masses. And perhaps the new pride that developed in the "look" of the clear beer led in part to a major influx of glass steins into the marketplace soon after 1800. These glass steins usually carried enameled folk art designs.

The "straight up," cylindrical, pewter tankards had also become very popular at this time. Engraved or stamped designs were common, especially using the same type of *folk art* motifs. Occasionally, pewter steins from this period can be found with remnants of painted decorations. Considering the lack of durability of paint-on-pewter this type of decoration must have been done quite often to have resulted in as many examples as have survived.

Porcelain and silver steins in the early 1800's were still being made, always with the Renaissance and Baroque designs that still appealed to the wealthy.

The preference of the masses in the early 1800's was so clearly for glass and pewter that nearly all of the faience workshops were permanently closed. Most stoneware manufacturers stopped making steins and turned to everyday items such as bowls, jars, and wide-mouthed jugs.

The Villeroy and Boch firm of Mettlach has its origin in these times. Although the family was wealthy, the von Bochs had to appeal to the common tastes, with plates and other utilitarian items, in order to stay in business. However, as the Biedermeier period was drawing to a close, in 1850, the Mettlach factory, with its aristorcratic owners and classically trained artists, was ready to leap ahead with the upcoming change of artistic tastes.

During the early 1800's a great number of archeological expeditions had uncovered outstanding examples of Greek, Roman, and Renaissance art. By about 1850 the public had been so captivated by the beauty of these finds that they were ready to forsake the mundane, functional styles of the Biedermeier period.

1.3 The Golden Era, 1850 - 1910

By 1850 art students were being instructed entirely by copying the forms and designs of the archeological finds from the Renaissance and Classical periods. The new style that resulted has been called neo-Renaissance and neo-Classical, or more commonly, *Historicism*. As for beer steins, the white clays of the Koln area were again used to make stoneware steins with Renaissance allegorical motifs. These steins have gray salt-glazed relief decorations, often with porcelain inlaid lids.

Later on, a major resurgence in stoneware steins was begun when Reinhold Hanke of the Westerwald region began remaking blue and purple saltglaze pieces with Historicistic decorations. Molds were used to avoid the expense of the labor-intensive originals. These were no longer unique steins, they were "mass-produced" as the seams in the molds clearly attest. But there was an artistic advantage to using molds, and this was exploited to the

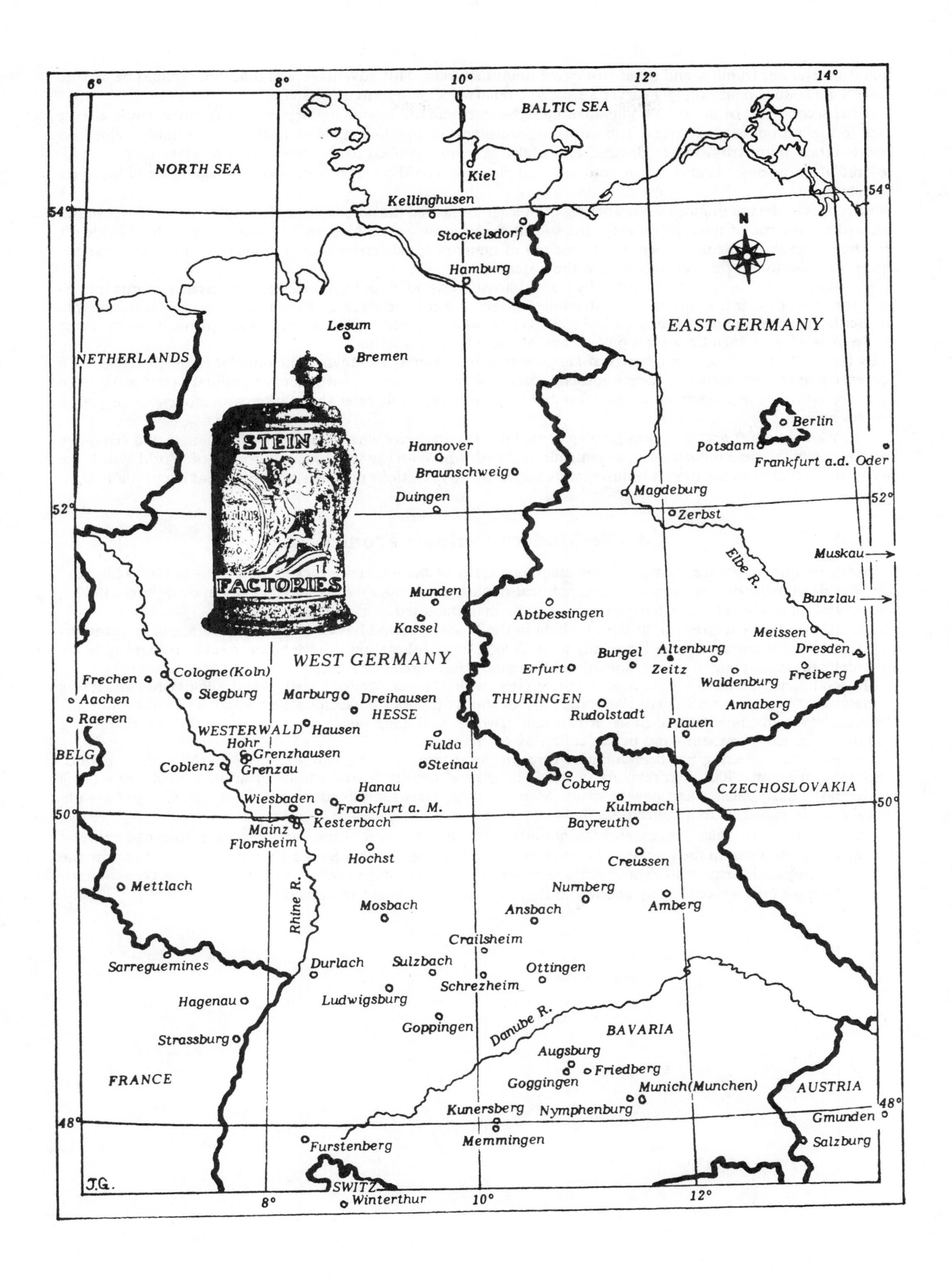
BALTIC SEA
NORTH SEA
Kiel
Kellinghusen
Stockelsdorf
Hamburg
N
EAST GERMANY
Lesum
Bremen
NETHERLANDS
STEIN
FACTORIES
Berlin
Potsdam
Frankfurt a.d. Oder
Hannover
Braunschweig
Magdeburg
Duingen
Zerbst
Muskau
Elbe R.
Bunzlau
Munden
Abtbessingen
Kassel
Meissen
Dresden
Burgel
Altenburg
WEST GERMANY
Erfurt
Zeitz
Freiberg
Waldenburg
Frechen
Cologne (Koln)
Aachen
Siegburg
Marburg
Dreihausen
THURINGEN
Annaberg
Raeren
HESSE
Rudolstadt
Plauen
WESTERWALD
Hausen
Hohr
Grenzhausen
Fulda
BELG
Coblenz
Grenzau
Steinau
Coburg
CZECHOSLOVAKIA
Hanau
Wiesbaden
Frankfurt a. M.
Kulmbach
Mainz
Kesterbach
Bayreuth
Florsheim
Hochst
Creussen
Mettlach
Nurnberg
Amberg
Rhine R.
Mosbach
Ansbach
Crailsheim
Sarreguemines
Durlach
Sulzbach
Ottingen
Schrezheim
Hagenau
Ludwigsburg
Goppingen
Danube R.
BAVARIA
Strassburg
Augsburg
Friedberg
FRANCE
Goggingen
Munich (Munchen)
AUSTRIA
Kunersberg
Nymphenburg
Gmunden
Memmingen
Salzburg
Furstenberg
J.G.
SWITZ
Winterthur
6°
8°
10°
12°
14°
54°
52°
50°
48°

fullest by Hanke, Dumler, and other stoneware manufacturers. This advantage was that molds could be used to quickly reproduce painstakingly carved, elaborate reliefwork on hundreds of steins.

In the second half of the 1800's, glassmaking techniques had progressed to the point where molds could also be used to mass-produce glass steins. The surprising sturdiness of the thick molded glass steins no doubt helped accelerate their popularity. Other glassmakers' tricks were also applied to the production of glass steins. Multicolored glass overlays, acid etchings, staining, and pewter overlaid on glass were used to make some rather spectacular steins.

Advances in the use of moisture-absorbing plaster molds helped the porcelain stein manufacturers. These molds allowed for the use of novel shapes, for the so-called *character* steins. Also, molds could be used to provide the *lithophane* scenes that can be seen on the bottom of many porcelain steins due to the variation in the thickness, and thus variation in the translucence, of the porcelain.

The Mettlach factory, with its classically trained artists, was quick to introduce the Renaissance motifs into its new line of relief steins. Experiments with colored glazes and colored clays led to some new brightly colored types of Mettlach steins, the *mosaic* and *etched* types. These were popular enough so that many of the laborers of the day were willing to spend a week's pay on one of these beautiful steins.

By the 1900's the designs and motifs of Historicism had begun to lose favor. The popular steins then had town scenes, occupational emblems, common social scenes, or remembrances, particularly to military service days. To meet these diverse new demands a great number of potters began to enter the market with stoneware or glazed pottery steins.

A new art style, *art nouveau,* was gaining some limited popularity when, around 1910, political and economic turmoil threw the stein industry into a tremendous slowdown. With the subsequent outbreak of World War I, the materials and labor of the pewter industry were converted to munitions products, and stein making virtually ceased.

1.4 The Modern Period - From 1920

Production of stoneware, glass, and porcelain, especially *character,* steins picked up sharply in the 1920's. Except for slowdowns during economic and political disturbances, notably the early 1930's and the early 1940's, substantial quantities of steins have continued to be manufactured.

The only major new direction in stein making in the Modern period has been the introduction of tremendous numbers of relief pottery steins. Especially after World War II these steins have become easily recognizable for their colorful hand-painted glazes, sometimes too gaudy and carelessly applied for most collectors' tastes.

The modern period owes a great debt to Historicism, with its reverence for Classical and Renaissance art. It was in that earlier period, from 1850 to 1900, that most of the great public museums were started. The public, not just the art intellectuals, now wanted to see artistic masterworks, including Renaissance steins. Public appreciation of antique steins led to museum and public collecting of steins.

Antique stein collecting has been a major force in the shaping of stein manufacturing in the modern period. Beginning in about 1900, then reviving in the 1920's, good quality reproductions of antique steins were being made, particularly faience and pewter steins. Many of these early reproductions are clearly marked and are obviously not intended to fool collectors.

The exceptions to this, Renaissance stoneware, early pewter, and some rare faience pieces had reached remarkably high prices in the marketplace, even at the turn of the century. So these are the steins that require the closest scrutiny to determine authenticity. It has really only been since the 1960's or 1970's that most types of antique steins have been valued highly enough so that reproductions might be considered.

2. Production of Steins

It would not be practical to make each of the Sections of this book self-contained. So to the extent that there are common elements to the production of the various different types of steins, these will be discussed in this Section. Also, to the extent that several of the Sections contain steins made from the ceramic materials, the description of the production of these have been brought forward into this Section.

2.1 Pewter Mountings

Pewter can contain as much as 90% tin, with the remainder made up of copper, zinc, bismuth, antimony, or, occasionally, *small* quantities of lead. Pewter is a very workable metallic alloy that melts at a relatively low temperature. It thus requires little in the way of special demands on the pewter workshop or the pewter craftsman.

In fact with regard to its undemanding nature it is only rivaled by lead: lead melts at an even lower temperature than pewter. Nevertheless ever since the inception of the "covered container" laws pewter has been the common choice for the material of a stein's mountings. One reason for this is that lead has a tendency to get very dark, powder, pit, and scale. And an even more important reason why pewter is always used for stein mountings, instead of lead, is that lead has been known since the Middle Ages to be unacceptable for holding food or drink because of its toxicity to humans.

The various parts of a stein's mounting are shown in the accompanying figure, though rarely will a stein contain all the elements shown in that mounting.

Because of the low melting temperature for pewter, pewter mountings can be fastened to most steins with little risk of damaging the already completed body of the stein - whether it is ceramic or glass. The fastening of the pewter mounting to the handle of the stein is generally accomplished in one of two ways. The most common method has been to wrap a leather strap around the handle, cover it with clay, then pull the strap out to leave a mold for the melted pewter. Occasionally wax has been used, covered with clay, then burned out by the molten pewter - the so-called *lost wax* process.

The purpose of the *footring* has always been to protect the bottom of the stein from chipping, cracking, or other damage. Because of their susceptibility to damage, virtually all faience steins, even modern replicas, have had footrings. Footrings will also occasionally be found on glass steins, even up to c.1900.

Also of interest is an understanding of the making of the *hinge*. Before 1860 the outside of the hinge was *closed* over, requiring a good deal of labor; after about 1860 the hinge was drilled and the pin set right in through all the teeth. The hinge pin of these more modern steins thus generally shows on the outside of the hinge.

The most common method for making *lids* and *footrings* has been to *cast* them, then trim away excess pewter by working these pieces on a lathe. This lathework will leave spinmarks on the inside, and often also the outside, of the lids and footrings. Up until about 1900 pewter has been quite expensive compared to labor. Older types of lids that are cast with a "heavy hand" and not slimmed down on the lathe, are usually reproductions.

The old types of ball *thumblifts,* commonly used in the 1700's, were made by soldering together two cup-shaped pieces of pewter. This saved on both weight and expense. Earlier types of thumblifts, from the 1600's, were generally solid, small figurals; most often used were shells, and single and double acorns. Thumblifts of the early 1800's ran the whole range from hollow vase-like devices to small solid balls and figurals. Toward the end of the 1800's the thumblifts were commonly bas-relief decorated tabs or figurals.

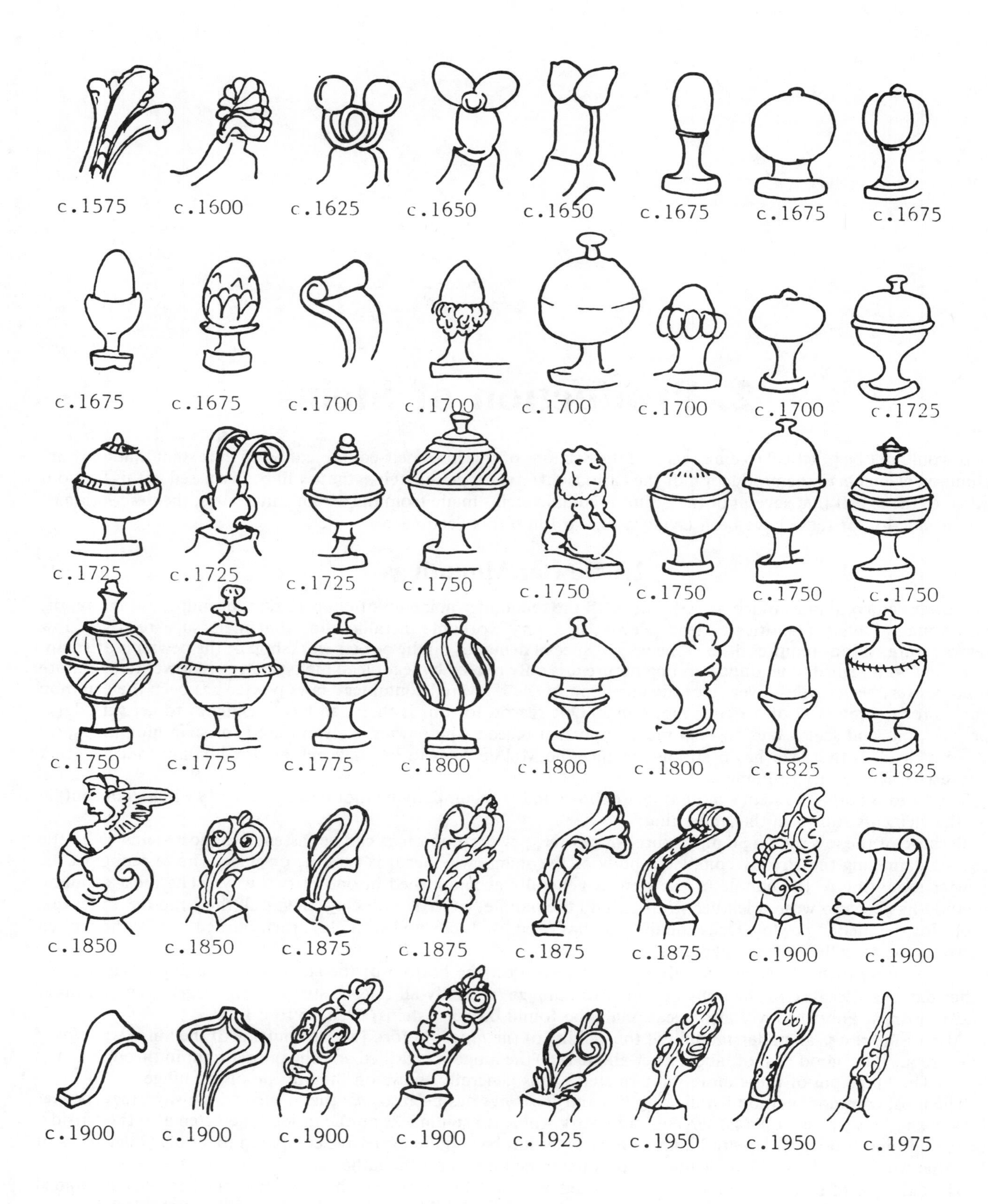

Thumblifts, or thumbpieces, of styles that have been popular in various time periods.

Patina can best be described as something that will be lost if pewter is cleaned with an abrasive material. *Patina* encompasses both the evidence of *wear* and the *color* that comes from aging. It gives old pewter a uniformly soft appearance, virtually impossible to reproduce exactly.

A check for possible repairs on a stein should thus begin with a careful examination of the strap, the hinge, and the patina, or age, color, and "use" of the pewter.

Being relatively soft, pewter mountings are easily marked with stamps that may give some information about the age and origin of a stein. On early steins these "touchmarks" were the registered symbols of the master pewterers. Reference books that identify touchmarks can be examined at many museums and some libraries.

The result of such touchmark searches, however, are often disappointing, so many of the original pewter guild records have been lost. On the average it seems that the city of the pewterer may be identifiable about one-third of the time, the name of the pewterer perhaps one-tenth of the time.

Dates that occur on touchmarks, and for that matter on lids, can be deceiving. Touchmark dates usually represent the date the pewter guild was founded, often 1708, or the date the master first registered his symbol.

Some of the names and symbols that occasionally occur on pewterwork of the last hundred years are discussed in Section 5.

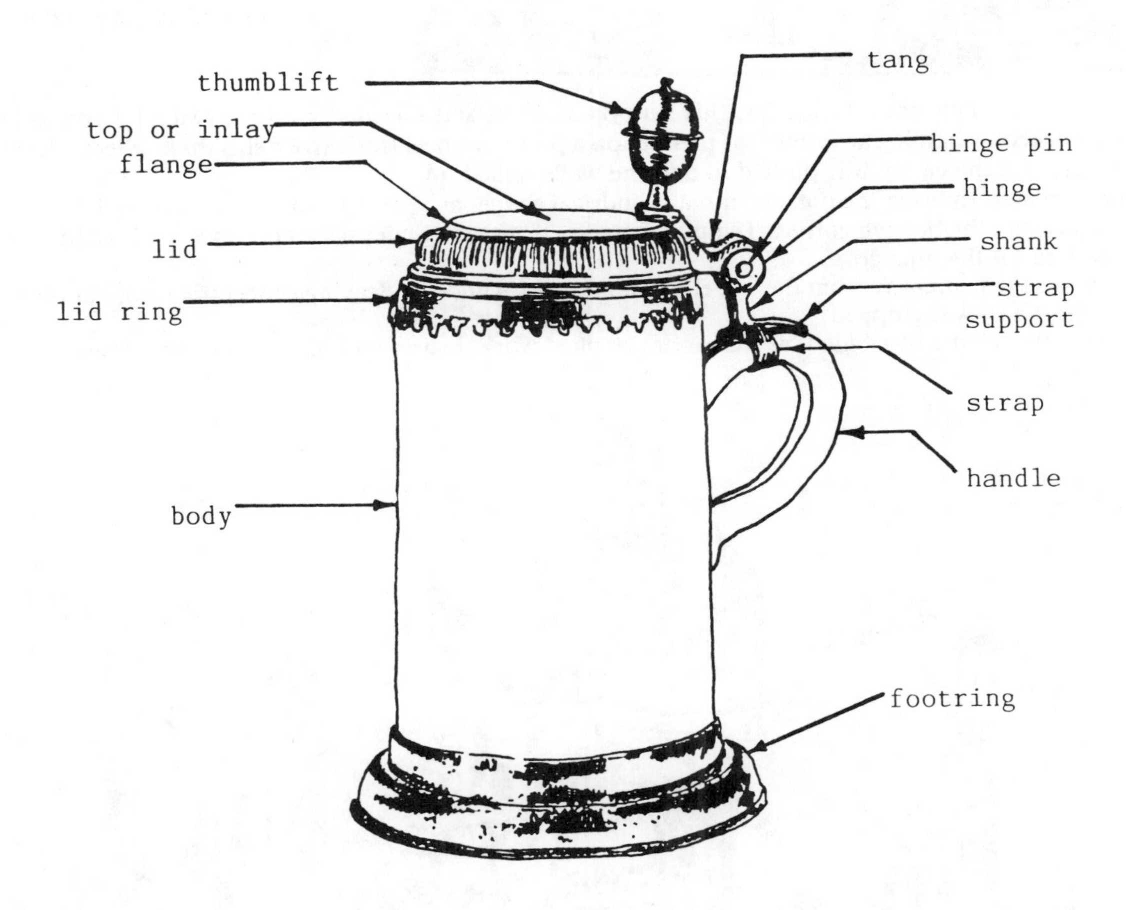

The most common names for the various parts of a stein's *mountings*.

2.2 Hand-Thrown Ceramics

Earthenware, Hafnerware, pottery, stoneware, *Steingut* or fine stoneware, porcelain, and the other ceramics all differ in only two respects: *firing temperature* and *recipe,* that is to say, the type of clay and other additives. As far as stein production is concerned, the ceramic pieces were basically either *hand-thrown* or *molded.*

In either case, production began by making sure all ingredients were in clay or powder form - some grinding may have been necessary. The proportions called for in the *recipe* were then measured out and dumped into a vat with water. The resulting *slurry* was thoroughly mixed and strained to remove impurities.

Two different mechanisms that were used as early potter's wheels.

In the case of the hand-thrown articles, this slurry was dried and kneaded until the "hump" would hold its shape when worked by hand. The *hump* was then set on a potter's wheel (for early steins these wheels were turned by apprentices) and the cavity was pushed in and the walls pulled up.

Scrapers were used to bring the outside into a cylindrical shape, as well as to carve excess materials away from the inside, especially the bottom corner. Templates, called *ribs,* were then used to produce the lip and any bands that were desired on the outside.

The hump was then cut away from the wheel by pulling a wire under it, leaving concentric whorls, or by using a knife, once the wheel was stopped.

At this point the handle was added, as well as any applied work, incising, or glazing, and the "mug" was ready for firing.

While he drives the potter's wheel, an early potter's apprentice watches the master potter.

2.3 Slip Molded Ceramics

It is not known exactly when slip molding was invented, but it had become an important stein making technique by the late 1800's.

The *slurry* was prepared in the same manner as described previously. The drying, however, was not accomplished in a mill or other separate process, instead it took place *right in the mold.*

The molds were made of *plaster* which slowly drew the moisture out of the *slip,* or slurry, that was right against it. The longer the slip was kept in the mold the thicker the dried portion of the slip became. After a prescribed number of hours the excess slip was poured out and the plaster mold was disassembled.

Because of the effort and expense involved in making the plaster mold and the time consumed in the process, slip molded steins are generally made of finer materials, like porcelain. Because slip molding could accommodate almost any kind of shape it helped to make possible the mass production of the oddly shaped *character* steins, shown in Section 14.

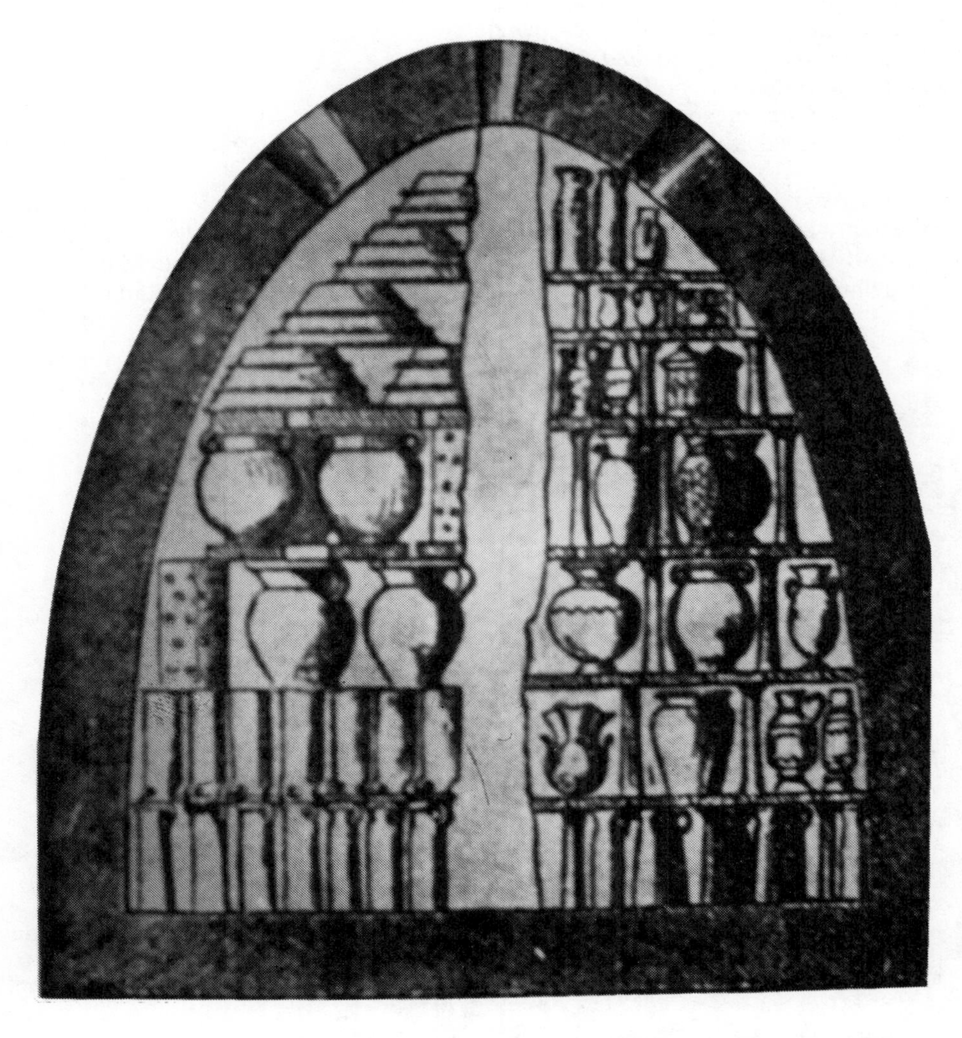

Cross-section of kiln showing a method of stacking the wares; the exhaust vents at the top were also used to pour in the approximately 400 pounds of salt at peak temperature.

2.4 Stein Marks

A large percentage of steins are *not* marked with the name of the manufacturer. There are several conjectures as to why this is so. It could be that, as with the earliest steins, the merchants preferred that their customers not be able to contact the manufacturers directly, and thus they persuaded makers to use only an identifying mold number. It is also known that the Europeans, particularly the Germans, have always been somewhat reluctant to discuss where they purchased items, just as Americans have always been reluctant to discuss price. Whatever the reason, it has made the study of stein producers very difficult, in many cases this study has to begin with the location of old catalogs.

Artists' names on steins are even scarcer. Except in the case of some Mettlach steins, a collector would be fortunate to locate the artist's initials somewhere in a stein's design. In the Renaissance revival of the 1800's artists were taught to aspire to the Classics, and as copyists not to sign their names. Perhaps this tradition continued from then through to the modern era.

Aside from the Mettlach factory, which had an elaborate marking system that is described in *The Mettlach Book,* pp. 19-22, there is little that can be learned from markings on the bottom of steins. The accompanying four pages show symbols that have been identified with particular manufacturers or distributors and dates.

The following are a few other markings that can occasionally be found, and what they mean:

GERMANY, or *Made in Germany,* indicates that the stein was meant to be exported to the United States or elsewhere outside Germany; this mark was required after the 1891 *Marking Law* and used until World War II.

WEST GERMANY, a mark used after World War II.

MUSTERSCHUTZ means *protected against copying.*

GESCHUTZT means *protected* or *patented.*

Gesetzlich Geschutzt translated as *legally protected.*

Gegen Nachbildung Geschutzt means *protected against copying.*

Reg. U.S. Pat. Off., registered at the U.S. Patent Office, was put on some items intended for sale in the United States.

Incised numbers most often denoted the manufacturer's catalog number of the mold that was used.

Painted numbers usually represent the decoration number.

Steins have occasionally been examined that carried paper labels with prices, export information, or even the manufacturer's or distributor's names. Of course it is rare that any of these will be found to help identify *antique* steins.

Obviously a highlight of the day when "the young, cook's maiden from the castle visits this potter in Grenzau, 1591."

J.u.H. Schilz Schilz
Karl Merkelbach III
Hohr-Grenzhausen

GEGR. 1876
Walter Merkelbach
Hohr-Grenzhausen

Marks and years of use for some of the important stein manufacturers.

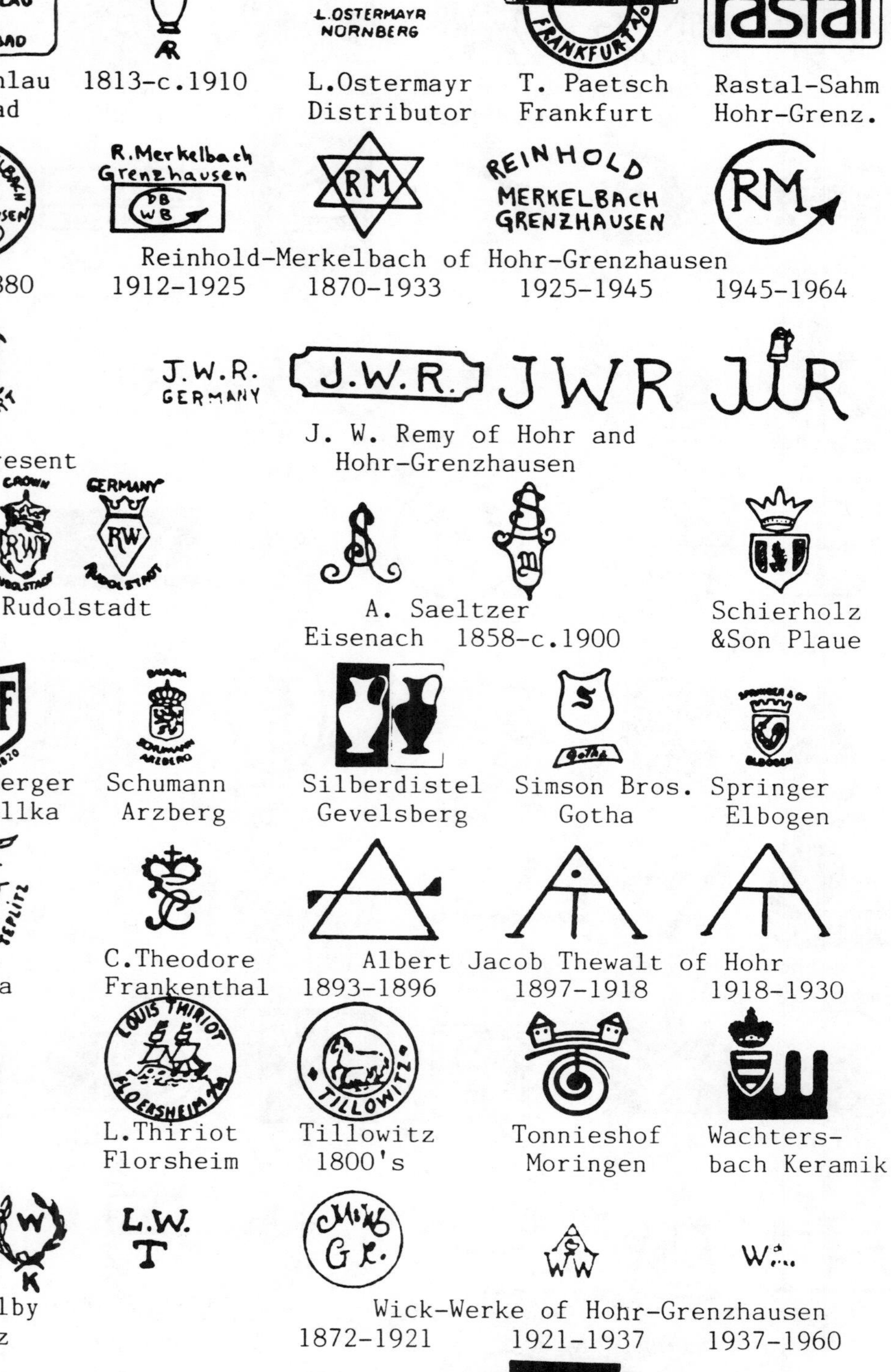
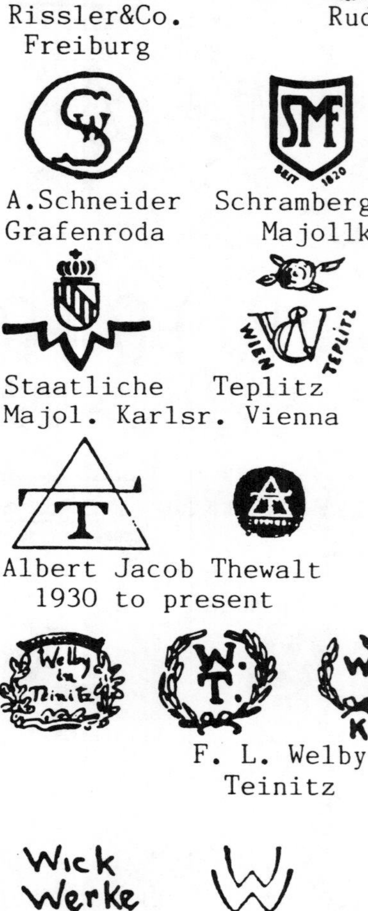
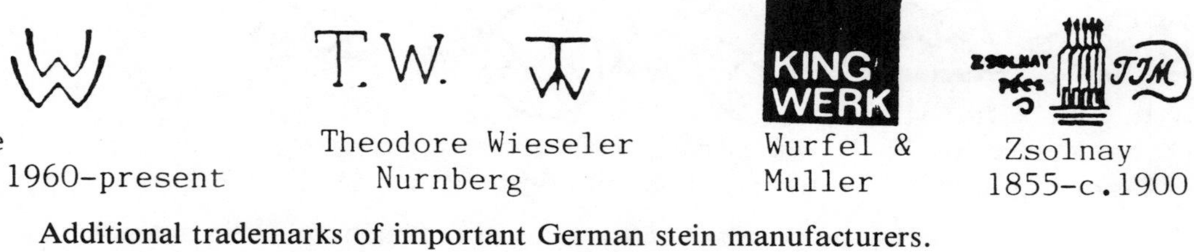

Additional trademarks of important German stein manufacturers.

Marks used by the Villeroy and Boch, Mettlach factory, and some of its other factories.

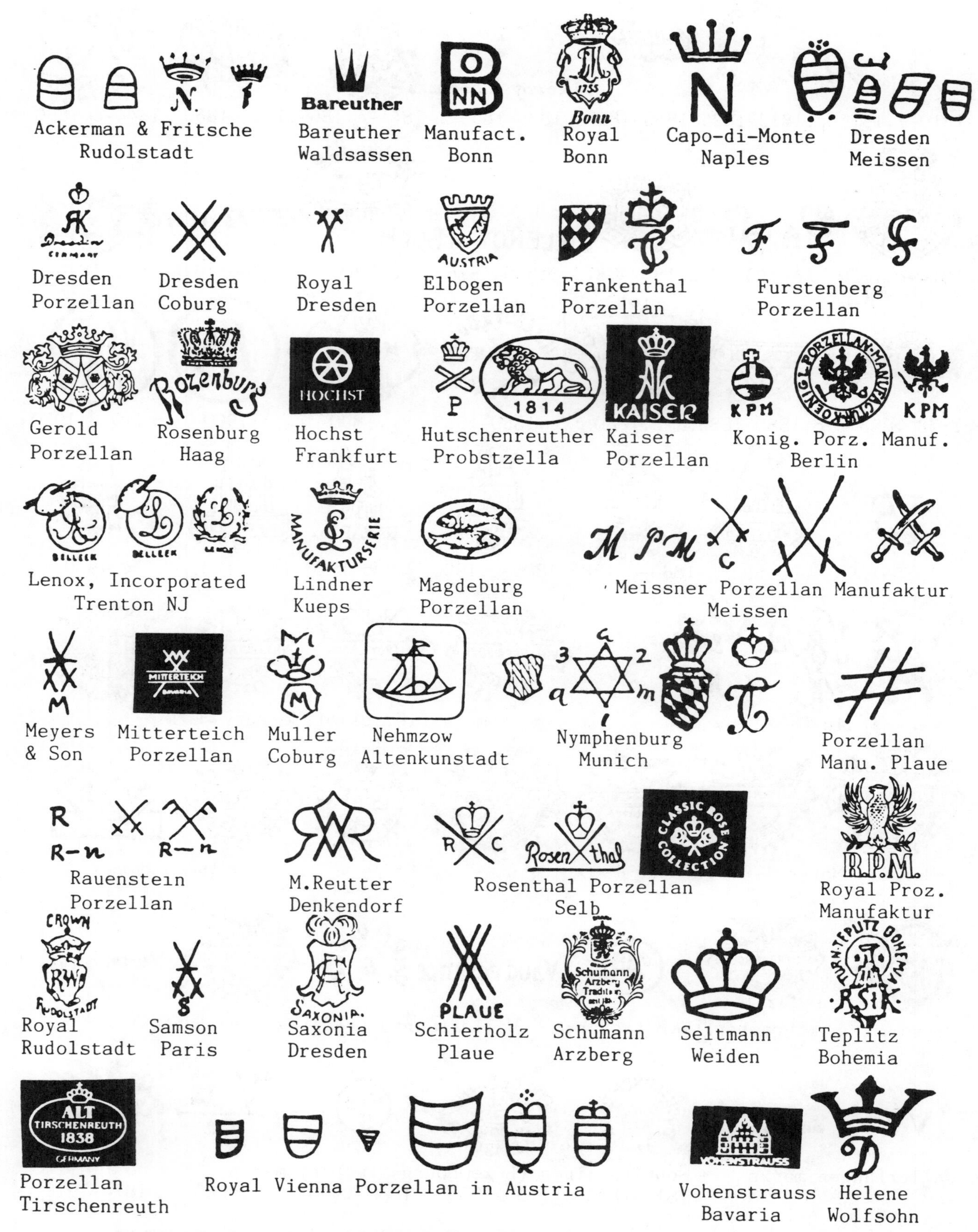

Marks used by other stein manufacturers, including the most common known porcelain marks.

3. Early Stoneware

The early history of stoneware steins is virtually the same as the early history of steins, as discussed in Section 1, since stoneware was for some time the only really important material used to make steins. There is a very short chapter in the history of stein making that does precede stoneware and this is related now.

3.1 Earthenware and Hafnerware

Earthenware vessels, especially in a *baluster* shape, were common in the Rhineland area in the 1400's. They were made by firing clay to about 800°C (1500°F) to drive off all the moisture. The resulting pottery was not durable and the surface was quite porous. None of these early pieces has been found with evidence of having had a lid.

Hafnerware, on the other hand, has been found with lids, that is to say, in the true beer stein form. Hafnerware is an earthenware that has been covered by a lead glaze, to make it non-porous, and to somewhat increase its durability.

Hafnerware had long been used to make stove tiles and other useful household items. Some decorative glazes have been found on Hafnerware steins, and examples can be found that date from the 1500's to the 1700's. Most of these are from Austria or Southern Germany. They are quite uncommon, however, and do not deserve any more discussion in this kind of general book.

3.2 Stoneware

The most common of the stoneware steins are those from the Westerwald region. Again, some of the history of these steins was discussed in Section 1. The remainder of this section, thus, will concentrate on some of the production techniques, factories and their styles, and some information for collectors.

Stoneware is a product of clay that has been heated so intensely, about 1200°C (2200°F), that the clay has vitrified into stone. It is hard to scratch, even with steel, and is impervious to liquids. Glazes have, thus, been added only for aesthetic reasons.

The furnace designs required to obtain such heat, took some time to evolve. But it is really the *special clay* that is required that prevented earlier discovery of stoneware. Stoneware clay must be very plastic, free from metallic and alkali impurities, and must fire with little (5% or less) shrinkage, and no warping or cracking. Stoneware clays, sometimes called "white gold," were originally mined out of potholes the sides of which were supported by saplings. These clays are still being mined today, but now using extensive shaft and tunneling techniques.

The old method for mining stoneware clay out of potholes that had sides supported by saplings; modern mining uses shaft and tunnel techniques.

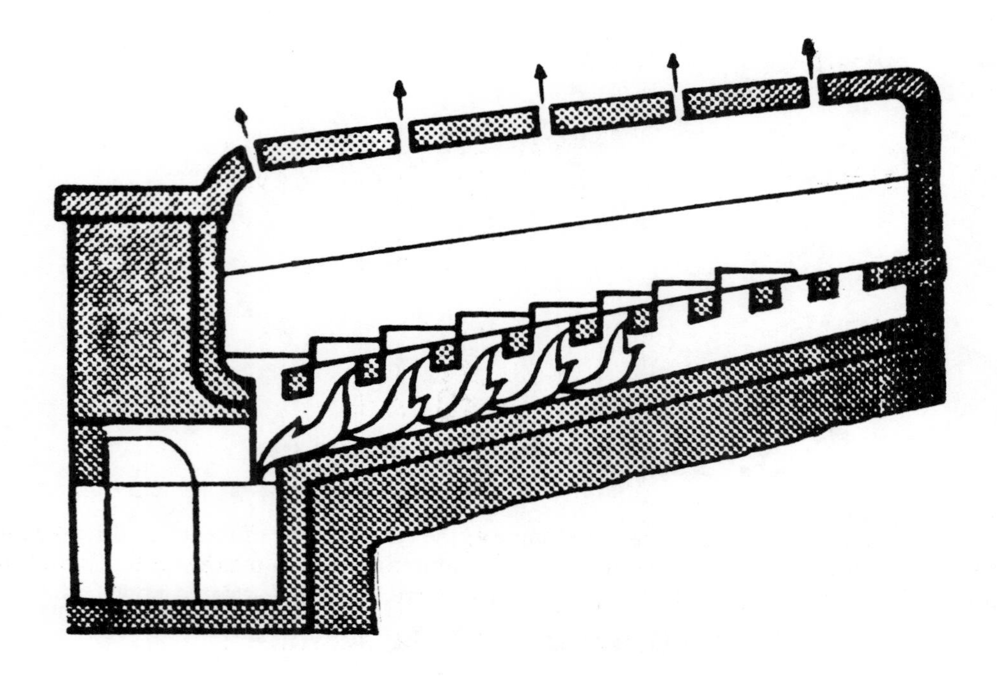

A more modern furnace, or kiln, design with a less vertical transfer of heat than the older upright configurations.

3.3 Stoneware Factories

Although the major deposits of stoneware clays have been in the Westerwald region, these did not become important until the 1600's. Before that time and even after the Westerwald area began production, there have been several regional stein producers that had their own distinctive styles and decorative techniques. Examples from most of these factories are shown in the following pictures, so only brief characterizations of steins produced by these factories are listed here:

Siegburg; early 1500's to late 1500's; white stoneware; clear glaze; slender and tall styles with Renaissance relief decorations; after 1600 the style became much like Westerwald.

Cologne-Frechen; early 1500's to 1600; gray stoneware; clear or "leopard" speckled-brown saltglazes; jug shapes, then later cylindrical; bearded man, allegorical, or smooth decor.

Raeren; about 1550 to early 1600's; gray stoneware; clear and blue or brown saltglazes; jug shapes and cylindrical; chip-carving (patterns of vertical creases) with allegorical scenes; then later bands with coat of arms.

Waldenburg; middle 1500's to late 1600's; gray stoneware; brown glazes with applied decor of allegorical scenes and coat of arms.

Westerwald; 1590 to about 1700; gray stoneware; clear, blue and purple saltglazes; jug shapes with applied decorations; 1670 to about 1800 - trend toward cylindrical shapes, first with applied shields and portraits, then in early 1700's with applied diamond-shape decorated bands, later with applied relief, stamped, scratch incised, zig-zag, and chip-carved designs.

Cruessen; early 1600's to middle 1700's; brown stoneware; saltglaze and often many colors of enamel; chocolate background color from the combination of the clay, so-called *black salt,* and particular wood used for fuel; squat cylindrical and pear shapes; relief decor, chip-carving, coat of arms, portraits, religious, hunt scenes, and mythological decorations.

Annaberg; middle 1600's to early 1700's; dark brown to grayish brown stoneware; saltglaze and various colors of enamel; squat cylindrical and pear shapes; chip-carving, relief decor, and organic designs.

Freiberg; middle to late 1600's; grayish to olive stoneware; saltglaze and enamels; cylindrical shapes with much chip-carving and stamped designs, often with checkerboard types of decorations.

Duingen; 1600's to about 1800; light brown stoneware; various brown saltglazes; plain bands with an occasional coat of arms.

Muskau; late 1600's to 1700's; gray stoneware; brown, blue and purple saltglazes; pear and cylindrical shapes with crudely scratched or stamped organic decorations.

Altenburg; 1700's to early 1800's; gray stoneware; light brown and creamy white glazes; tall cylindrical shapes with designs often made from many applied "pearls" of glazes stoneware, usually depicting folk art designs.

Bunzlau; 1700's; cream stoneware-earthenware; pear and bulbous shapes; brown glazes with occasional cream-colored applied *bisque* decorations, sometimes with smooth "melon" ribs.

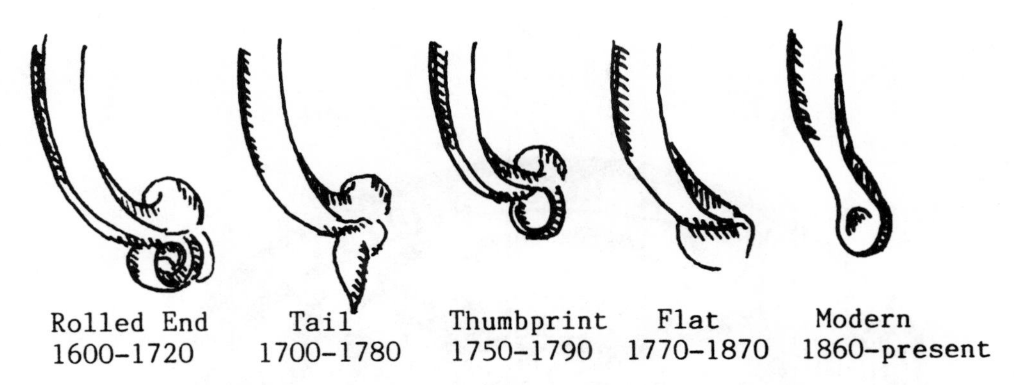

The potter's treatment of the lower end of the handle changed significantly over time, and can sometimes be used to help date Westerwald steins.

3.4 Collecting Early Stoneware

Few of the early stoneware steins were signed by the artist. Some of the famous Raeren and Westerwald steins from around 1590 are signed. Some of the Creussen steins are signed in the bottom with the letters of the artist's name cryptically combined into a clustered stick pattern. Occasionally a Westerwald stein, especially one with a *GR* design *(Georgius Rex,* made for export to England) uses a central applied design that has come from an initialed mold. These are virtually the only identifying marks that will be found on any of these old stoneware steins. The reason, as explained previously, is that the stein merchants did not want customers identifying and requesting, or contacting, specific stein makers.

Of interest to some collectors is the area within the broad *Westerwald* region that was responsible for certain steins. It is true that the vast majority of Westerwald steins were produced in the Hohr, Grenzau, and Grenzhausen cluster of neighboring villages. Westerwald-type steins are also known to have been produced in Steinau, other Hessen villages, Siegburg and Raeren (later than the original famous steins), and even possibly from around the Frechen area. The pictures in this Section identify a couple of the major style variations that are known to have come from specific villages. Examination of leaf designs, deer, ropework, checkerboarding, zig-zag incising, and some floral stamps will help in the identification of similar steins.

There *are* early stoneware steins that come to the marketplace; actually more than one might at first expect. A collector should be aware of several things before considering such a purchase. Reproductions are usually easily identified, but there can be some fakes that are convincing after a cursory examination. So look inside and out at all of the parts of the stein, including the pewterwork.

A second important thing to note is that there are *considerable* differences between the prices of different stoneware steins, as the information later in this Section clearly shows. Note also that the value of these steins does not strictly follow age, aesthetic appeal, size, rarity of type, or any other immediately apparent criteria -although each of these will have some bearing on the value. It is important to study the styles and values of the steins pictured.

Finally, it should be noted that the effect of condition on value is difficult to generalize. Some collectors, especially those who have previously collected mass-produced steins, are very fastidious about the condition of old stoneware pieces. On the other hand, long-time collectors and museums tend to place more emphasis on the aesthetic and technical quality of the stein *compared to others* of the *same* type. Each of these old stoneware steins is one-of-a-kind, and damage ought to be considered with this in mind.

There are no particularly dominant strategies for collecting old stoneware steins. Some collectors attempt to acquire examples of all of the various types. Others concentrate on one particular region, and this is usually the Westerwald region because these are encountered most frequently. Whatever the strategy it is always better to concentrate on quality, as these are the pieces that disappear from the marketplace first, and are most sought after by other collectors and museums who are always looking to *upgrade* their collections.

Coat-of-arms adopted by the Westerwald Potters Guild in the 1700's.

a. Stoneware, Siegburg, dtd. 1589, $2000.

b. Stoneware, Siegburg, middle 1500's, $3000.

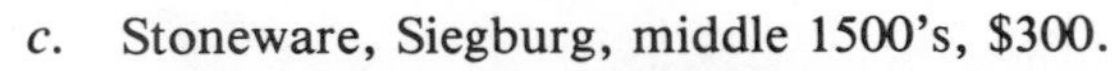

c. Stoneware, Siegburg, middle 1500's, $300.

d. Stoneware, Siegburg, cream colored, applied panels, c.1580, $3000.

e. Stoneware, Altenburg, white glaze, middle 1700's, $3000.

a. Stoneware, 1.5L, Altenburg, early 1700's, $1500.

b. Stoneware, 1.5L, Altenburg, middle 1700's, $2500.

c. Stoneware, 1.0L, Altenburg, late 1700's, $2000.

d. Stoneware, 1.0L, Altenburg, early 1700's, $1800.

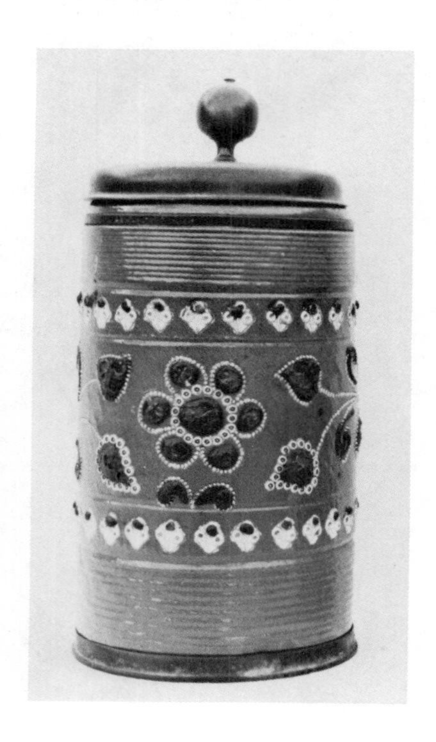

e. Stoneware, 1.0L, Altenburg, middle 1700's, $2000.

f. Stoneware, 1.0L, Altenburg, c.1750, $1800.

a. Stoneware, 1.0L, Altenburg, middle 1700's, $2400.

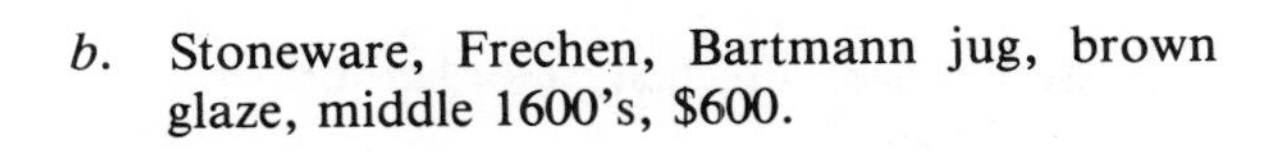

b. Stoneware, Frechen, Bartmann jug, brown glaze, middle 1600's, $600.

c. Stoneware, Frechen, Bartmann jug, brown glaze, early 1600's, $2500.

d. Stoneware, Raeren, middle 1700's, $800.

a. Stoneware, Frechen, mottled brown glaze, gold-plated silver mountings, late 1600's, $8500.

b. Stoneware, Annaberg, figure, brown glaze with enamels, c.1680, $3500.

c. Stoneware, Muskau, cut and stamped decor, c.1700, $2000.

d. Stoneware, Muskau, late 1600's, $1000.

e. Stoneware, Muskau, late 1600's, $2000.

f. Stoneware, Muskau, late 1600's, $3500.

a. Stoneware, Annaberg, late 1600's, $3500.

b. Stoneware, Annaberg, late 1600's, $3500.

c. Stoneware, Annaberg, late 1600's, $3000.

d. Stoneware, Annaberg, portrait with cherry borders, brown and enamel painted, c.1670, $2500.

e. Stoneware, Annaberg, couple, brown glaze with enamel painting, late 1600's, $3000.

f. Stoneware, Freiberg, gray with enamel painting, chip-carved and stamped decor, 1667, $5000.

a. Stoneware, Muskau, late 1600's, $2500.

b. Stoneware, Muskau, late 1700's, $800.

c. Stoneware, Creussen, dtd. 1693, $4000.

d. Stoneware, Altenburg (Duingen), middle 1700's, silver lid, $800.

e. Stoneware, Raeren, early 1700's, dtd. 1719 on body, $1200.

f. Stoneware, Duingen, early 1700's, $600.

g. Stoneware, Raeren, late 1700's, $300.

a. Earthenware, Bunzlau, double eagle, brown glaze with applied cream-colored decor, c.1760, $1500.

b. Earthenware, Bunzlau, double eagle, brown glaze with applied cream-colored decor, c.1760, $1500.

c. Stoneware, Muskau, brown and black glaze, cut and applied decor, late 1700's, $1000.

d. Stoneware, Muskau, middle 1700's, $600.

e. Earthenware, Bunzlau, seal of Hamburg, middle 1700's, $1500.

a. Stoneware, .5L, Westerwald, gray saltglaze, applied decor, c.1680, $1200.

b. Stoneware, 1.25L, Westerwald, gray saltglaze, stamped, applied, and zig-zag decor, c.1780, $1600.

c. Stoneware, .75L, Westerwald, gray saltglaze, applied decor, c.1700, $800.

d. Stoneware, 1.0L, Westerwald, gray saltglaze, cut and applied decor, c.1690, $1000.

e. Stoneware, .4L, Westerwald, blue, purple, and gray saltglaze, applied decor, c.1710, without lid $700, with lid $1100.

f. Stoneware, .75L, Westerwald, blue, purple, and gray saltglaze, applied decor, c.1700, $1300.

g. Stoneware, 1.0L, Westerwald, Hausen-style, blue and gray saltglaze, cut, stamped, and applied decor, c.1770, $1000.

h. Stoneware, .5L, Westerwald, blue, purple, and gray saltglaze, applied decor, c.1680, $1200.

a. Stoneware, .5L, Westerwald, Hausen-style, blue and gray saltglaze, cut, stamped, and applied decor, c.1780, $650.

b. Stoneware, .5L, Westerwald, Hausen-style, blue and gray saltglaze, cut, stamped, and applied decor, c.1790, $800.

c. Stoneware, 2.5L, Westerwald, blue, purple, and gray saltglaze, cut, stamped, and applied decor, c.1780, $2200.

d. Stoneware, 1.0L, Westerwald, blue and gray saltglaze, cut, stamped, and applied decor, c.1760, $1000.

e. Stoneware, .5L, Westerwald, blue, purple, and gray saltglaze, cut, stamped, and applied decor, c.1790, $1000.

f. Stoneware, .5L, Westerwald, Hausen-style, blue, purple, and gray saltglaze, cut, stamped, and applied decor, c.1790, $650.

g. Stoneware, .5L, Westerwald, blue, purple, and gray saltglaze, cut, stamped, and applied decor, c.1780, $800.

h. Stoneware, .5L, Westerwald, blue, purple, and gray saltglaze, cut and applied decor, c.1780, $900.

a. Stoneware, .5L, Westerwald, blue and gray saltglaze, cut, stamped, and zig-zag decor, c.1725, $1300.

b. Stoneware, .5L, Westerwald, Steinau-style, blue and gray saltglaze, cut decor, c.1790, $750.

c. Stoneware, .75L, Westerwald, Steinau-style, blue and gray saltglaze, cut and stamped decor, 1788, $850.

d. Stoneware, .5L, Westerwald, Hausen-style, blue and gray saltglaze, cut decor, c.1790, $550.

e. Stoneware, .5L, Westerwald, Steinau-style, blue and gray saltglaze, cut, stamped, and applied decor, c.1770, $1000.

f. Stoneware, .5L, Westerwald, blue and gray saltglaze, cut, applied, and zig-zag decor, c.1740, note inlaid lid, $3000.

g. Stoneware, 1.0L, Westerwald, Hausen-style, blue and gray saltglaze, cut and applied decor, c.1770, $1100.

h. Stoneware, .75L, Westerwald, Hausen-style, blue and gray saltglaze, cut and stamped decor, c.1780, $800.

a. Stoneware, .5L, Westerwald, blue and gray saltglaze, cut and stamped decor, c.1755, $750.

b. Stoneware, .75L, Westerwald, Steinau-style, blue and gray saltglaze, cut, stamped, and zig-zag decor, c.1750, $1000.

c. Stoneware, 1.0L, Westerwald, Hausen-style, blue and gray saltglaze, cut decor, c.1760, $900.

d. Stoneware, .5L, Westerwald, blue and gray saltglaze, cut decor, c.1770, $600.

e. Stoneware, .4L, Westerwald, Hausen-style, blue and gray saltglaze, cut decor, c.1775, $600.

f. Stoneware, .5L, Westerwald, Hausen-style, blue and gray saltglaze, cut decor, c.1775, $600.

g. Stoneware, 1.0L, Westerwald, Hausen-style, blue and gray saltglaze, cut decor, c.1775, $750.

h. Stoneware, 1.0L, Westerwald, Hausen-style, blue and gray saltglaze, cut decor, c.1775, $750.

a. Stoneware, .25L, Westerwald, Georgius Rex for export to England, blue and gray saltglaze, cut and applied decor, c.1730, always without lid, $400.

b. Stoneware, .75L, Westerwald, Georgius Rex, blue and gray saltglaze, cut and applied decor, c.1730, always without lid, $600.

c. Stoneware, 1.5L, Westerwald, Prince William of Orange of Holland, signed PR, blue, purple, and gray saltglaze, cut and applied decor, 1687, $1700.

d. Stoneware, 1.0L, Westerwald, Georgius Rex, blue and gray saltglaze, cut and applied decor, c.1720, $500.

4. Faience

Antique faience pieces can be found with Dutch, French, English, Italian, German and all sorts of other origins as well as in innumerable shapes: drinking vessels, utensils, and endless numbers of purely decorative items. *Faience* is a tremendously large field of study. However, the focus here on *steins,* and thus primarily on the *German* faience factories, makes this history and discussion more manageable.

4.1 History of Faience

About the year 800 A.D. Chinese porcelain made its way to the Middle Eastern and European royal courts. Despite major efforts to produce this *white gold* outside China, it was not until 1709 that Johann Bottger and Ehrenfried von Tschirnhaus were able to produce porcelain in Meissen. The 900 or so years of that search produced steadily more attractive substitutes, of which *faience* was perhaps the most convincing.

Faience, as it was originally produced beginning about the 1400's in Faenza, Italy, succeeded in reasonably imitating the white background that gave the Chinese porcelain its contrast and clarity. From the 1400's faience spread slowly through France to the Northern European countries, and slowly across the Alps into Switzerland and Austria.

Beginning in the 1600's the then frequent Dutch trade with East Asia brought relatively large quantities of Chinese porcelain to Europe. In the middle of the 1600's, however, revolts in the Ming empire cut off the Chinese supply. The Dutch quickly supplied this disrupted market with wares from its *faience* works. Religious changes in the Netherlands had pushed some of these potters into Germany, and in 1661 at Hanau and 1666 at Frankfurt, Germany faience production began to supply the waiting German market.

The first of these German, so-called *porcellaine,* steins were unabashed replicas of the authentic Chinese pieces. Their decor included Oriental people in Oriental costume in the midst of Oriental landscapes. The colors were Ming blue on porcelain-like, pure white. Often these steins had finely tooled silver lids, as had been made for the expensive imports.

Predictably, once the stein decor could be controlled by European artists, blank white faience bodies were sold by the factories to private artists, called *Hausmalers,* who provided decorations. Included were many of the day's finest artists, who painted steins on commission or free-lance, and the results were often magnificent. Every color of glaze was used as well as the scenes and designs most fashionable in this late-Renaissance and early-Baroque period.

By 1700, with Germany fragmented into hundreds of principalities, many rulers found it profitable to sell licenses or to franchise faience works and exclude imports. Thus, factories were started in almost all the locations where the clay and firewood were available.

The invention of European porcelain in 1709 only slowly began to influence the faience stein market. Initially it was almost as expensive as Chinese porcelain. However, by about 1725, when production began to pick up and a white ground was available, some major shifts began to take place:

(1) the best Hausmalers moved away from faience and began working in porcelain,
(2) the silver lids, often gilded as well, now went only on the porcelain steins,
(3) the cheaper factory decorations and pewter mountings opened up the faience stein market to an eager middle class,
(4) the larger narrow-necked, *Enghalskrug,* and pear, *Birnkrug,* shapes increasingly gave way to the more masculine, cylindrical, *Walzenkrug,* shape in individual sizes of half liter and full liter.

To be sure, even until about 1770, there were first-rate artists that stayed at the faience factories. After 1800, though, faience steins were definitely not up to their former quality. In the Biedermeier period, 1800 to 1850, the middle classes had turned to the unpretentious, sturdier materials: pewter and thick glass.

Somewhat after the end of the Biedermeier period there began an undercurrent of collecting the antique faience items. A number of crude reproductions were made around 1900, common types were pear-shaped. In the 1920's some excellent reference books brought collecting out of the selected circles, and something of a faience revival occurred. This revival is easy to understand, faience and porcelain have always provided the stein artist with a freedom of color and a white paper-like background unavailable elsewhere.

Another resurgence of good reference books in the 1950's seemed to sharpen the interests of museums, especially in works from their localities. Steins from the 1600's and from Hausmalers have largely moved from private collections into museums. Now, the majority of the nice faience steins that come to the marketplace were made in the 1700's.

Identifying the workshop and possibly even the artist is of great interest to the collectors. The fact that so many pieces are unsigned or, at best, cryptically signed, is an important part of the history of faience (as well as stoneware) steins. All of the guild systems were very strong in the 1600's and into the 1700's. The guild systems afforded the few master craftsmen with:

(1) cheap labor in the form of apprentices and journeymen,
(2) absolute control on the numbers of shops, so the master craftsmen could stay well-to-do, and
(3) quality and quantity control.

A worker who provided clay or wood to an unguilded potter could lose supplies from the bakers', butchers', and other guilds. Pewterer's guilds would attach mountings only to steins from guilded potters.

And most importantly, merchants' guilds bought steins only from potters' guilds. In return, the merchants required that the steins not be marked. They didn't want buyers to know how to contact the best potters directly, and thus lose their commissions!

Some of the cryptic bottom marks that were used are shown in this Section. Also the pictures in this chapter should help in identifying the styles of different factories and painters. A number of faience books are listed in Section 15 that will provide additional information on glazes, styles, and colors of clays used at the different factories.

It must be noted, however, that there are few *certainties* in faience identification. Some artists are known to have been at *three* different factories in one ten-year period. And, of course, glazes and motifs often moved with the artists. Constant empirical experimentation with clay recipes, slightly different temperatures, even different kinds of wood could change the color of the fired earthenware. Thus, it is often much easier to identify a stein with a region, than with a specific factory. These regions include:

(1) Western German
- Florsheim 1765-1922
- Frankfurt am Main 1666-1772
- Fulda 1741-1758
- Hanau 1661-1806
- Hochst 1746-1758
- Kassel 1680-1777
- Kelsterbach 1758-1835
- Koln 1770-1820
- Wiesbaden 1770-1797

(2) Central German
- Berlin 1678-1786
- Braunschweig 1707-1807
- Frankfurt a.d. Oder 1763-1795
- Hannoversch - Munden 1732-1854
- Magdeburg 1754-1785
- Potsdam 1740-1796
- Wrisbergholzen 1735-1834

(3) Thuringen
- Abtbessingen 1739-1791
- Coburg 1739-1786
- Dorotheenthal 1707-1806
- Dresden 1708-1784
- Erfurt 1717-1792
- Zerbst 1721-1796

(4) Eastern German
- Glinitz 1767-1800
- Proskau 1763-1793

(5) Upper Plains
- Amberg 1759-1910
- Ansbach 1710-1839
- Bayreuth 1714-1835
- Nurnberg 1712-1840
- Sulzbach 1752-1774

(6) Wurttemberg
- Crailsheim 1720-1827
- Goppingen 1741-1812
- Ludwigsburg 1757-1824
- Schrezheim 1752-1852

(7) Swaben
- Augsburg 1678-1754
- Friedberg 1754-1768
- Goggingen 1748-1752
- Kunersberg 1745-1846
- Ottingen 1735-1846
- Schrattenhoffen 1735-1846

(8) Upper Rhine
- Hagenau 1709-1781
- Strassburg 1721-1781

(9) Baden
- Durlach 1723-1840
- Mosbach 1770-1828

(10) Seas
- Hamburg 1625-1655
- Kellinghausen 1763-1860
- Kiel 1763-1787
- Lesum 1756-1800
- Stockelsdorf 1772-1786

(11) Austria
- Gmunden 1582-1820
- Salzburg 1590-1790

Those with a still unquenched interest in faience factory identification might begin to accumulate a collection of reference texts, such as some of those listed in the bibliography in Section 15.

4.2 Faience Stein Production

Faienciers always located themselves near woods and clay. They experimented with the clay, mixed it with some other earths, sand, lime, and silicic acid, until a recipe was found that would be reasonably resistant to flaking, cracking, and crazing, when glazed.

Once a suitable clay recipe was established, that mixture was combined with water, strained, then dried until workable. The thrower would then fashion a basic shape and let the piece dry further, until "leather hard." The handle was then attached and a first firing to about 700°C drove off the water and left a hard porous, so-called *bisque,* body.

This body was then dipped in a glaze made from tin oxide, powdered glass, and a flux. At this point, factories generally decorated the pieces with pigments that could withstand high temperatures: cobalt blue, manganese violet, antimony yellow, copper green, and sometimes iron red. The second firing, to about 1000°C, melted the tin oxide and pigments into a smooth porcelain-like finish.

Occasionally wares were sent to the second firing with only the white glaze. Afterward, these blanks were then decorated with a far greater variety of low-temperature glazes, even gold leaf, and were fired a third time to about 750°C. Often the pieces for the third firing were set behind protective *muffle bricks* while other wares received the intensely hot second firing. These *muffle-fired* decorations, as were used by the Hausmalers, can be felt or seen as lying on top of the background glaze.

A 1794 print showing the dip glazing of faience ware with the white tin oxide mixture.

Most factories could not be bothered with the third firing; they usually accomplished all the decorations with pigments that could stand the second firing, or occasionally (such as with some Ansbach or Schrezheim steins) just *cold-painted* the decorations. After much use such cold-painted decorations became very messy, and are often totally removed to make a plain faience stein (usually leaving a plain turquoise background).

Sprinkling of faience wares with an overglaze by using a paape brush, from a 1794 print.

4.3 Collecting Faience

At best, faience, with its porous earthenware body, is not particularly durable. Even with the original protective lid and footring, old faience steins almost always have nicks, hairline cracks, or worse damages. Of course, collectors generally have an aversion to buying glued together pieces. Such steins aside, the age and aesthetic quality of steins are more important than absolutely *perfect* condition.

Most reproductions can be spotted easily, as the decorations are usually very crudely painted. Reproductions also generally have *cast* lids and thumblifts, rather than carefully handspun and soldered pewterwork. Old lids occasionally can be found fastened to reproduction bodies, but the patina and file marks around the strap or shaft will almost inevitably show what has been done.

There are not many faience collecting strategies of note. However, shape is often of concern in developing a strategy for collecting. Collectors who collect steins from many different types of materials seem to prefer the cylindrically shaped faience steins, which appear more in place with the other kinds of steins. On the other hand, collectors who concentrate totally on *faience,* more often relish the *earlier* narrow-necked and pear-shaped forms. Very few faience stein collectors try to concentrate on a particular motif or factory; it is much more popular to actively seek diversity.

The faience steins shown on the following pages have been identified by several experts and are reasonably accurate. Still a substantial amount of uncertainty exists regarding the factories. It can take many days of aesthetic and chemical analyses to ascertain the origin of some faience steins. For this reason, the ''possibly'' and ''probably'' have been included in the following descriptions.

Unless otherwise noted, the prices have been set presuming these steins are in reasonably good shape, such as a couple of hairlines and some minor chipping of the handle. For a stein that has chunks missing, the value will be down closer to that of the pewter mountings, perhaps as little as $100 or $200.

An early inn or tavern scene, from an early 1800's woodcut by L. Richter.

Abtsbessingen	Amberg	Ansbach
Bayreuth	Berlin	Braunschweig
Coburg	Crailsheim	Dorotheenthal
Erfurt	Florsheim	Frankenthal
Frankfurt a.d. Oder	Frankfurt a.M.	Friedberg
Fulda	Glinitz	Goggingen
Goppingen	Hamburg	Hanau
Hannoversch-Munden	Hochst	Kellinghusen
Kelsterbach	Kiel	Kunersberg

Factory and artist marks used on the bottom of some faience steins.

Lesum	Ludwigsburg	Magdeburg
Mainz	Marburg	Mosbach
Munden	Niederweiler	Nurnberg
Offenbach	Ottingen	Poppelsdorf
Potsdam	Proskau	Reval
Rheinsberg	Rudolstadt	Schleswig
Schrattenhofen	Schrezheim	Stockelsdorf
Stralsund	Strassburg	Sulzbach
Wiesbaden	Wrisbergholzen	Zerbst

Additional faience marks; almost all faience marks were painted under the glaze.

a. Faience, .5L, possibly Ansbach, middle 1700's, $600.

b. Faience, 1.0L, Hanau, early 1700's, $800.

c. Faience, .5L, Hanau or Bayreuth, middle 1700's, $800.

d. Faience, .25L, Hanau or Bayreuth, middle 1700's, $600.

e. Faience, .25L, redware or ironware, c.1700, $800.

f. Faience, 1.5L, redware or ironware, c.1700, $2000.

a. Faience, .5L, Bayreuth, late 1700's, $850.

b. Faience, .5L, Bayreuth, late 1700's, $1100.

c. Faience, .5L, possibly Erfurt, late 1700's, $1100.

d. Faience, .5L, probably Bayreuth, late 1700's, $950.

e. Faience, .5L, probably Berlin, middle 1700's, $1000.

f. Faience, .5L, Bayreuth, late 1700's, $1000.

g. Faience, .5L, probably Salzburg, c.1800, $700.

h. Faience, .5L, Ansbach or Kunersberg, floral, middle 1700's, $1300.

a. Faience, .5L, Upper Plains region, late 1700's, $1300.

b. Faience, .5L, unknown factory, late 1700's, $1000.

c. Faience, .5L, Thuringen region, late 1700's, $1000.

d. Faience, .5L, Thuringen region, late 1700's, $1000.

e. Faience, .5L, unknown factory, Duingen style decoration, middle 1700's, $800.

f. Faience, .75L, unknown factory, middle 1700's, $800.

a. Faience, .5L, Bayreuth, c.1780, $1200.

b. Faience, .5L, possibly Thuringen region, late 1700's, $1200.

c. Faience, .5L, Bayreuth or Hanau, c.1780, $1000.

d. Faience, .5L, Ansbach, c.1780, $1700.

e. Faience, .5L, Gmunden, late 1700's, $800.

f. Faience, .5L, possibly Thuringen region, c.1770, $2000.

g. Faience, .5L, Thuringen region, late 1700's, $1500.

h. Faience, .5L, possibly Ansbach, late 1700's, $2500.

a. Faience, .5L, Swaben region, middle 1700's, $3000.

b. Faience, .5L, Berlin - Funcke factory, middle 1700's, $2000.

c. Faience, .5L, probably Schrezheim, c.1800, $800.

d. Faience, .5L, Bayreuth or Erfurt, late 1700's, $1200.

e. Faience, .5L, Crailsheim, c.1800, $2000.

f. Faience, .5L, Ansbach, middle 1700's, $2500.

g. Faience, .5L, Dorotheenthal, late 1700's, $1200.

h. Faience, .5L, Frankfurt Oder, middle 1700's, $1200.

a. Faience, .5L, Central German region, late 1700's, $800.

b. Faience, .5L, probably Sachsen, c.1780, $950.

c. Faience, .5L, unknown factory, c.1780, $950.

d. Faience, .5L, possibly Thuringen region, late 1700's, $2000.

e. Faience, .5L, Bayreuth, c.1790, $1500.

f. Faience, .5L, Central German region, c.1790, $1200.

g. Faience, .5L, Thuringen, c.1780, $1800.

h. Faience, .5L, Thuringen region, late 1700's, $1600.

a. Faience, .5L, probably Berlin, FWR stands for Friedrich Wilhelm Rex, middle 1700's, $2000.

b. Faience, .5L, probably Ansbach, baker's emblem, late 1700's, $2000.

c. Faience, .5L, unknown factory, tailor's emblem, late 1700's, $2000.

d. Faience, .5L, Thuringen region, Chinese scene, c.1750, $1400.

e. Faience, .5L, Thuringen region, late 1700's, $1500.

f. Faience, .5L, Erfurt, late 1700's, $1500.

a. Faience, .5L, unknown factory, c.1760, $1000.

b. Faience, .5L, unknown factory, middle 1700's, $1000.

c. Faience, .5L, Bayreuth or Erfurt, c.1760, $1500.

d. Faience, .25L, probably Erfurt, middle 1700's, $900.

e. Faience, .5L, Bayreuth, c.1770, $1500.

f. Faience, .5L, Thuringen region, late 1700's, $900.

g. Faience, .5L, Upper Plains or Thuringen region, middle 1700's, $1200.

h. Faience, .5L, Upper Plains or Thuringen region, middle 1700's, $1200.

a. Faience, 1.0L, Central German region, middle 1700's, $1800.

b. Faience, .5L, Thuringen, late 1700's, $1200.

c. Faience, .5L, Braunschweig, c.1800, $600.

d. Faience, .5L, Thuringen or Berlin, c.1780, $1200.

e. Faience, .5L, Hanau, marked *H,* exotic bird, early 1700's, dtd. 1733, $3000.

a. Faience, .5L, possibly Berlin, c.1770, $2000.

b. Faience, .5L, Thuringen, late 1700's, $1500.

c. Faience, .5L, unknown factory, middle 1700's, $2500.

d. Faience, .5L, Proskau, harp player, c.1790, $3000.

e. Faience, .5L, probably Frankfurt Oder, late 1700's, $1200.

f. Faience, .5L, Hanau, c.1760, $2000.

g. Faience, .5L, probably Schrezheim, late 1700's, $1000.

h. Faience, .5L, Thuringen, c.1780, $1200.

a. Faience, .5L, possibly Frankfurt am Main, early 1700's, $4000.

b. Faience, .5L, Bayreuth, c.1790, $1500.

c. Faience, .5L, Crailsheim, middle 1700's, $4000.

d. Faience, .5L, Crailsheim, middle 1700's, $4000.

e. Faience, .5L, creamware, c.1790, $1000.

f. Faience, .5L, Erfurt, middle 1700's, $1200.

g. Faience, .5L, Thuringen, scholar, c.1790, $1300.

a. Faience, .5L, Thuringen region, c.1780, $1500.

b. Faience, .5L, Thuringen region, late 1700's, $1700.

c. Faience, .5L, Thuringen region, c.1780, $2500.

d. Faience, .5L, Thuringen region, c.1790, $2500.

e. Faience, .5L, Erfurt, c.1740, $1300.

f. Faience, .5L, possibly Ansbach, middle 1700's, $1300.

g. Faience, .5L, Erfurt, c.1800, $1600.

h. Faience, .5L, unknown factory, middle 1700's, $1500.

a. Faience, .5L, Crailsheim, middle 1700's, $4000.

b. Faience, .5L, Crailsheim, c.1760, $2000.

c. Faience, .5L, Bayreuth, late 1700's, $2000.

d. Faience, .5L, Crailsheim, late 1700's, $2000.

e. Faience, .5L, Crailsheim, middle 1700's, $4000.

f. Faience, .5L, Crailsheim, c.1800, $1500.

g. Faience, .5L, Crailsheim, late 1700's, $4000.

a. Faience, .5L, Nurnberg, marked *I...*, crescent moon Madonna, by G.F. Kordenbusch, 1765, $3000.

b. Faience, .5L, Potsdam, marked *P/R,* nobleman, c.1780, $2000.

c. Faience, 1.0L, Thuringen region, middle 1700's, $2000.

d. Faience, .5L, Thuringen region, princess, c.1770, $2000.

e. Faience, .5L, Kunersberg, middle 1700's, $5000.

f. Faience, .5L, Gmunden, late 1700's, $1200.

g. Faience, .5L, Gmunden, late 1700's, $1000.

h. Faience, .5L, Goggingen, early 1700's, $3000.

a. Faience, .5L, Nurnberg, middle 1700's, $3000.

b. Faience, .25L, Nurnberg, late 1700's, $2000.

c. Faience, .15L, Nurnberg, late 1700's, $2000.

d. Faience, .5L, Nurnberg, middle 1700's, $3000.

e. Faience, .5L, Nurnberg, oasis scene, middle 1700's, $4000.

f. Faience, .25L, Nurnberg, Saint, middle 1700's, $2000.

a. Faience, .5L, Berlin, late 1700's, $2000.

b. Faience, .5L, Berlin, early 1700's, $4000.

c. Faience, .5L, Proskau, late 1700's, $3000.

d. Faience, .4L, creamware, c.1800, $800.

e. Faience, .4L, creamware, c.1800, $800.

f. Faience, .5L, creamware, c.1800, $1000.

g. Faience, .5L, creamware, c.1800, $900.

a. Faience, 1.0L, possibly Salzbach or Gmunden, late 1700's, $800.

b. Faience, .5L, Gmunden, c.1800, $600.

c. Faience, 1.0L, Gmunden, late 1700's, $600.

d. Faience, .5L, unknown factory, c.1780, $2000.

Courtesy of The Stroh Brewery Co.

Upper Row:

a. Stoneware, .5L, Raeren, brown saltglazed, applied relief medallion, early 1700's, $1200.

b. Earthenware, .5L, dark brown lead glazed, late 1700's, $800.

c. Enameled glass, .5L, amber glass, flowers, late 1800's, pewter lid, $350.

Lower Row:

d. Stoneware, .5L, Altenburg or Duingen, leadglazed, tan and brown, middle 1700's, $350.

e. Earthenware, 12'' ht, Saxony, iron red lead glaze, early 1700's, $2000.

f. Earthenware, .5L, Wetterau-Hessen, reddish brown glaze, sunburst design, late 1700's, $1500.

Courtesy of The Stroh Brewery Co.

Upper Row:

a. Stoneware, 5½'' ht, Creussen, saltglazed with enameled 6 Apostles and Lamb, late 1600's, $5000.

b. Stoneware, 7'' ht, Creussen, saltglazed with enameled 12 Apostles and coat of arms, late 1600's, $10,000.

c. Stoneware, 6½'' ht, Creussen, saltglazed with enameled 12 Apostles and coat of arms, dtd. 1690, $6000.

Lower Row:

d. Stoneware, 7'' ht, Creussen, saltglazed with enameled 12 Apostles and Lamb, late 1600's, $8000.

e. Stoneware, 9¾'' ht, Annaberg, lead glazed with enameled queen and palmettes, pressed and applied relief, late 1600's, $3500.

f. Stoneware, 11¼'' ht, Annaberg, lead glazed with enameled Virgin and Child, pressed and applied relief, late 1600's, $4000.

Courtesy of The Stroh Brewery Co.

Upper Row:

a. Stoneware, 7¼" ht, Creussen, saltglazed with enameled 12 Apostles and Christ, late 1600's, $10,000

b. Stoneware, 7½" ht, Creussen, saltglazed with enameled Electors and coat of arms, middle 1600's, $8000.

c. Stoneware, 7¼" ht, Creussen, saltglazed with enameled hunt scene, late 1600's, $10,000.

Lower Row:

d. Stoneware, 8½" ht, Creussen, saltglazed with enameled 12 Apostles and Christ, late 1600's, $8000.

e. Stoneware, 9½" ht, Creussen, saltglazed with enameled 12 Apostles and Lamb, late 1600's, $8000.

f. Stoneware, 8½" ht, Creussen, saltglazed with enameled planetary symbols, dtd. 1668, $12,000.

Courtesy of The Stroh Brewery Co.

Upper Row:

a. Stoneware, 5½" ht. Freiberg, enameled, pressed and applied relief, late 1600's, $4000.

b. Stoneware, 1.0L, Westerwald, blue saltglaze, incised and applied relief, c.1770, $1200.

c. Stoneware, 1.0L, Westerwald, blue saltglaze, incised and applied relief, c.1770, $1000.

d. Stoneware, 5¼" ht, Westerwald, blue saltglaze, incised design, middle 1700's, stoneware lid, $2000.

Lower Row:

e. Stoneware, 11½" ht, Siegburg, saltglazed, applied relief panels of knights and coat of arms, late 1500's, pewter mountings added c.1800, $4000.

f. Stoneware, .5L, Muskau, blue saltglaze, tailor's occupational, incised design, early 1700's, $800.

g. Stoneware, 1.0L, Westerwald, blue saltglaze, birds and boars incised, late 1700's, $1100.

h. Stoneware, 1.0L, Westerwald or Raeren, blue saltglaze, rampant lion applied relief medallion, middle 1700's, silver lid, lip ring and base, $2000.

Courtesy of The Stroh Brewery Co.

Upper Row:

a. Faience, .5L, unknown factory, middle 1700's, $1200.

b. Faience, .5L, possibly Florsheim, 1700's, $900.

c. Faience, 1.0L, Hanau, early 1700's, $1200.

Lower Row:

d. Faience, 1.0L, Dorotheenthal, mkd. *RL,* middle 1700's,.$2000.

e. Faience, 1.0L, Bayreuth, middle 1700's, $2500.

f. Faience, 1.0L, unknown factory, late 1700's, $1400.

Courtesy of The Stroh Brewery Co.

Upper Row:

a. Faience, .5L, Schrezheim, mkd. *C,* St. George slaying dragon, late 1700's, $2000.

b. Faience, .5L, Schrezheim, *S. Catharina,* late 1700's, $2400.

c. Faience, .5L, Crailsheim, gardening, middle 1700's, $4000.

Lower Row:

d. Faience, 1.0L, Erfurt, middle 1700's, $2000.

e. Faience, 1.0L, Erfurt, mkd. *A,* hunter and dog chasing game, middle 1700's, $2400.

f. Faience, 1.0L, probably Berlin, mkd. *C,* middle 1700's, $2500.

Courtesy of The Stroh Brewery Co.

Upper Row:

a. Faience, .5L, Schrezheim, baker's occupational, c.1700, $1400.

b. Faience, .5L, Berlin, middle 1700's, $2000.

c. Faience, .5L, possibly Schrezheim, late 1700's, $1400.

Lower Row:

d. Faience, 1.0L, Thuringen region, middle 1700's, $1500.

e. Faience, 1.0L, Thuringen region, middle 1700's, $1500.

f. Faience, 1.0L, Proskau, smoker, late 1700's, $3000.

Courtesy of The Stroh Brewery Co.

Upper Row:

a. Faience, .5L, Hannoversch-Munden, tailor's occupational, late 1700's, $600.

b. Faience, .5L, Erfurt, late 1700's, $1200.

c. Faience, .5L, Potsdam, late 1700's, $1000.

Lower Row:

d. Faience, .5L, Nurnberg, mkd. *K,* middle 1700's, $3000.

e. Faience, 1.0L, Erfurt or Thuringen, late 1700's, $1500.

f. Faience, 1.0L, Abtsbessingen, mkd. *4P,* $1000.

Courtesy of The Stroh Brewery Co.

Upper Row:

a. Faience, .5L, Nurnberg, middle 1700's, $2000.

b. Faience, .5L, Nurnberg, Virgin Mary, c.1740, $2500.

c. Faience, .5L, Erfurt, late 1700's, $1500.

Lower Row:

d. Faience, 1.0L Nurnberg, architectural scenes, middle 1700's, $4000.

e. Faience, .5L, Goggingen, nobleman's crown, c.1750, $1500.

f. Faience, 1.0L, Nurnberg, possibly St. Peter, middle 1700's, $3000.

Courtesy of The Stroh Brewery Co.

Upper Row:

a. Faience, .5L, Schrezheim, flowers, early 1800's, $800.

b. Faience, .5L, possibly Ansbach, 1700's, $1000.

c. Faience, .5L, possibly Schrezheim, late 1700's, $700.

Lower Row:

d. Faience, .5L, Bayreuth, mkd. *BP,* middle 1700's, pewter mountings more recent, $1000.

e. Faience, .5L, Austrian, probably Gmunden, c.1800, $400.

f. Faience, .5L, Dorotheenthal, Oriental scene, mkd. *K,* middle 1700's, $1200.

Courtesy of The Stroh Brewery Co.

Upper Row:

a. Glass, .5L, ruby flashed over clear, late 1800's, inlaid lid, $150.

b. Opaline glass, .5L, German blown glass, enameled floral design, c.1800, pewter base & lid, $800.

c. Blown glass, .5L, ruby flashed over clear, fluted body, late 1800's, $200.

d. Porcelain, .5L, Nymphenburg, enameled garlands, late 1700's, pewter lid & base, $3000.

Lower Row:

e. Biedermeier glass, .5L, enameled farm scene, early 1800's, $1000.

f. Engraved glass, 1.0L, floral designs and well driller's occupational, gold decorations, early early 1700's, pewter lid & base, $2000.

g. Porcelain, 1.0L, late 1800's, inlaid lid, $275.

h. Porcelain, 1.0L, Copenhagen, vertical grooves, floral pattern, middle 1700's, silver lid & base, $1000.

Courtesy of The Stroh Brewery Co.

Upper Row:

a. Wood, 8'' ht, Scandinavian, carved with typical three feet, painted, early 1700's, $2000.

b. Wood, .5L, probably German, carved birch bark, town scene, late 1800's, wood inlaid lid, $250.

c. Lichtenhainer, 6½'' ht, pewter inlaid oak slats, early 1700's, $2200.

d. Lichtenhainer, 6½'' ht, pewter inlaid oak slats, early 1700's, $2200.

Lower Row:

e. Wood, 9¼'' ht, Norwegian, burl, early 1700's, lid, thumblift and feet are carved lions, $1200.

f. Pewter, 12½'' ht, guild flagon, cooper, dtd. 1756 as founding of guild, c.1870, $550.

g. Pewter, 1.0L, German, straight-up tankard or *Walzenkrug,* engraved with wriggle work and Saxony crest and crown, late 1700's, $700.

Courtesy of The Stroh Brewery Co.

Upper Row:

a. Silver, 8'' ht, American, hand hammered, *Gorham Sterling Silver Co.,* late 1800's, $1500.

b. Silver, 7'' ht, probably German, relief, 1800's, $1500.

Lower Row:

c. Pewter, 1.0L, German or Swiss, straight-up tankard, engraved with wriggle work, lid dtd. 1860, early 1800's, $500.

d. Pewter, 12½'' ht, German flagon, brewer's occupational, dtd. 1706, probably c.1870, $400.

e. Pewter & Wood, 9'' ht, Swedish copy of Lichtenhainer style, pewter inlaid oak slats, late 1800's, $400.

Upper Row:

a. Mettlach 1723, .5L, etched, Mettlach, inlaid lid, $1800.

b. Mettlach 2391, .5L, etched, Lohengrin stein, inlaid lid; 1.0L, $2100; .5L, $900.

c. Mettlach 2134, .5L, etched, inlaid lid, $1600; .3L, $800.

d. Mettlach 1786, .5L, etched & glazed, St. Florian stein, pewter lid; 1.0L, $975; .5L, $725.

Lower Row:

e. Mettlach 2917, .5L, etched & relief, Munich, inlaid lid; 1.0L, $3300; .5L, $2300.

f. Mettlach 2718, .5L, etched & glazed, David and Goliath stein, inlaid lid; 1.0L, $3400; .5L, $2300.

g. Mettlach 2894, .5L, etched, Heidelberg Student stein, inlaid lid, $2100.

h. Mettlach 2765, .5L, etched, Knight on White Horse stein, inlaid lid; 1.0L, $3600; .5L, $2600.

Upper Row:

a. Mettlach 2027, .5L, etched, Gambrinus stein, inlaid lid; 1.0L, $1350; .5L, $950.

b. Mettlach 2074, .5L, etched, Bird in the Cage stein, inlaid lid, $1500.

c. Mettlach 2583, .5L, etched, Egyptian stein, inlaid lid; 1.0L, $1900; .5L, $1350.

d. Mettlach 1724, .5L, etched, Fireman stein, inlaid lid, $1650.

Lower Row:

e. Mettlach 2382, 1.0L, Thirsty Knight stein, inlaid lid, $975; .5L, $775.

f. Mettlach 2778, 1.0L, etched, Carnival stein, inlaid lid, $1900; .5L, $1400; .25L, $750.

g. Mettlach 2829, 1.0L, etched & relief, Rodenstein, inlaid lid, $2400; .5L, $1700.

h. Mettlach 2204, 1.0L, etched, Blue Max stein, inlaid lid, $975; .5L, $525.

a. Cut overlaid glass, .5L, English cameo glass, probably Webb, late 1800's, glass inlaid lid, $8000.

Courtesy of Stroh Brewery Co.

c. Ivory, 16'' ht, 1800's, silver lid & base, $8000.

b. Silver, .5L, Russian, marked P. Ovchinnikov, 1893, gilded, enamel, $18,000.

5. Pewter

Some information on pewter is presented in Subsection 2.1 on Pewter Mountings. History and production information can be found there. This Section provides additional detail and pictures of steins that have been made entirely of pewter. Unfortunately it is not possible to treat the popular areas of American and English pewter tankards. There are, however, many fine references in that field, often combined with discussions of other pewter utensils, and these are usually available at libraries and museums.

5.1 History of Pewter Steins

For centuries pewter was the most popular material for food and drink utensils. Pewter does not tarnish, rust, break, and of great importance in the stein business, it does not give a taste to beer, as do copper, silver, and iron. It was not until the 1700's that stoneware took over the prominent position of pewter as the material-of-choice for most steins.

The shaping and decoration of pewter is so easy that there have been many very different techniques that have been used in pewter stein making. In the 1500's pewter steins were either decorated in cast or hammered *relief* or by *engraving* or incising. The handles were S-shaped relatively thin, straps of pewter. Motifs commonly contained allegorical scenes within arcades or bands. At that time the most outstanding relief pewter steins were being produced in Saxony and Nurnberg. The quality of the *engraved* decoration on pewter steins from the 1500's and 1600's usually depended on whether the pewterer did it himself, or sent it to a specialist, such as a copper-plate engraver.

The next innovation in pewter stein design came in the late 1600's with the so-called *Lichtenhainer* steins. They are not really made using *anchored-grooves* as their name suggests, but are simply pewter strips laid into carved oak staves. Since these steins, mainly from Kulmbach or Scandinavian areas, are primarily *wood,* they are pictured and described further in Section 7.

Occasionally pewter steins from the 1600's and 1700's are found gilded, but this is not common. Enameling of pewter steins, however, may have been somewhat more popular, especially in the 1700's and early 1800's when pewter steins were having trouble competing with the more colorful faience, stoneware, and glass steins.

Around 1800, and especially in the following *Biedermeier* period, many pewter steins were produced in the *Walzenkrug* shape, that is cylindrical with the height about twice the width. Tiny zigzag, or *wrigglework,* engraving was quite popular then, in Germany and Switzerland, and the designs were typically "folk art," as was the fashion in that period.

After 1850, in the *Historicism* period, the neo-Renaissance designs abounded in pewter steins: cartouches, masks, fruit bundles, garlands, and other classical devices arranged in panels or covering the stein bodies.

At the beginning of this century, pewter steins made their last important stylistic change when they were often used to capture the sinuous lines of the *art nouveau* period.

It is probably true that the outstanding metalworking artists have always worked with silver or gold, rather than pewter. However, pewter steins from the 1600's by Gunther, Wiegold, Wildt, and other top artists are as eagerly sought as any metal tankards.

Regional differences in shape can help in the identification of steins. *Rorken,* or footed vase shapes, are more commonly from northern Germany. Pear-shaped pewter steins are often from Schlesien, Bohemia, Hungary, or southern Germany. Also from southern Germany, as well as Austria and Switzerland, come the tall, tapered pewter steins.

5.2 Production and Marks

Due to the scarcity and great expense of pewter in early times, designs were often hammered into molds, to save material that would be lost in casting. Lids, handles, and thumblifts were also often made in separate pieces and soldered together. Early molds were usually made from mixtures of calves' hair and clay, except for complicated molds which were often made of stoneware. Metal molds began to be used in the late 1500's, for complicated relief pieces. They slowly gained popularity among craftsmen until, by the 1800's, iron molds had become very popular for the making of pewter steins.

Touchmarks can frequently be used to identify the origin of pewter steins made between 1600 and 1800. Not only are the master pewterer's touchmarks often visible, but the town's touchmark is commonly seen on steins, especially on those from the middle 1700's. Although touchmarks are known to have been used even in the 1500's, few very early steins are marked.

During the 1800's pewterers began using their full name when they stamped steins, often with their city's name as well - thus removing much of the mystery of touchmark identification.

Pewter comes in three basic types, or recipes. The best *genuine (Lautere)* pewter has a light color, is lead-free tin with small additions of copper, brass, or bismuth. *Probezinn,* or *proved* pewter, occasionally called *Reichsprobe, Probe,* or similar names, contains about a ten to one ratio of tin to lead. *Low (geringen)* pewter has a six to one ratio. Beginning in the 1700's a fourth type of pewter was developed when *antimony* was added to pewter alloys to make a very different material, *Britannia metal;* some examples are shown in Section 7.

This *quality* of the pewter is often found stamped on steins. Sometimes *KL* is used for *genuine (klar und lauter = clear and pure); X* is for *Probezinn;* or sometimes just the ratio appears, like *10:1.* In the 1800's it is common to see *Feinzinn,* or *Englishzinn* for lead-free pewter - in the 1700's this was often represented by a touchmark that had an *angel* with a sword and balance or a palm frond and trumpet.

One final mark of importance, *KAYSERZINN,* or *KZ.* This is an antimony-pewter alloy used by the *Kayser* factory from the late 1800's to the early 1900's.

5.3 Collecting Pewter

A great deal of the reproduction of early styles was undertaken in the Historicism period. These were not originally intended as "fakes," but the removal of the manufacturer's name quickly converts them to fakes. Most of these reproductions make extensive and unfaithful use of casting, often in sand or gypsum/plaster molds which are not as sharp as originals. Knowledge of marks, purities, and the study of originals will greatly help the beginning collector in identifying these reproductions.

Pewter can get "sick," either with a black flaking "disease" or a powdering disease. In either case the pewter may slowly be eaten away until there are actually holes in it. Leaving steins wrapped in accidently dampened newspapers (which contains sulfur) will greatly accelerate the damage done by these diseases. *Polishing* (and the darkening, if desired) or transplants are virtually the only ways to arrest these diseases, which can, incidently, be spread to neighboring pieces.

a. Stamped, engraved pewter, 1.0L, Normandy, early 1700's, $750.

b. Engraved pewter, 1.0L, Saxony, dtd. 1829, $500.

c. Relief pewter, .5L, Germania, late 1800's, $225.

d. Relief pewter, 1.0L, early 1800's, copy of early 1600's style, $500.

e. Plain pewter, 1.0L, Saxony, late 1700's, $450.

f. Engraved pewter, 1.5L, late 1700's, $500.

Opposite:

a. Relief pewter, 1.5L, blacksmith, c.1870, $500.

b. Relief pewter, 1.5L, baker, c.1870, $500.

c. Relief pewter, 1.5L, carpenter, c.1870, $500.

a. Engraved pewter, 1.0L, Swedish, made by F. Santesson, early 1900's, $375.

b. Engraved pewter, 1.0L, Saxony, painted decoration, early 1800's, $600.

Opposite:

d. Relief pewter, 1.5L, Ferdinand and his dog, c.1870, $550.

e. Relief pewter, 1.5L, knight, c.1870, $450.

f. Relief pewter, 1.5L, knight, c.1870, $450.

a. Relief pewter, 1.5L, c.1870, $475.

b. Relief pewter, 1.5L, knight, c.1870, $475.

c. Relief pewter, 1.5L, tailor, c.1870, $550.

Opposite:

e. Relief pewter, .5L, Alpine scenes, c.1870, $275.

f. Relief pewter, .5L, mkd. *L. Lichtinger,* Imperial eagle, c.1880, $300.

g. Relief pewter, .5L, mkd. *W. Roeder,* c.1890, $200.

h. Relief pewter, .3L, c.1900, $175.

a. Relief pewter, .5L, stag, c.1900, $200.

b. Relief pewter, .5L, hunter, c.1900, $250.

c. Relief pewter, .5L, Munich scene, c.1900, $225.

d. Relief pewter, .5L, Falstaff and Bardolph, c.1900, $225.

a. Engraved pewter, 1.0L, late 1800's, $175.

b. Relief pewter, .5L, c.1900, $225.

c. Relief pewter, .3L, c.1900, $150.

d. Relief pewter, .5L, c.1900, $175.

e. Relief pewter, 1.5L, Imperial eagle, c.1900, $450.

f. Relief pewter, 2.0L, mkd. *Osiris,* c.1900, $225.

g. Relief pewter, 1.0L, Falstaff scene, c.1900, $350.

h. Engraved pewter, .5L, c.1900, $275.

a. Relief pewter, .25L, *St. Louis* souvenir, dtd. 1904, $150.

b. Relief pewter, .25L, *Anaconda, Montana* souvenir, c.1900, $125.

c. Relief pewter, .25L, *Santa Barbara* souvenir, c.1900, $125.

d. Relief pewter, .25L, c.1900, $100.

e. Relief pewter, .2L, *Winnepeg, Canada* souvenir, c.1900, $75.

f. Relief pewter, .1L, *Chicago* souvenir, c.1900, $100.

g. Relief pewter, 1.0L, mascaroons and cartouches, dtd. 1898, $425.

h. Relief pewter, 1.0L, Bacchus and revellers, late 1800's, $375.

i. Relief pewter, .5L, mascaroons and eagles, late 1800's, $300.

j. Relief pewter, .5L, hunter, c.1900, $250.

a. Relief pewter, .5L, mkd. *Orivit,* king, knight, lady in panels, late 1800's, $550.

b. Relief pewter, .5L, *University of Pennsylvania* souvenir, c.1900, $175.

c. Relief pewter, .5L, *Pfalz* souvenir, c.1900, $200.

d. Relief pewter, .5L, hunter, c.1900, $200.

e. Relief pewter, .5L, woman sharpshooter, c.1900, $250.

f. Relief pewter, 1.5L, courting and dancing, c.1900, $275.

g. Relief pewter, 1.0L, forest scenes, c.1900, $275.

6. Glass

The tremendous variety of ways glass has been used to produce beer steins makes it very difficult to select general comments and representative pictures. Some references listed in Section 15 can be used for more specifics, unfortunately these concentrate on the earliest glass steins, with little available on glass steins made after 1850.

6.1 History of Glass Steins

The variety of ways to use glass is certainly due to the fact that it is a material that has been known and loved for thousands of years and thus it has received the attention of many innovative craftsmen.

Glass steins are known to have been made in the 1530's and 1540's. A couple of examples that exist have large *finials* but no thumblifts. It seems possible that the thumblifts, which became popular shortly thereafter, may have been finials *displaced* to make it easier to open the lid.

So few glass steins exist from the 1500's and 1600's that it is difficult to generalize about their materials, shapes, or decorations. The glass was sometimes greenish to brownish in color, sometimes it was milk glass. Some had applied glass *prunts,* others were enameled, with portraits or heraldic symbols. The enameled steins show the influence of French and Italian Renaissance designs, which is readily explainable because it was the French who had re-introduced the lost art of enameling to the Germans in the 1400's, with the Italian influence coming in the middle 1500's.

Enameling glass just involves the painting of powdered colored glass, flux, and a vehicle onto glass, then heating at a low enough temperature to fuse the design to the glass. So-called *cold* painting, with lacquers or oil paints, is known to have been used on early glass steins. It is not durable, however, and may account for some now-plain glass bodies in rather elaborate old mountings.

From the late 1600's to about 1800 milk glass was a commonly used *porcelain substitute.* Milk glass was made by mixing tin oxide, the same white coloring agent as used in faience, into the raw materials for the glass. The early decorations on milk glass steins, as on many enameled clear items of this period, were similar to those appearing on the faience steins of those times: first the Chinese motifs, then the so-called Indian and German flowers, and finally the genre scenes. Like the faience steins, these motifs turned from Baroque to folk art by about 1800.

Also in the 1700's some spectacular engravings were being cut into clear and colored glass steins, steins that were almost always cylindrically shaped. Common themes were floral, heraldic, hunting, portraits, celebrations, cities, and some of the earlier themes were mythological or religious.

Silver and pewter mountings were about equally in use on glass steins from around 1700. Somewhat later the *pewter* mountings became far more common. By then, silver mountings were apparently reserved only for spectacular glass steins, such as those that were ornately engraved (often diamond-cut) or those of ruby or cranberry glass (made using *gold* as the coloring agent in the glass).

During the Biedermeier period, 1800 to 1850, glass steins began to move from the cylindrical, *Walzenkrug,* shape into a shape tapered slightly toward the top and often also pulled into a partial pedestal near the base. Folk art enameled designs were used, often with wedding scenes or small panels with inscriptions about weddings or remembrances. These were probably the most popular steins, of any kind, of this period.

The next period, Historicism, brought a strong interest in the Renaissance enameled decorations, occasionally on cut colored glass. Glass that was cut or engraved through one or more different colored layers, gained in popularity through the middle 1800's. Subsection 6.2 relates the techniques used to make these steins, often depicting deer, forests, buildings, geometric patterns, or other folk themes. Geometric patterns gained by deep cutting or mold blown techniques were also popular in the middle 1800's.

About 1870 elaborate pewter piercework or lattice overlays began to be constructed right over colored glass steins. Toward 1900 the pewterwork became more elaborate and comprehensive, often including the handle, so that the colored glass *cup* could be separately manufactured and dropped into the pewter "shell."

Enameled decorations on steins continued to be popular in the late 1800's and early 1900's, but the themes changed from neo-Renaissance to those of more *social* significance. Also during this period there developed a strong interest in *clear* glass steins of every reasonable shape; cylindrical, pedestal, pear, vase, conical, spherical, and all combinations. These may have included adding prunts, cutting, engraving, etching, enameling, or adding *rigaree* ribbons.

Such steins have continued to be popular until today, although the hand work has generally disappeared. Occasionally these modern glass steins will carry an enameled design, which has been printed or silkscreened onto a *decal* that was then fired onto the stein. As with stoneware, there are still a few (a very few) craftsmen who are making steins using some of the old glass making techniques.

6.2 Production

Glass is the product of a silicic acid (often from sand) and an alkali (often from soda and ash). It must be brought to a temperature of about 1100°C (2000°F) in order to form a "melt." Great amounts of wood are required if wood is to be used as fuel, which has caused most "glasshouses" to be located in forests. Some coal-fired glass furnaces were used, but these only became common in the 1800's. Some time after 1900 electricity became the most popular energy for glass furnaces.

For the earliest glass steins, a long pipe, called a *punty* or *pontil,* was used to take a blob of glass from the furnace, which was then pressed, spun, drawn, and/or blown into a cylindrical shape. The end was trimmed off, and the handle was formed and pressed into place. When somewhat cooled, the "mug" was broken away from the pipe leaving a *pontil mark* on the bottom. This mark often has its rough edges ground smooth, but is clearly visible on glass steins made preceding about 1870, and on the fewer and fewer hand-made steins since then.

A new *mold blown* technique was developed in about 1840. Glass steins of this type were made by putting a partially blown and shaped blob of glass *into a mold,* then further blowing it until it touched the sides and picked up the pattern of that mold. Steins from three-part molds or dip molds have soft contours, unlike sharper pressed or cut glass, and they will still have pontil marks. These mold blown glass steins can also be identified by hollows and patterns similar to those on the *outside,* that exist, to some extent, on the corresponding places *inside* the steins.

Sand spots, bubbles or "seeds," swirls, or streaks may often be seen in these steins, as in all earlier hand-made glass. The sizes are usually regular, such as quarter, half, and whole liters. The lids are the same as those that are characteristic of most steins made roughly from 1840 to 1880, that is, porcelain inlaid, cut glass inlaid, and heavy steepled pewter occasionally with faceted colored glass "jewels."

In the middle of the 1800's the demand for glass bottles and jars generated *tremendous* economic incentive for the invention of bottle-making machines. The widespread use of coal as an abundant furnace fuel made possible such mass production. By the 1870's *automatic* machinery had replaced the mold blown processes. Nearly always using clear glass, these steins are usually seen with the same types of lids as the mold blown steins. Into the 1900's, the pewter lids became markedly less heavy and less ornate.

Colors are imparted to glass intentionally or unintentionally by *metal oxides.* As mentioned previously, iron oxide in the sand and other raw materials imparts a greenish blue tinge. Metallic impurities in wood ash tend to produce a grayish green tint. Some of the intentional colors come from: cobalt oxide = royal blue; manganese oxide = violet; chromium oxides and nickel oxides = greens; tin oxide = milk or white; gold = cranberry; silver = gray; copper sulfate = turquoise; cadmium oxides = red; and so on. Most of these colors were available in the 1200's, long before stein making started, and were subsequently refined during the Medici's synthetic gem experiments and the improvements of stained glass windows.

Some other techniques are often used to affect the color of glass. If a blob of molten clear glass is touched to a blob of another color, usually red, blue, violet, green, or yellow, it will pick up a thin outer layer of that color. This layer can then be engraved, cut, or etched (with hydrofluoric acid) through to the clear glass. Some beautiful steins have been produced using multiple layers of this *overlaid* glass.

Clear or colored glass can also be *stained* with silver nitrate or some other stains that are fired into the surface layers of the glass. These stains are always in the range from light yellow to orangish yellow - and they can be engraved, cut, or etched through to clear, similar to the techniques used on overlaid glass.

Flashed glass has a thin layer of a clear enamel fired onto its surface, most often this is a ruby color with a slight bluish surface sheen. Flashed glass is easily cut through to clear to provide decorative effects - often scenes of spas, buildings, or deer.

Of these three types of surface colors, the *overlay* is the richest, most even, and most difficult to produce. Compared to the other two techniques, it can easily be identified by its noticeable *thickness* at all places where it has been cut through.

As beautiful as colored glass can be, the quest for a formula for any specific color pales in comparison to the fanatical search for a perfectly *clear* glass. The materials required to make a glass of so-called *superior brilliance* requires that the raw materials have to be surprisingly pure. Even stirring the raw materials for glass with an *iron* tool will be enough to impart to the glass that common greenish blue tinge of iron oxide.

A 1601 woodcut with the following poem:
"The brewermaid is usually seen
With empty barrels rumbling aft.
These empty vessels she'll clean and rinse
Then at the brewery refill with draft."

In the middle 1800's it became common to mask this iron oxide tint with small quantities of manganese oxide -but this ''decolorizer'' becomes unstable in sunlight and changes to light purple. During World War I manganese became a *strategic mineral* and was replaced by the straw-coloring selenium. Since the late 1920's, whenever a reasonably clear glass was desired, without the expense of using a *crystal* recipe, traces of selenium (straw-colored) and cobalt (bluish) have been mixed to yield a glass with a very light gray color. Clear glass steins can often be identified with these periods by looking into the edge of the base, or the lip, for a *concentrated* view of the color of the glass.

6.3 Collecting Glass Steins

The Historicism of the 1800's brought about the reproduction of many Renaissance enameled glass pieces, however, few were steins (mostly beakers and pokals, often with the Imperial Eagle motif). Streaks and seeds in the glass, and great attention to detail in the originals, are the best ways of identifying age. Enameled names of manufacturers who reproduced the steins can be expected to have been polished off.

The most difficult copies to detect are those that use authentic old glass bodies, originally decorated very sparsely or polished clean, and then enameled using old designs. To properly bake such enamel designs onto a stein, however, requires the removal and reattachment of the mountings - which can usually be easily detected.

The same types of problems are encountered in the identification of reproduced engraved glass steins. And the same solutions exist, examining the detail of the engraving, replaced lids, and so on.

Care of glass steins is simple, but important. To protect against damage from heat, they should be kept out of direct sunlight and away from fireplaces, stoves, and furnace vents when these are in use. Especially vulnerable are the very old and very thin-walled steins.

Since there is such a great variety of glass steins, most glass stein collectors tend to specialize in a particular type or types. Many of these types can be recognized by those that are nicely *grouped* together in the following pictures. Again, with such a great variety there are some types of steins that don't come up for sale very often. This makes it difficult for many collectors to accumulate a good ''feel'' for prices, thus this Section has a somewhat more comprehensive selection of pictures.

a. Milk glass, .5L, enameled horse, c.1800, pewter lid & base, $1200.

b. Milk glass, .5L, enameled Holy Child, c.1800, pewter lid & base, $1400.

c. Milk glass, .5L, engraved and enameled design, early 1800's, pewter lid & base, $800.

d. Milk glass, .5L, enameled flower, dtd. 1795, pewter lid & base, $900.

e. Milk glass, .5L, enameled design, early 1800's, pewter lid & base, $800.

f. Milk glass, .5L, enameled design, early 1800's, pewter lid & base, $800.

g. Milk glass, .5L, enameled flowers, c.1800, pewter lid & base, $900.

h. Milk glass, .5L, enameled flowers, c.1800, pewter lid, $600.

a. Engraved glass, 1.0L, dtd. 1771, pewter lid & base, $1000.

b. Engraved glass, 1.0L, late 1700's, pewter lid, $800.

c. Engraved glass, 1.0L, middle 1700's, pewter lid & base, $900.

d. Engraved glass, .5L, knight on horse, c.1800, pewter lid & base, $1000.

e. Engraved glass, .5L, man and woman, c.1800, pewter lid & base, $900.

f. Engraved glass, 1.0L, eagles with butcher emblem, inlaid glass medallion, late 1700's, pewter lid & base, $1800.

a. Engraved glass, 1.0L, *St. Mathias,* late 1700's, pewter lid & base, $1700.

b. Engraved glass, .5L, late 1700's, pewter lid, $900.

Courtesy of Cypress Antiques

c. Swirl glass, 1.0L, clear and white glass, early 1800's, pewter lid, $1300.

d. Enameled glass, 1.0L, late 1700's, pewter lid & base, $2000.

e. Biedermeier glass, 1.0L, cobalt blue glass, gold and white enamel, early 1800's, pewter lid & base, $900.

a. Enameled glass, 1.0L, horse, c.1800, pewter lid & base, $1200.

b. Enameled glass, 1.0L, birds, c.1800, pewter lid & base, $1000.

c. Biedermeier glass, 1.0L, enameled flowers, early 1800's, pewter lid & base, $700.

d. Biedermeier glass, .5L, enameled flowers, middle 1800's, pewter lid, $350.

e. Biedermeier glass, 1.0L, Saxony, enameled flowers, middle 1800's, pewter lid, $500.

f. Biedermeier glass, 1.0L, Saxony, enameled flowers, middle 1800's, pewter lid, $500.

g. Biedermeier glass, 1.0L, Saxony, enameled flowers, middle 1800's, pewter lid, $550.

h. Biedermeier glass, 1.0L, Saxony, enameled flowers, middle 1800's, pewter lid & base, $500.

a. Biedermeier glass, 1.0L, enameled, middle 1800's, pewter lid, $700.

b. Biedermeier milk glass, 1.0L, enameled flowers, early 1800's, pewter lid, $500.

c. Biedermeier glass, 1.0L, cobalt blue glass, gold and white enamel, early 1800's, pewter lid, $700.

d. Biedermeier glass, 1.0L, cobalt blue glass, early 1800's, pewter lid & base, $850.

e. Biedermeier glass, .5L, cobalt blue glass, enameled, early 1800's, pewter lid, $400.

f. Biedermeier glass, 1.0L, orange glass, enameled, early 1800's, pewter lid & base, $900.

g. Enameled glass, .5L, green glass, middle 1800's, pewter lid & base, $450.

h. Enameled glass, .3L, green glass, Hans Sachs, late 1800's, pewter lid & base, $375.

a. Cut overlaid glass, .3L, blue and white on clear, middle 1800's, porcelain inlaid lid, $700.

b. Cut overlaid glass, .5L, blue and white on clear, middle 1800's, glass inlaid lid, $750.

c. Cut overlaid glass, .5L, blue and white on clear, middle 1800's, glass inlaid lid, $750.

d. Cut overlaid glass, .5L, white on green, middle 1800's, porcelain inlaid lid, $650.

e. Cut overlaid glass, .5L, white on clear, middle 1800's, glass inlaid lid, $550.

f. Cut overlaid glass, .5L, pink and white on clear, middle 1800's, silver-plated lid, $600.

g. Cut overlaid glass, .5L, pink and white on clear, middle 1800's, glass inlaid lid, $700.

h. Cut overlaid glass, .5L, pink and white on clear, English cameo glass, probably Webb, late 1800's, glass inlaid lid, $8000.

a. Swirl glass, .5L, blue and white, Venetian style, early 1800's, glass inlaid lid, $1100.

b. Cut overlaid glass, .5L, white on blue, red and gold enamel, middle 1800's, porcelain inlaid lid, $1300.

c. Cut overlaid glass, .5L, white on clear, enameled spa scenes, middle 1800's, glass inlaid lid, $700.

d. Cut overlaid glass, .5L, white on clear, enameled, middle 1800's, glass inlaid lid, $800.

e. Cut overlaid glass, .5L, black and white on clear, late 1800's, pewter lid, $800.

f. Cut overlaid glass, .5L, blue and white on clear, middle 1800's, silver-plated lid, $700.

g. Cut overlaid glass, .5L, blue and white on clear, middle 1800's, glass inlaid lid, $700.

h. Cut overlaid glass, .5L, blue and white on clear, middle 1800's, silver lid, $650.

a. Cut overlaid glass, .5L, pink on clear, middle 1800's, glass inlaid lid, $600.

b. Cut overlaid glass, .5L, white on clear, middle 1800's, glass inlaid lid, $600.

c. Cut overlaid glass, .5L, white on pink, middle 1800's, glass inlaid lid, $650.

d. Cut overlaid glass, .25L, pink and white on clear, middle 1800's, porcelain inlaid lid, $650.

e. Cut glass, .5L, late 1800's, silver lid, $350.

f. Enameled glass, .5L, pink flashed color, dtd. 1867 on lid, glass inlaid lid, $250.

g. Cut overlaid glass, .5L, white on clear, enameled flowers middle 1800's, silver-plated lid, $650.

h. Cut overlaid glass, 1.0L, white and pink on clear, middle 1800's, porcelain inlaid lid, $750.

a. Engraved glass, 1.5L, red flashed over clear, late 1800's, glass inlaid lid, $800.

b. Engraved glass, .5L, yellow stained clear glass, deer, late 1800's, glass inlaid lid, $400.

c. Engraved glass, .5L, ruby flashed over clear, architectural views, late 1800's, glass inlaid lid, $225.

d. Engraved glass, .5L, building, late 1800's, silver-plated lid, $175.

e. Engraved glass, .75L, deer, late 1800's, pewter lid, $900.

f. Engraved glass, .5L, deer, late 1800's, glass inlaid lid, $275.

g. Engraved glass, .5L, deer, late 1800's, glass inlaid lid, $275.

h. Engraved glass, .5L, red flashed over clear, hunter in field, late 1800's, glass inlaid lid, $400.

a. Cut glass, .5L, red flashed over clear, buildings on side panels, late 1800's, glass inlaid lid, $350.

b. Cut overlaid glass, .5L, red over clear, middle 1800's, glass inlaid lid, $700.

c. Engraved and cut glass, .5L, red flashed over clear, deer, late 1800's, glass inlaid lid, $750.

d. Engraved and cut glass, .5L, blue flashed over clear, horses, late 1800's, glass inlaid lid, $900.

Courtesy of Cypress Antiques

e. Engraved glass, .5L, boot shape, stag, late 1800's, glass inlaid lid, $800.

f. Engraved and cut glass, .5L, red flashed over clear, deer, late 1800's, glass inlaid lid, $750.

g. Engraved and cut glass, .5L, blue flashed over clear, horses, late 1800's, glass inlaid lid, $900.

a. Cut overlaid glass, .5L, white on clear, enameled flowers and buildings, middle 1800's, glass inlaid lid, $600.

b. Enameled glass, .5L, green, blue, white and gold enamel, late 1800's, silver-plated lid, $375.

c. Enameled glass, .5L, green glass, blue, red and yellow enamel, c.1900, art nouveau pewter lid, $200.

d. Enameled glass, .5L, amber glass, late 1800's, pewter lid, $350.

e. Engraved glass, .5L, yellow stained clear glass, early 1800's, pewter lid, $375.

f. Cut and engraved glass, .5L, yellow stained clear glass, early 1800's, pewter lid, $375.

g. Cut overlaid glass, .5L, red on clear, middle 1800's, gilded lid, $900.

h. Bohemian glass, .5L, red, middle 1800's, gold on silver mountings & overlay, $900.

a. Amber glass, .5L, blue applied rigaree bands and prunts, late 1800's, pewter lid, $325.

b. Enameled glass, .5L, amber glass, flowers, late 1800's, silver lid, $350.

c. Enameled glass, .5L, amber glass, flowers, late 1800's, glass inlaid lid, $350.

d. Enameled glass, .5L, white enamel, late 1800's, glass inlaid lid, $375.

e. Enameled glass, .5L, flowers, clear rigaree at foot, prunts, late 1800's, pewter lid, $300.

f. Enameled glass, .5L, knight, late 1800's, glass inlaid lid, $350.

g. Enameled glass, .5L, amber glass, prunts on base, late 1800's, pewter lid, $350.

h. Glass, .5L, transfer decoration, prunts, late 1800's, pewter lid, $350.

Courtesy of Cypress Antiques

a. Enameled glass, .5L, hops and wheat stalks, late 1800's, glass inlaid lid, $400.

b. Enameled glass, .5L, hops decor, late 1800's, pewter lid, $350.

c. Enameled glass, .5L, art nouveau water lilies and pads, c.1900, pewter lid, $450.

d. Enameled glass, .5L, enameled flowers, prunts, late 1800's, glass inlaid lid, $400.

e. Enameled glass, .3L, blue glass, boy, frequently called Mary Gregory glass, late 1800's, glass inlaid lid, $225.

f. Enameled glass, .3L, blue glass, girl, late 1800's, glass inlaid lid, $225.

g. Enameled glass, .5L, white enamel, late 1800's, prism glass inlaid lid, $350.

h. Enameled glass, .3L, late 1800's, pewter lid, $275.

a. Enameled glass, 1.5L stein and matching amber glasses, c.1870, pewter base, lid & overlay, $1000.

b. Enameled glass, 2.0L, crest, prunts, late 1800's, glass inlaid lid, $650.

a. Enameled glass, 2.0L, enameled knight, late 1800's, pewter lid, $700.

b. Enameled glass, 3.0L, amber glass, knights, prunts, c.1900, pewter lid, $500.

Opposite:

c. Enameled glass, 2.0L, green glass, flowers, prunts, late 1800's, glass inlaid lid, $650.

d. Enameled glass, 2.0L, green glass, crest, prunts, late 1800's, glass inlaid lid, $475.

e. Enameled glass, 2.0L, amber glass, bird and flowers, late 1800's, pewter lid, $350.

c. Enameled glass, 1.0L, late 1800's, Viking helmet pewter lid, $350.

d. Cut overlaid glass, 1.0L, blue and white on clear, gold and red enamel, middle 1800's, gilded lid, $900.

a. Glass, .5L, late 1800's, pewter lid, base & overlay, $350.

b. Glass, .5L, c.1900, pewter lid, base & overlay, $275.

c. Enameled glass, .5L, Bock and flowers, late 1800's, pewter lid, $300.

d. Enameled glass, 1.0L, musicians, late 1800's, Viking helmet pewter lid, $375.

e. Enameled glass, .5L, amber glass, Munich Child, late 1800's, pewter lid & base, $350.

f. Enameled glass, .125L, amber glass, Munich Child, late 1800's, pewter lid, $150.

g. Enameled glass, .125L, amber glass, Munich Child, late 1800's, pewter lid, $150.

h. Enameled glass, .5L, amber glass, Munich Child, late 1800's, pewter lid & base, $375.

a. Cut glass, .5L, c.1800, pewter lid & base, $550.

b. Cut glass, .5L, late 1800's, pewter lid & base, $250.

c. Cut glass, .5L, late 1800's, pewter lid & base, $250.

d. Glass, .5L, green prunts, late 1800's, green glass lid overlaid with pewter, pewter base, $300.

e. Enameled glass, .5L, amber glass, enameled rifles and target, dtd. 1890, pewter lid, $300.

f. Amber glass, .5L, c.1900, pewter lid and overlaid pewter medallion of farmer with wagon, $400.

g. Cranberry glass, .5L, threaded design, late 1800's, pewter lid and base, $400.

h. Cranberry glass, .5L, inverted thumbprint pattern, late 1800's, pewter lid, $375.

a. Cranberry glass, .5L, late 1800's, pewter lid & base, $450.

b. Cranberry glass, .5L, late 1800's, pewter lid, base & overlay, $425.

c. Amber glass, .5L, late 1800's, pewter lid, base & overlay, $400.

d. Cranberry cut glass, .5L, late 1800's, pewter lid & base, $450.

e. Cranberry glass, .5L, late 1800's, cranberry glass insert in pewter lid, pewter base & overlay, $450.

f. Cranberry glass, .5L, dtd. 1893, pewter lid, base & overlay, $400.

g. Turquoise glass, .5L, c.1900, pewter lid & base, $325.

a. Amber glass, .5L, late 1800's, pewter lid & base, $325.

b. Amber glass, .5L, inverted thumbprint pattern, late 1800's, pewter lid, base & overlay, $400.

c. Amber glass, .5L, prunts, late 1800's, pewter lid & base, $350.

d. Green glass, .5L, late 1800's, green glass insert in pewter lid, pewter base & overlay, $475.

e. Amber glass, .5L, late 1800's, pewter lid, base & overlay, $400.

f. Green glass, 1.0L, dtd. 1894, pewter lid, base & overlay, $550.

g. Green glass, .5L, late 1800's, pewter lid, base & overlay, $400.

a. Cranberry glass, .5L, late 1800's, pewter lid, base & overlay, $450.

b. Cranberry glass, .5L, late 1800's, pewter lid, base & overlay, $475.

c. Cranberry glass, .5L, late 1800's, gilded lid, base & overlay, $600.

d. Enameled glass, .5L, Alpine decoration, late 1800's, pewter lid, $225.

e. Glass, .5L, transfer decoration, late 1800's, pewter lid, $175.

f. Enameled glass, .5L, flowers, c.1900, pewter lid, $175.

g. Enameled glass, .5L, flashed metal alkali coating, flowers, prunts, dtd. 1894, pewter lid, $250.

a. Enameled glass, 1.0L, Bavarian crest, late 1800's, winged helmet pewter lid, $475.

b. Enameled glass, 1.0L, amber glass, Defregger tavern scene, prunts, late 1800's, pewter lid, $450.

c. Green glass, .5L, prunts, late 1800's, pewter lid, $250.

d. Green glass, .3L, late 1800's, pewter lid, base & overlay, $350.

e. Cut glass, 3.0L, late 1800's, pewter lid, $500.

f. Glass, 2.0L, green prunts, late 1800's, pewter lid, $550.

a. Cut and engraved glass, .5L, flowers, late 1800's, silver-plated lid, $200.

b. Glass, .5L, faceted, late 1800's, silver-plated lid with helmet finial, $400.

c. Pressed glass, .5L, etched bust of Hindenburg, c.1900, pewter lid, $275.

d. Cut glass, .5L, dtd. 1848, pewter lid, $225.

e. Pressed glass, .5L, etched Bock, late 1800's, glass inlaid lid, $250.

f. Glass, .5L, lower half threaded, rigaree bands, late 1800's, pewter lid, $200.

g. Cut glass, .5L, late 1800's, pewter lid with Pickelhaube finial, $375.

a. Cut glass, .5L, middle 1800's, porcelain inlaid lid, $150.

b. Pressed glass, .5L, c.1900, porcelain inlaid lid, $75.

c. Pressed glass, .5L, c.1900, pewter lid, $75.

d. Pressed glass, .5L, c.1900, copper and pewter lid, $125.

e. Pressed glass, .5L, c.1900, porcelain inlaid lid, $75.

f. Pressed glass, .5L, c.1900, porcelain inlaid lid, $100.

g. Pressed glass, .5L, c.1900, porcelain inlaid lid, $100.

h. Pressed glass, .5L, c.1900, pewter lid, $75.

a. Enameled glass, 2.0L, amber glass, cavalier, late 1800's, pewter lid, $375.

b. Enameled glass, 2.5L, green glass, *Trumpeter from Sackingen,* late 1800's, pewter lid, $425.

c. Enameled glass, 2.5L, amber glass, flowers, late 1800's, pewter lid, $325.

d. Mold blown glass, .5L, c.1860, pewter lid, $125.

e. Mold blown glass, .5L, c.1860, red glass jewel inlaid lid, $125.

7. Unusual Materials

Included in this Section are steins made from silver, wood, ivory, and miscellaneous materials. Either because of expense or because of their form, none of these materials lended themselves to mass production processes. They were hand worked, often with great detail, and mostly fell into their period of decline at the beginning of the 1800's. Each has an interesting history, but they are now encountered by collectors so infrequently that they do not deserve extensive discussions.

7.1 Silver Steins

Silver is often considered the most valuable material to be regularly used in stein making. Gold was virtually never used because it was too soft to make a serviceable material for utensils.

Early silver steins or silver mountings usually show traces of having been *gilded.* This was apparently not intended as a *deception,* rather it was just a means of avoiding the polishing that was made necessary by the oxidation of exposed silver. Beginning in the 1700's, gilding was no longer commonly used, with silver being appreciated for its own qualities, regardless of the polishing required.

Silver is often *alloyed,* usually with copper, to reduce its cost and increase its strength. The purity of the silver in the earliest days of stein making was stamped according to the number of *sixteenths* representing the fraction of silver, for example 11 or 12. In more recent times this fraction has been changed to *thousandths,* such as 825.

Silver steins of the 1500's and early 1600's were decorated with hand-hammered relief and/or engravings. They were often tall, slim, and tapered toward the top. They were used for beer, cider, and wine, which were most often drunk *warm,* sometimes *hot.* With silver's high conductivity of heat, it was important that thumblifts be made thin and handles hollow (also reducing the cost and weight of silver steins).

Silver tankards were the first steins, in middle 1600's, to consistently use the *Walzenkrug,* or cylindrical shape, about twice as high as wide. These steins were most often just engraved.

Toward the end of the 1600's casting techniques provided deep and elaborate relief. However this type of stein faded quickly, in favor of simpler engraved designs again, which carried right through to the 1800's.

The 1800's began a period of *revivals,* especially of earlier cast pieces. In 1884 a marking rule was passed requiring that a crescent moon, crown, and purity be stamped on all German silver steins. This can be very helpful in identifying some of the later reproductions.

Identifying authentic early silver steins requires some understanding of styles, techniques, and marks, especially goldsmiths' marks, which should be sharp, not smooth as on many reproductions. It also should be noted that reproductions made during the late 1800's, the Historicism era, were not intended as "fakes" and often carried marks clearly identifying their manufacturer and period. When it appears that marks have been polished out, extra scrutiny should be used.

7.2 Wooden Steins

Wood was one of the most popular materials for making beer *beakers* in the Middle Ages. Wood began its downfall in the 1500's, due to the difficulties involved in making a durable hinge for a lid. Occasionally, good examples are seen of all-wooden steins, and when they are from the 1600's the carving is generally very detailed and in high relief.

As mentioned in Section 5, the pewter mounted and pewter inlaid wooden steins were first popular from the late 1600's to the middle 1700's. The *Lichtenhainer* name given to these steins is actually derived from the popular beer brewed in this region around Kulmbach. Natural motifs, such as plants and animals, dominate the inlaid designs on these steins.

Beginning in the early 1800's some very nice all-wooden steins were being produced in Norway and other Scandinavian countries. These are usually found made from birch burl with feet and thumblifts often in the shape of lions. Earlier examples have bodies carved with plant forms; later examples generally have smooth sides.

Two new types of wooden steins are noteworthy from the era around 1900. The St. Louis Silver Co. produced several types of steins made from oak staves and held together with silver-plated overlays and mountings. Also at the time, a number of lathe-produced steins were made, often put together from separate pieces, with bodies carrying woodburnt decorations.

7.3 Other Materials

Horn, amber, stone, coconuts, various metals such as hammered brass, and many other materials have been used to make steins. Of particular note among these are the *ivory* steins, which received the attention of some great craftsmen.

Ivory steins were not really possible until the Dutch East Indies Trade Co. began to bring African ivory to Europe in the 1600's. Steins were carved in Nurnberg and the vicinity, usually in high relief. When the drilling, carving, and filling were finished the scenes were polished with wood ashes and oil.

Checks, or cracks, and discolorations have hurt the appearance of most ivory steins, but the workmanship is still evident. Toward the 1700's the scenes, for the most part, changed from the cherubs and mythological scenes to hunts, battles, and city scenes.

Checks in the ivory are not good indicators of *age,* as they can be produced by soaking in hot water then quickly drying. A yellowish to orangish color may be a sign that a piece was ''torched'' or buried (in dung) to simulate patina. Authentic old ivory steins are, however, often as *white* as originals, due to the bleaching action of light. Very fine workmanship on carvings and on mountings can be another good way to recognize old steins, in fact, of almost any type.

Some of the tools and equipment that were in a metalwork shop of the late 1500's.

a. Ivory, 17'' ht, 1800's, $4500.

a. Ivory, 9½" ht, 1800's, brass lid & base, $3200.

b. Ivory, 9" ht, 1700's, silver lid & base, $2400.

c. Ivory 8½" ht, 1800's, brass lid & base, $2800.

d. Ivory, 11" ht, 1700's, silver lid & base, $4000.

e. Ivory, 10½" ht, 1700's, silver lid & base, $4400.

f. Ivory, 9½" ht, 1800's, $2500.

a. Ivory, 14'' ht, 1800's, $5500.

b. Ivory 14'' ht, 1700's, silver lid & base, $6500.

c. Ivory, 15'' ht, Italian, 1800's, $3000.

d. Ivory, 11'' ht, 1700's, gold on silver lid & base, $6000.

Courtesy of Cypress Antiques

a. Ivory 16'' ht, dtd. 1538, silver lid & base, $15,000.

b. Wood, 1.5L, 1700's, silver lid & base, $4500.

a. Wood, 1.0L, Norwegian, burl, c.1800, $500.

b. Wood, .75L, Norwegian, burl, c.1800, $600.

c. Wood, 1.0L, Irish, painted leaves, early 1800's, $650.

d. Wood, 2.0L, dtd. 1714, $950.

e. Wooden drinking horn, .5L, c.1900, $400.

Courtesy of Cypress Antiques

a. Wood, 1.5L, probably Swedish, 1700's, $1300.

b. Wood, 1.5L, probably Swedish, 1700's, $1600.

c. Wood, 1.5L, Norwegian, c.1900, $750.

d. Wood, 1.5L, Norwegian, c.1900, copy of earlier style, $600.

a. Wood, 1.5L, Norwegian, burl, early 1700's, $950.

b. Wood, 1.5L, Norwegian, burl, early 1700's, $950.

c. Lichtenhainer, .5L, wood & pewter, 1600's, $2500.

Courtesy of Cypress Antiques

d. Wood, .5L, Norwegian, burl, c.1800, $600.

e. Wood, 2.0L, Norwegian, burl, early 1700's, $1200.

f. Wood & pewter, 1.5L, Norwegian, late 1800's, $550.

Courtesy of Cypress Antiques

a. Wood, 1.5L, Norwegian, burl, late 1800's, $700.

b. Wood, 1.0L, Norwegian, burl, middle 1700's, $750.

c. Wood & pewter, 1.0L, German, late 1800's, $450.

d. Wood & pewter, 1.5L, probably northern German, late 1800's, $650.

e. Wood & pewter, .5L, German, late 1800's, $400.

a. Wood, 1.5L, St. Louis Silver Co., c.1900, silver-plated mountings, $275.

b. Wood, 1.0L, St. Louis Silver Co., c.1900, silver-plated mountings, $225.

c. Wood, .5L, St. Louis Silver Co., c.1900, silver-plated mountings, $175.

d. Wood, 2.0L, St. Louis Silver Co., c.1900, silver-plated mountings, $300.

e. Britannia metal, 2.0L, bronze patina, Pan and three maidens, late 1800's, $700.

f. Brass and blown glass, 1.5L, bronze patina, amber glass, Bock finial, late 1800's, $1200.

a. Bronze, 1.5L, middle 1800's, $2500.

b. Britannia metal, 1.5L, late 1800's, bronze patina, $1200.

c. Silver, 1.0L, Russian, marked *Pavel Ovchinnikov, Moscow,* late 1800's, $3500.

a. Silver, .3L, gold dore, Egyptian turquoise and rubies, probably 1700's, $4000.

b. Silver, 1.5L, late 1700's, $4000.

c. Silver, .5L, Austrian, early 1900's, $800.

d. Silver, 1.5L, 1700's, $3500.

e. Silver, 1.5L, 1800's, $2000.

f. Silver, .5L, marked *Charles Nephew & Co., Calcutta,* late 1800's, $600.

a. Silver, .5L, English, late 1800's, $700.

b. Silver, 1.0L, Norwegian, dtd. 1815, $1400.

c. Silver, 1.0L, gold dore lining, late 1800's, $900.

d. Silver, .5L, Nurnberg, late 1700's, $1800.

e. Silver, 2.0L, Norwegian, King Olaf's death in 1387, dtd. 1905, $3000.

a. Silver, 1.0L, English, 1800's, $1600.

b. Silver-plated, .5L, late 1800's, $400.

Courtesy of Cypress Antiques

c. Silver, .5L, Russian, dtd. 1861, $2500.

d. Silver-plated, 1.5L, late 1800's, $600.

Courtesy of Cypress Antiques

e. Serpentine, .4L, early 1700's, silver lid & base, $3500.

f. Horn, .5L, late 1800's, silver lid & base, $700.

a. Enamel, .75L, Austrian, 1800's, $3000.

b. Enamel, 1.0L, Austrian, 1800's, $3500.

c. Enamel, .5L, Austrian, early 1800's, $2800.

Courtesy of Cypress Antiques

d. Enamel, .5L, blue, white and gold, early 1800's, $2500.

8. Porcelain

In the Transition Period, Subsection 1.2 of the first chapter, and in Subsection 4.1, History of Faience, there are some important discussions about the origins of European porcelain steins. This Section will provide additional information on porcelain steins.

There were three basic reasons why Oriental porcelain steins were not important after the discovery of porcelain making in Europe, and price (originally about the same) was not a factor. First, the *kaolin,* or white clay, available in Europe produced a *harder* porcelain than the so-called *softer* Oriental varieties. Second, the cobalt oxide available in Europe was naturally purer, and resulted in sharper, less diffused, blue decorations. And, most importantly, the European artists and decorators knew best how to appeal to European tastes. Thus the Oriental chapter in the history of steins virtually closed in the beginning of the 1700's soon after the successful experiments of Johann Bottger and Walter von Tschirnhaus in 1708 and 1709 in Meissen.

8.1 History of Porcelain Steins

The shape of most porcelain steins is the *Walzenkrug,* a shape that was probably initiated with the silver steins of the 1600's, and a shape which was popularized by the faience and stoneware steins of the 1700's. Unlike those faience and stoneware steins, however, *pewter* mountings are rarely found on early porcelain steins. The expense of the porcelain made *silver,* often gilded, the material of choice of lids, thumblifts, and footrings. Porcelain lids, or inlays, became increasingly common until they were exclusively used in the 1800's. In turn, these lids were finally replaced altogether by steepled pewter lids in the late 1800's.

At first, Bottger was unable to make a *white* porcelain and a few steins were produced in the early *brown* color. These were mostly very plain steins, with occasional examples engraved or decorated with gold. Once the *white* porcelain had been developed a few *relief* steins were made in those earliest days, but these gave way when they could not be made to match the intricate details of the glaze decorations.

Artists who decorated porcelain in the early 1700's were often quite famous in their time. Until about 1730, though, they seemed to follow the customary Oriental motifs, as if they were producing reproductions. Soon after 1730, however, these Oriental designs quickly lost favor to the more fashionable Renaissance and Baroque scenes and decorative devices, including exotic floral motifs.

Toward the end of the 1700's the so-called *German flowers,* painted in a very naturalistic style, became popular. Copies of famous paintings, often executed by *Hausmalers,* the independent, individual decorators, were common themes around 1800.

Also at this time, *transfer-printing,* or the print-under-glaze, techniques, were brought from England. Decorations could thus be cheaply mass produced, and these were often used on porcelain *mugs* of this period. Apparently the expensive silver mountings of the true porcelain *steins* were rarely mixed with the cheap, new, transfer decoration techniques; at least not until the late 1800's.

By the late 1800's transfer printing and pewter lids were commonplace on porcelain steins as a view of the end of this Section's pictures, and the Occupational and Regimental Sections show.

8.2 Production and Collecting

Porcelain recipes are composed of kaolin, feldspar, some quartz, and traces of various other materials, such as whiting. Once prepared, the materials could either be worked on a potter's wheel or, for relief sections or unusual shapes, thinned to a slip and poured into a gypsum or plaster mold. Section 2 describes these processes in more detail. Handles, relief areas, or separately constructed portions of the stein were then ''glued'' together with additional slip.

Once air-dried to a leather-hard consistency the stein bodies received a bisque firing to about 900°C (or about 1600°F). The glazes used to decorate porcelain steins merely use coloring agents or dyes mixed into the porcelain slips. These glazes soaked into the porous surfaces and required a *sure* hand for good decorations. This decoration was completed before the second firing, to about 1400°C (about 2500°F). In a process similar to that described in Subsection 4.2, porcelain bodies could receive a third, *lower* temperature firing, which allowed for the use of a myraid of low-temperature colors of glaze, as well as gold. Here, too, this process was called *muffle-painting* and *muffle-firing.*

Porcelain collectors would be advised to become familiar with the porcelain marks shown at the end of Section 2. Comparing the *consistency* of the *ages* of the mark, the design, and the lid, will provide good protection against the mistaken purchase of reproductions. *Signed* pieces, especially those signed by famous artists, should be suspect, and subject to extra scrutiny. Reproductions are also often crudely executed, and a visit to a museum, or a fine collection, will show the quality that should be expected of various eras. The most common reproductions of porcelain steins have been the porcelain character steins produced after World War II. Examinations of the marks and the cruder decorations, often full color, should remove any doubts about authenticity.

a. Porcelain, 1.0L, mkd. *Meissen,* hand-painted, dtd. 1738 on lid, late 1800's, porcelain lid, $1700.

b. Porcelain, 1.0L, mkd. *Meissen,* hand-painted, late 1800's, porcelain lid, $2000.

c. Porcelain, 1.0L, mkd. *Meissen,* hand-painted, late 1800's, porcelain lid, $2000.

d. Porcelain, 1.0L, mkd. *Meissen,* hand-painted, late 1800's, porcelain lid, $1700.

e. Porcelain, 1.0L, mkd. *Meissen,* hand-painted, late 1800's, porcelain lid, $2400.

f. Porcelain, .75L, mkd. *Meissen,* hand-painted, late 1800's, porcelain lid, $2200.

Courtesy of Cypress Antiques

a. Porcelain, 1.0L, mkd. *Nymphenburg,* hand-painted, dtd. 1756, gilded lid, $8000.

b. Porcelain, 1.0L, mkd. *Meissen,* hand-painted, late 1800's, porcelain lid, $1800.

c. Porcelain, 1.0L, mkd. *Meissen,* hand-painted, late 1800's, porcelain lid, $2000.

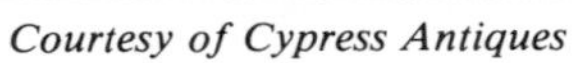

Courtesy of Cypress Antiques

Courtesy of Cypress Antiques

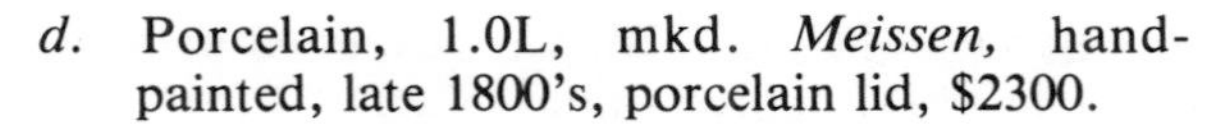

d. Porcelain, 1.0L, mkd. *Meissen,* hand-painted, late 1800's, porcelain lid, $2300.

e. Porcelain, .5L mkd. *Meissen,* hand-painted, late 1800's, porcelain lid, $2000.

f. Porcelain, 1.0L, mkd. *Meissen,* hand-painted, c.1750, porcelain inlaid lid, $6000.

a. Porcelain, 1.0L. mkd. with beehive, hand-painted, c.1900, porcelain lid, $2500.

Top of lid

b. Porcelain, 1.0L, mkd. with beehive, hand-painted, c.1900, porcelain lid, $2500.

c. Porcelain, .05L, mkd. *Dresden,* hand-painted, c.1900, porcelain inlaid lid, $500.

d. Porcelain, .05L, mkd. with beehive, hand-painted, c.1900, porcelain inlaid lid, $500.

a. Porcelain, .5L, mkd. with beehive, hand-painted, c.1900, porcelain inlaid lid, $1300.

b. Porcelain, .5L, mkd. with beehive, hand-painted, *Phaedra,* c.1900, porcelain inlaid lid, $1500.

c. Porcelain, .5L, mkd. with beehive, hand-painted, c.1900, porcelain inlaid lid, $1300.

d. Porcelain, .25L, mkd. with beehive, hand-painted, c.1900, porcelain inlaid lid, $900.

e. Porcelain, .5L, mkd. with beehive and *Germany,* hand-painted, c.1900, porcelain inlaid lid, $1300.

f. Porcelain, .5L, mkd. with beehive, hand-painted, c.1900, porcelain inlaid lid, $1300.

g. Porcelain, .5L, mkd. with beehive, hand-painted, c.1900, porcelain inlaid lid, $1200.

h. Porcelain, .5L, mkd. with beehive, hand-painted, c.1900, porcelain inlaid lid, $1300.

a. Porcelain, .5L, mkd. with beehive, hand-painted, c.1900, brass mountings, $1300.

b. Porcelain, .5L, mkd. with beehive, hand-painted, c.1900, porcelain inlaid lid, $1500.

c. Porcelain, .25L, mkd. with beehive, hand-painted, c.1900, porcelain lid, $850.

d. Porcelain, .5L, mkd. with beehive, hand-painted, c.1900, porcelain inlaid lid, $1500.

e. Porcelain, .5L, mkd. with beehive, hand-painted, *Meine et Amor,* c.1900, porcelain inlaid lid, $1500.

f. Porcelain, .25L, mkd. with beehive, hand-painted, *Reflexion,* c.1900, porcelain inlaid lic, $800.

g. Porcelain, .25L, mkd. with beehive, hand-painted, *Erbluth,* c.1900, porcelain inlaid lid, $800.

a. Porcelain stein, .5L, mkd. *HR 188,* hand-painted, Wilhelm II, c.1900, pewter lid, $450.

b. Porcelain stein, .5L, mkd. *HR 160,* etched, c.1900, pewter lid, $325.

c. Porcelain stein, .5L, mkd. *HR 188/20,* hand-painted, c.1900, pewter lid, $200.

d. Porcelain stein, .3L, mkd. *HR 181/73,* hand-painted, c.1900, pewter lid, $225.

e. Porcelain stein, .5L, mkd. *HR 182,* etched, c.1900, pewter lid, $325.

f. Porcelain stein, 1.5L, mkd. with crown over N, relief and hand-painted, c.1900, porcelain lid, $750.

g. Porcelain stein, .4L, mkd. *T & V France,* hand-painted, c.1900, porcelain inlaid lid, $600.

a. Porcelain, .5L, unmarked, bisque glaze, Wagner, c.1900, porcelain inlaid lid, $500.

b. Porcelain, .5L, unmarked, bisque glaze, Beethoven, c.1900, porcelain inlaid lid, $500.

c. Porcelain, .5L, unmarked, horses, lithophane, c.1900, pewter lid, $100.

d. Porcelain, .5L, unmarked, deer, lithophane, c.1900, pewter lid, $125.

e. Porcelain, .5L, unmarked, *Sangerrunde, d. B.B. Munchen,* lithophane, c.1900, pewter lid, $150.

f. Porcelain, .5L, unmarked, *Radfahrer Club Huglfing,* lithophane, dtd. 1920, pewter lid, $150.

a. Porcelain, .5L, unmarked, *Lindau im Bodensee,* lithophane, c.1900, pewter lid, $100.

b. Porcelain, .5L, unmarked, man and woman, lithophane, c.1900, pewter lid, $125.

c. Porcelain, .5L, unmarked, *Trumpeter from Sackingen,* lithophane, c.1900, pewter lid, $150.

d. Porcelain, .5L, unmarked, hunter, c.1900, pewter lid & base, $175.

e. Porcelain, .5L, unmarked, bowling, lithophane, c.1900, pewter lid, $200.

f. Porcelain, .5L, unmarked, Lohengrin, lithophane, c.1900, pewter lid, $200.

g. Porcelain, 1.0L, unmarked, Lohengrin, lithophane, c.1900, pewter lid, $225.

h. Porcelain, 1.0L, unmarked, people talking, lithophane, c.1900, pewter lid, $200.

a. Porcelain, .5L, unmarked, photo, lithophane, c.1900, pewter lid, $100.

b. Porcelain, .5L, unmarked, flowers, lithophane, c.1900, pewter lid, $100.

c. Porcelain, .5L, unmarked, flowers, lithophane, c.1900, pewter lid, $100.

d. Porcelain, .5L, unmarked, flowers, lithophane, c.1900, pewter lid, $100.

e. Porcelain, .5L, unmarked, hunters and game warden, lithophane, c.1900, pewter lid, $200.

f. Porcelain, .5L, unmarked, secret society, lithophane, c.1900, pewter lid, $150.

g. Porcelain, .5L, unmarked, *Gruss aus Landshut,* lithophane, c.1900, pewter lid, $125.

h. Porcelain, 1.0L, unmarked, zither, lithophane, c.1900, pewter lid, $175.

a. Porcelain, 1.0L, mkd. with crown over N, Capo di Monte, relief, white, late 1700's, porcelain lid, $1800.

b. Porcelain, 1.0L, unmarked, Capo di Monte, relief, late 1800's, porcelain lid, $500.

c. Porcelain, .5L, mkd. with crown over N, Capo di Monte, relief, middle 1700's, porcelain lid, $1600.

9. Mettlach

Ever since they were first produced in about 1850, Mettlach steins have been cherished as very high quality art objects. *The Mettlach Book,* with information, pictures, and prices similar to this book's, has been devoted entirely to Mettlach ware. Most of that book is relevant to the interests of stein collectors. A little of that information is repeated here; those with a greater interest should seek out that reference.

9.1 Mettlach History

Mettlach, from the Latin word for *mid-lakes,* is a small village on the Saar River in what is now the far western part of West Germany, near both Luxembourg and France. Although the ceramic products made here were produced by the Villeroy and Boch Company, V&B, they have commonly been called *Mettlach* wares. Apparently this was done partly to avoid confusion with the very different products made at the eight V&B factories in other cities, and partly because the name Mettlach dominates the important incised *old tower* or *castle* trademark used by the Mettlach factory.

Pierre-Joseph Boch, the founder of the family pottery business, had a son Jean Francis Boch who studied chemistry and mineralogy at the Ecole des Sciences in Paris. After Jean Francis completed his studies he began searching for a place to begin a pottery so he could make use of his education. Utilizing the fortunes of his family and of his wife, Rosalie Buschmann, in 1809 he purchased for their Boch-Buschmann firm the old Benedictine Abbey of Mettlach, including its expansive central buildings and its famous old tower.

The government had imposed a condition on the sale of the buildings that the abundant hard coal resources, and not the scarce wood, must be used to fire the kilns. This presented a tremendous obstable because it required the invention of a coal-burning kiln, which was only accomplished in 1816, but did result in a far superior and more uniform firing.

Mettlach innovations did not come solely through necessity. Water power was harnessed for turning the potters' wheels and for the clay preparation machinery. These novel labor-saving advances helped the enterprise cope with the skyrocketing wage demands of the new middle class that followed the French Revolution. Other advances came when the copper plate engraving and transfer printing techniques from Staffordshire England were brought to Mettlach in 1820, and excellent common wares were produced that appealed to the newly monied middle class. Art studios, archives, museums, art schools, and famous artists were all brought to Mettlach in an effort to further promote the artistic accomplishments of the factory.

With the business then in the hands of Jean Francis' son Eugene, in 1836 a merger with Nicholas Villeroy's factory was undertaken in order to eliminate the only significant competition that had arisen in the region. This created the Villeroy and Boch Company. Soon after this there was a loosening of the hold of the Empire and Biedermeier styles that demanded only mundane wares, and Mettlach found a market for the decorative relief beakers and steins, in the style of Historicism, which they then produced in great numbers.

The golden age of Mettlach lasted approximately from 1880 to 1910, during which, using guarded secret techniques, the etched, glazed, and cameo wares were at the pinnacle of their productions. New design lines and an explosion of color were then brought into the production of the Mettlach items. An extensive display at the 1885 Antwerp World's Fair propelled Mettlach into the forefront of the ceramics field, with reviewers using descriptions such as *Vollkommenes* = perfection, and *geradezu unerreicht* = frankly unrivalled. Production quantities continued to grow until at its height the Mettlach plant employed about 1250 people.

About 1909, and certainly by the time of the First World War, business seems to have slacked off considerably. Researchers of this subject tend to blame unfavorable economic circumstances and a lack of skilled labor. In 1921 a great fire destroyed molds, production records, and formulas for the production processes and materials, including the 30 colored clay slips, 150 under-glaze colors, and 176 colored hard glazes. From 1925 until the early 1930's some few etched and PUG articles were again being produced at the Mettlach plant. Although the Mettlach factory continued to produce tiles, dishes, plumbing fixtures, and other wares, there was almost a fifty year lapse before they recently revived the stein and plaque manufacturing. Although some of the most desirable steins and plaques have been reproduced, the processes and materials were obviously different. The quality of these reproduced pieces is admirable but they are so noticeably inferior to the original chromolith items that most collectors would rather have comparably priced antique PUGs.

9.2 Production Techniques

The Villeroy and Boch Company produced steins and other wares that were, almost without exception, both original in design and in production technique. The majority of V&B steins have certain common characteristics. They were made from a very hard impervious stoneware material which was homogeneous and vitrified. A pure white, porcelain-like glaze was applied to all insides, except those marked BAVARIA which are a gray color inside and out. The same general type of stoneware that formed the bodies of the wares was also used in the decorations on the etched, relief, and mosaic items. Mold marks are generally not visible, indicating a very careful cleaning of the seams after the body was formed, or the use of potters' wheels to form or clean the bodies.

The earliest steins produced at Mettlach were bas-relief in style, commonly called *relief.* The earliest decorations usually consisted of green or brown leaves and vines, eventually evolving into figures and other more decorative relief scenes. These earliest relief steins were produced from the 1840's through the early 1880's, when diversification into a variety of other production methods took place.

The design on the relief wares seems to have been produced in two ways. Rarely it appears that the relief has been applied by hand; the common method was apparently to form the design in a full-bodied mold. After an opaque tan relief material was set into the mold, a colored background stoneware-slip was painted into the mold, usually of a light blue, green, brown, grey, or coral red color.

Cameo and relief ware are often confused with each other. Their production processes seem to be quite similar, except that (1) the cameos do not protrude as far from the body as the reliefs, thus calling for closer tolerances, and (2) the material used in the cameo reliefwork is a more translucent, porcelain-like material that allows for shadings of background colors to show through the thinnest portions of the relief. The resultant product is similar to the gemstone and shell cameos, from which they get their name.

The simplest steins to produce were the *print under glaze,* or PUG steins. After blank body was formed, fired, and glazed, a decal-type, or transfer printed, scene was applied and the body was covered with an additional coat of transparent glaze, and refired. Actually the process could best be described as print between glazes. After the final firing the transfer scene had become an integral part of the product.

The decorations on the Mettlach *faience, Delft,* and *Rookwood* steins were primarily accomplished, with a few possible exceptions, via hand painting.

When the name *Mettlach* is recognized, it is mostly associated with the *etched* or *chromolith* steins. With no tangible evidence other than *autopsies* of broken pieces, there have been a number of theories advanced to explain the process for making the chromolith products.

There are some elements that are common to many of the chromolith theories. The design is generally recognized to be a separate section which was applied and fused to the body with pressure and great heat. The hard white glaze on the interior was applied separately and vitrified during one of the firings. While it would appear that the design materials were wrapped around the body, there are some knowledgeable researchers who feel that the body could have been poured into the design.

A *reverse painting* theory seems to be picking up more support lately, and it claims the following. A flat or curved tray was developed which had the etched lines in reverse, that is protruding, from its surface. Colored clay slips were hand painted onto this, perhaps plaster or metal, tray. Colors for which atomizer sprayed shadings were required, were sprayed after all other colors had been painted, and then painted over with the solid background color. An eighth inch, or so, layer of slip or moist stoneware was then placed on the tray and the decoration was lifted from the design tray and set into the appropriate portion of a body or a body mold. The rest of the body had already, or was then, poured or hand worked into its mold, which was then cleaned on a potter's wheel.

In virtually all theories it is believed that the handle was applied separately on most of the steins. Bases were sometimes also applied, but the frieze bands are generally felt to be integral to the body of steins. After the decoration had been fired it is usually believed that the black lines, that form the distinctive outlining in the decoration, were produced by rubbing a black glaze into the incised lines.

The so-called *art nouveau* wares are *etched* with the bold sinuous designs that became so popular at the beginning of the 20th Century. The designs are often dominated by either a blue and tan or a rust and green color scheme. The *mosaic* wares generally followed the relief era and preceded the etched era. Although some mosaic pieces contain etched sections, for the most part they were totally decorated with colored glazes on surfaces that are actually quite complex compared to the usual etched pieces. The *glazed* wares are similar to mosaics but have no protrusions from the surface. The relative undesirability of many of the mosaic and glazed pieces is due more to the simple, repetitive, floral and geometric design than to a disenchantment with the results of the techniques themselves.

Estimations of the number of steins originally produced are fraught with uncertainties. A *tremendous* number of steins were destroyed over the years, particularly during the wars. There are any number of soliders who have recalled machine-gunning hundreds of shelves full of steins throughout Germany — apparently this had become an important cathartic form of cultural vandalism for the invading forces. This destruction has made the U.S. inventory an importatnt fraction of the current world supply. Based partly upon the extrapolation back from recent observations, and partly from the use of cost and wage figures, it seems improbable that the *average* production of Mettlach wares could have exceeded 2000 examples. The *most common* items, however, definitely had more than 2000 produced, perhaps 10,000 or more. In the case of the *extremely rare* steins it seems unlikely that more than 100 were ever produced.

9.3 Marks

Many of the trademarks used by Villeroy & Boch, Mettlach are shown at the end of Section 2. Fortunately, throughout the important Mettlach period from about 1880 to 1910 the factory marked their products consistently and profusely. Of course some of these marks are of little importance to collectors because they were intended for the identification of individual craftsmen and for quality control purposes. However, some of the marks *are* interesting to collectors and these are the ones described here.

A most important mark is the one that shows the *form* number, sometimes called the *mold* or *stock* number; it is the large Arabic number impressed into the base or back of Mettlach wares. This is generally a three- or four-digit number and is usually located below the trademark. Even when the trademark is not present the distinctive crisp style of the form number can be used, together with an examination of quality, to identify Mettlach items.

A *decoration* number was used for identifying the design on PUG, Rookwood, and some faience products. This number was stamped on PUGs and Rookwoods, and painted on faiences, usually in black or blue, and generally occurred with *Geschutzt* (patented) or DEC. (abbreviation for *Dekoration?).*

The exact year of production can often be discerned from the marks on an item. All of the known dating systems are described in *The Mettlach Book*. The most important date code is the two-digit incised number that often is located to the right and below the trademark, as can be seen in the Figure. Items made from 1882 to 1887 have an 82 to 87 incised inside a small rectangle. For 1888 and after the rectangle was not used, so for example 88 is 1888, 95 is 1895, 00 is 1900, 05 is 1905, and so on.

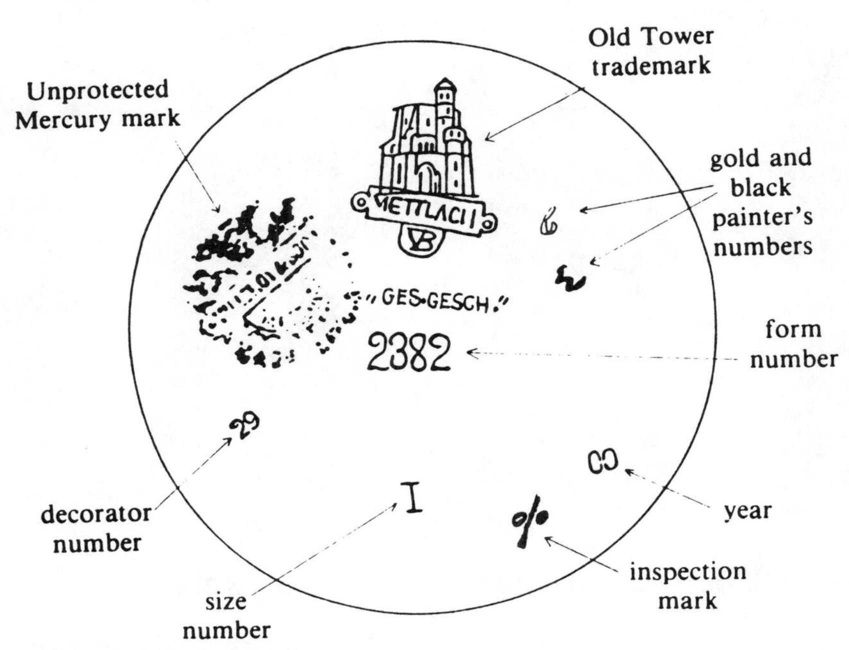

Bottom of a well-marked Mettlach stein: a 1.0 liter 2382 made in 1900, the MADE IN GERMANY barely visible around the bottom of the Mercury mark indicated that this stein was probably exported.

a. Mettlach 171, .5L, relief, inlaid lid, $175; .25L, $150.

b. Mettlach 1184, .25L, relief, inlaid lid, $170.

c. Mettlach 1266, .25L, relief, inlaid lid; .5L, $180; .25L, $140.

d. Mettlach 2211, .3L, relief, inlaid lid, $165.

e. Mettlach 485, 1.0L, relief, inlaid lid, $340; .5L, $275.

f. Mettlach 812, .5L, relief, inlaid lid; 1.0L, $340; .5L, $275.

g. Mettlach 2182, .5L, relief, inlaid lid, $275.

h. Mettlach 2278, .5L, relief, inlaid lid, $275.

a. Mettlach 1121, .3L, mosaic, inlaid lid, $325.

b. Mettlach 1155, .5L, mosaic, inlaid lid, $325.

c. Mettlach 1224, .6L, mosaic, inlaid lid, $375.

d. Mettlach 1261, .5L, mosaic, inlaid lid, $300.

e. Mettlach 1059, .5L, relief, inlaid lid, $200.

f. Mettlach 1062, .5L, mosaic, inlaid lid, $375.

g. Mettlach 1068, .6L, mosaic, inlaid lid, $350.

h. Mettlach 1105, .5L, relief, inlaid lid, $275.

a. Mettlach 284, .5L, hand-painted, pewter lid, $225.

b. Mettlach 406, .5L, hand-painted, Albrecht Durer, pewter lid, $375.

c. Mettlach 2140, .5L, PUG, Signature stein, inlaid lid, $375.

d. Mettlach 2222, .5L, PUG, Signature stein, inlaid lid, $375.

e. Mettlach 280, .5L, hand-painted, fraternal crest, pewter lid, $275.

f. Mettlach 280, .5L, hand-painted, fraternal crest, pewter lid, $250.

g. Mettlach 280, .5L, hand-painted, Gambrinus, pewter lid, $450.

h. Mettlach 406, .5L, hand-painted, pewter lid, $450.

a. Mettlach 1533, .5L, tapestry, pewter lid; 1.0L, $350; .5L, $300.

b. Mettlach 1641, .5L, tapestry, pewter lid; 1.0L, $350; .5L, $300.

c. Mettlach 1642, .5L, tapestry, pewter lid; 1.0L, $350; .5L, $300.

d. Mettlach 1662, .5L, tapestry, pewter lid; 1.0L, $375; .5L, $325.

e. Mettlach 2018, .5L, character, Pug Dog, stoneware lid, $975.

f. Mettlach 2036, .5L, character, Owl, stoneware lid, $950.

g. Mettlach 2069, .5L, character, Monkey, stoneware lid, $1600.

h. Mettlach 2106, .5L, etched & relief, inlaid lid, $1600.

a. Mettlach 1010(1909), .5L, PUG, pewter lid, $200.

b. Mettlach 1077(1526), .5L, PUG, pewter lid, $170.

c. Mettlach 1098(1526), .5L, PUG, pewter lid, $250.

d. Mettlach 961(2179), .25L, PUG, pewter lid, $170.

e. Mettlach 726(1909), .5L, PUG, pewter lid, $300.

f. Mettlach 732(1909), .5L, PUG, pewter lid, $290.

g. Mettlach 983(1909), .5L, PUG, pewter lid, $290.

h. Mettlach 1143(1909), .5L, PUG, pewter lid, $320.

a. Mettlach 1073(1909), .5L, PUG, pewter lid, $290.

b. Mettlach 1102(1909), .5L, PUG, pewter lid, $300.

c. Mettlach 1109(1909), .5L, PUG, pewter lid, $300.

d. Mettlach 1181(1909), .5L, PUG, pewter lid, $300.

e. Mettlach 626(280), .5L, PUG, pewter lid, $225.

f. Mettlach 1212(1909), .5L, PUG, pewter lid, $290.

g. Mettlach 1055(2271), .5L, PUG, pewter lid, $285.

h. Mettlach 1110(1526), 1.0L, PUG, pewter lid, $340.

a. Mettlach 1675, .5L, etched, Heidelberg, inlaid lid, $550.

b. Mettlach 1742, .5L, etched, Gottingen, inlaid lid, $550.

c. Mettlach 1863, .5L, etched, Stuttgart, inlaid lid, $575.

d. Mettlach 3200, .5L, etched, Heidelberg, inlaid lid, $650.

e. Mettlach 2277, .5L, etched, Nurnberg, inlaid lid, $550.

f. Mettlach 2829, 1.0L, etched & relief, Rodenstein, inlaid lid, $2400; .5L, $1700.

g. Mettlach 2828, .5L, etched & relief, Wartburg, inlaid lid; 1.0L, $2700; .5L, $1850.

h. Mettlach 2024, .5L, etched & glazed, Berlin, inlaid lid, $700.

a. Mettlach 2002, .5L, etched, Munich, inlaid lid; 1.0L, $625; .5L, $450.

b. Mettlach 2917, .5L, etched & relief, Munich, inlaid lid; 1.0L, $3300; .5L, $2300.

c. Mettlach 2585, .5L, etched & relief, Munich, inlaid lid; 1.0L, $1200; .5L, $700.

d. Mettlach 3043, .5L, etched & glazed, Munich, inlaid lid, $1600.

e. Mettlach 2204, .5L, etched, Blue Max stein, inlaid lid, $525.

f. Mettlach 2204, 1.0L, etched, Blue Max stein, inlaid lid, $975.

g. Mettlach 1956, 1.0L, etched, Prussian eagle, overlay bust of Wilhelm I, inlaid lid, $2500.

h. Mettlach 2727, .5L, etched & glazed, Printer occupational stein, inlaid lid, $1650.

a. Mettlach 2382, .5L, etched, Thirsty Knight stein, inlaid lid; 1.0L, $975; .5L, $775.

b. Mettlach 2580, .5L, etched, *Die Kannenburg* stein, inlaid lid; 1.0L, $1400; .5L, $900.

c. Mettlach 2765, .5L, etched, Knight on White Horse stein, inlaid lid; 1.0L, $3600; .5L, $2600.

d. Mettlach 2894, .5L, etched, Heidelberg Student stein, inlaid lid, $2100.

e. Mettlach 2391, 1.0L, etched, Lohengrin stein, inlaid lid, $2100; .5L $900.

f. Mettlach 2394, .5L, etched, Siegfried's youth, inlaid lid, $900.

g. Mettlach 2401, .5L, etched, Tannhauser in the Venusberg, inlaid lid; 1.0L, $1250; .5L, $900.

h. Mettlach 2402, .5L, etched, The courting of Siegfried, inlaid lid, $900.

a. Mettlach 1997, .5L, etched & PUG, George Ehert, inlaid lid, $300.

b. Mettlach 2900, .5L, etched, Argentina Quilmes stein, inlaid lid, $400.

c. Mettlach 1403, .5L, etched, inlaid lid, $500.

d. Mettlach 2959, .5L, etched, inlaid lid; 1.0L, $550; .5L, $450.

e. Mettlach 2238, .5L, etched, 7th Regiment Armory stein, inlaid lid, $1200.

f. Mettlach 2373, .5L, etched, St. Augustine (Florida) stein, inlaid lid, $700.

g. Mettlach 2871, 1.0L, etched, Cornell University stein, inlaid lid, $1100.

h. Mettlach 3135, .5L, etched, American Flag stein, inlaid lid, $1250.

a. Mettlach 1732, .5L, etched, inlaid lid, $925.

b. Mettlach 1934, .5L, etched, inlaid lid, $900.

c. Mettlach 2030, .5L, etched, inlaid lid, $950.

d. Mettlach 2031, .5L, etched, inlaid lid, $950.

e. Mettlach 2097, .5L, etched, inlaid lid, $525.

f. Mettlach 2581, .5L, etched, inlaid lid, $550.

g. Mettlach 2027, .5L, etched, Gambrinus stein, inlaid lid; 1.0L, $1350; .5L, $950.

h. Mettlach 2776, .5L, etched, Keeper of the wine cellar, inlaid lid, $800.

a. Mettlach 1856, .5L, etched & glazed, Postman stein, inlaid lid; 1.0L, $2100; .5L, $1650.

b. Mettlach 2075, .5L, etched & glazed, Telegrapher stein, inlaid lid, $1650.

c. Mettlach 2082, .5L, etched, William Tell stein inlaid lid; 1.0L, $2100; .5L, $1400; .3L, $1400.

d. Mettlach 2083, .5L, etched, Board Hunt stein, inlaid lid; 1.0L, $2100; .5L, $1400; .3L, $1400.

e. Mettlach 1379, .5L, etched, Architect stein, inlaid lid, $700.

f. Mettlach 1724, .5L, etched, Fireman stein, inlaid lid, $1650.

g. Mettlach 1914, .5L, etched, 4F stein, inlaid lid, $700.

h. Mettlach 2049, .5L, etched, Chess stein, inlaid lid, $2000.

a. Mettlach 2044, .5L, etched, inlaid lid, $650.

b. Mettlach 2051, .5L, etched, inlaid lid, $625.

c. Mettlach 2532, .5L, etched, inlaid lid, $550.

d. Mettlach 2520, .5L, etched, inlaid lid; 1.0L, $850; .5L, $675.

e. Mettlach 2528, .5L, etched, inlaid lid, $950.

f. Mettlach 2582, .5L, etched, Jester stein, inlaid lid; 1.0L, $1000; .5L, $800.

g. Mettlach 2716, .5L, etched, inlaid lid; 1.0L, $900; .5L, $650.

h. Mettlach 3220, .5L, etched, inlaid lid, $600.

a. Mettlach 1479, .5L, etched, inlaid lid, $525.

b. Mettlach 2282, .5L, etched, inlaid lid, $575.

c. Mettlach 2090, .5L, etched, Club stein, inlaid lid; 1.0L, $700; .5L, $575; .3L, $475.

d. Mettlach 2091, .5L, etched, St. Florian stein, inlaid lid, $850.

e. Mettlach 1725, .5L, etched, inlaid lid, $550; .25L, $350.

f. Mettlach 2235, .5L, etched, inlaid lid; 1.0L, $900; .5L, $600.

g. Mettlach 2599, 1.0L, etched, inlaid lid, $1100.

h. Mettlach 2768, .5L, etched, inlaid lid, $700.

a. Mettlach 2130, .5L, cameo, Gambrinus, inlaid lid, $700; also a relief version, $275.

b. Mettlach 2479, .5L, cameo, Hildebrand stein, inlaid lid, $900; .25L, $600.

c. Mettlach 2652, .25L, cameo, Rodenstein stein, inlaid lid; .5L, $900; .25L, $550.

d. Mettlach 2627, .5L, cameo, inlaid lid, $900; .3L, $600.

e. Mettlach 811(2140), .5L, PUG, *Grenadier-Regt. Nr.2,* pewter lid, $475.

f. Mettlach 886(2140), .5L, PUG, *Dragoner-Regt. Nr. 19,* pewter lid, $550.

g. Mettlach 801(2140), .5L, PUG, *Garde-Train-Bataillon,* pewter lid, $550.

h. Mettlach 1056(2140), .5L, PUG, *Infanterie-Regt. Nr. 119,* inlaid lid, $500.

a. Mettlach 2231, .5L, etched, inlaid lid, $550.

b. Mettlach 2640, .5L, etched, inlaid lid, $550.

c. Mettlach 2693, .5L, etched, inlaid lid, $675.

d. Mettlach 2780, .5L, etched, inlaid lid; 1.0L, $900; .5L, $675.

e. Mettlach 2833B, .5L, etched, inlaid lid, $450.

f. Mettlach 3000, .5L, etched, pewter lid; 1.0L, $400; .5L, $300.

g. Mettlach 3001, .5L, etched, pewter lid, $300.

h. Mettlach 3250, .5L, etched, inlaid lid, $450.

a. Mettlach 1916, 2.15L, etched, inlaid lid, $1450.

b. Mettlach 2799, 2.1L, etched, inlaid lid, $500.

c. Mettlach 1830, 3.0L etched, inlaid lid, $1600.

d. Mettlach 1734, 2.1L, etched, inlaid lid, $1200; 1.4L, $1200.

a. Mettlach 1469, 6.0L, etched, pewter lid, $1800.

b. Mettlach 2381, 3.0L, etched, no lid, $1800.

c. Mettlach 2383, 4.15L, etched, *Alexander and Diogenes,* inlaid lid, $3400.

Opposite:

e. Mettlach 1577, 4.5L, etched, pewter lid, $2000.

f. Mettlach 1578, 4.5L, etched, pewter lid, $2000.

g. Mettlach 1562, 5.65L, etched, *Trumpeter from Sackingen,* pewter lid, $1600.

a. Mettlach 2835, 2.65L, cameo, inlaid lid, $1450.

b. Mettlach 2107, 2.25L, etched, Gambrinus, inlaid lid, $1350; 1.5L, $1350.

c. Mettlach 2095, 2.5L, etched, inlaid lid, $2500.

a. Mettlach 2455, 6.8L, etched, Lohengrin's Arrival, pewter lid, $5800.

b. Mettlach 2126, 5.5L, etched, Symphonia stein, pewter lid, $4300.

c. Mettlach 2122, 3.8L, etched, Crusader stein, inlaid lid, $3400.

Opposite:

d. Mettlach 1815, 4.0L, mosaic, inlaid lid, $475.

e. Mettlach 1827, 3.0L, mosaic, inlaid lid, $400.

f. Mettlach 3082, 3.0L, hand-painted, fraternal crest, pewter lid, $425.

d. Mettlach 2921, 2.8L, etched, inlaid lid, $900.

a. Mettlach 2428, 2.75L, etched, inlaid lid, $1175.

b. Mettlach 2430, 3.0L, etched, inlaid lid, $1250.

c. Mettlach 1817, 3.1L, etched, pewter lid, $2500.

d. Mettlach 1851, 3.2L, etched, pewter lid, $2800.

a. Mettlach 955(2180), 3.3L, PUG, pewter lid, $675.

b. Mettlach 1075(2384), 2.25L, PUG, pewter lid, $700.

c. Mettlach 1143(2384), 2.25L, PUG, pewter lid, $625.

Opposite:

e. Mettlach 2205, 5.2L, etched, inlaid lid, $2500.

f. Mettlach 2206, 3.0L, etched, inlaid lid, $1200.

g. Mettlach 2784/6129, 2.2L, Rookwood style, pewter lid, $550.

h. Mettlach 2789/6134, .5L, Rookwood style, pewter lid, $400.

d. Mettlach 2284, 3.9L, relief, inlaid lid, $600.

a. Mettlach 5004, .5L, faience, pewter lid, $375.

b. Mettlach 5005, .5L, faience, pewter lid, $450.

c. Mettlach no number (5000 series), .5L, faience, Salzburg, pewter lid, $550.

d. Mettlach 5189, .5L, faience, pewter lid, $375.

e. Mettlach 5015, 1.3L, faience, pewter lid, $900.

f. Mettlach 5019, 1.0L, faience, pewter lid, $950; .5L, $425.

g. Mettlach 5023, 1.0L, faience, pewter lid, $1500.

10. Other Etched Ceramics

It is clear that the success of the Villeroy & Boch, Mettlach, so-called *etched* steins piqued the interest of many of the stein factories. The first Mettlach production steins to use the "inlaid clays" etched technique were made around 1879. They immediately captured the Grand Prizes at the world trade fairs. The Mettlach technique was often advertised as "secret," adding to the public interest in these steins, and thus the interest of other manufacturers.

It is not known which of the competitors was the first to follow Mettlach's lead in the etched steins, but it had certainly occurred by about 1890. In fact, by 1900 there were *etched* steins by Simon Peter Gerz, Marzi & Remy, J.W. Remy, A.J. Thewalt, Merkelbach & Wick, Matthias Girmscheid, and HR.

All of these factories had one thing in common, they produced etched steins in the same way, and it was not the *Mettlach* method. Rather than painting the colored slips *into* molds, these other factories had their decorators paint the colored slips directly onto the *outside* of their molded steins. The results lack the uniformity, clarity, and soft finish of the Mettlach etched steins.

It was obviously *easier* to decorate these steins from the *outside,* but not all of these manufacturers were looking to capture the "low end" of the etched stein market. For example, original price lists of HR etched steins show them at *higher* prices than the Mettlach etched steins. So, some of these manufacturers were obviously appealing to the *special order* market.

Another factory that produced etched steins was *Steinzeugwerke* of Hohr-Grenzhausen. The Steinzeugwerke, or literally Stoneware Works, was actually a *consortium* of several factories that banded together in 1912 and lasted until 1925. The major factories that joined the Steinzeugwerke were Reinhold Hanke, Reinhold Merkelback, Simon Peter Gerz, Walter Mueller, and Marzi & Remy, all of the Hohr-Grenzhausen area.

This consortium had no separate trademark, and the only way they have been identified has been through the examination of a supplementary catalog that shows these steins. This catalog shows that is was possible to purchase these steins plain, blue or brown saltglazed, sparsely painted, or fully painted.

Catalogs have also been found for some of these consortium companies, as well as other stein factories. They show many *etched* steins, and many *character* steins, that have yet to be "found." These provide a good indication of how exciting stein searching can be, as well as an indication of how much damage there was to steins during the two world wars.

The end of Section 2 shows the marks and dates of these *etched* stein factories. Books and articles about individual factories are listed in Section 15, the bibliography.

a. Gerz 1423, .5L, pottery, etched, Parsival Acts 1, 2 and 3, c.1900, inlaid lid, $275.

b. Gerz 1428, .5L, pottery, etched, Siegfried, c.1900, inlaid lid, $275.

c. Gerz 1421, .5L, pottery, etched, *Siegfried,* c.1900, inlaid lid, $275.

d. Gerz 1422, .5L, pottery, etched, *Lohengrin,* c.1900, inlaid lid, $275.

e. Gerz 1216, .5L, pottery, etched, c.1900, pewter lid, $175.

f. Gerz 1265, .5L, pottery, etched, hunter and dogs, c.1900, pewter lid, $175.

g. Gerz 1254, .5L, pottery, etched, c.1900, inlaid lid, $200.

h. Gerz 1210, .5L, pottery, etched, c.1900, inlaid lid, $200.

a. Gerz 1345BI, .4L, pottery, etched, sleigh ride, c.1900, inlaid lid, $225.

b. Gerz 1209, .4L, pottery, etched, c.1900, inlaid lid, $150.

c. Gerz 1219, .5L, pottery, etched, c.1900, pewter lid, $150.

d. Gerz 1214B, .3L, pottery, etched, c.1900, inlaid lid, $150.

e. Gerz 1334, 1.0L, pottery, etched, c.1900, pewter lid, $200.

f. Gerz 1318, 1.0L, pottery, etched, c.1900, inlaid lid, $225.

g. Gerz 1388, 1.0L, pottery, etched, c.1900, inlaid lid, $225.

h. Gerz 1389, 1.0L, pottery, etched, c.1900, inlaid lid, $225.

a. Gerz 1314B, .5L, pottery, etched, c.1900, inlaid lid, $225.

b. Gerz 1210, .5L, pottery, etched, c.1900, inlaid lid, $250.

c. Gerz 1220, .5L, pottery, etched, c.1900, inlaid lid, $175.

d. Gerz 275B, .3L, pottery, etched, c.1900, inlaid lid, $150.

e. Marzi & Remy 1765, .5L, pottery, etched, c.1900, inlaid lid, $300.

f. Marzi & Remy 1764, .5L, pottery, etched, c.1900, inlaid lid, $250.

g. Marzi & Remy 1615, .5L, pottery, etched, c.1900, inlaid lid, $250.

h. Marzi & Remy 1768, .5L, pottery, etched, c.1900, inlaid lid, $275.

a. Marzi & Remy 1635, .5L, pottery, etched, c.1900, inlaid lid, $225.

b. Marzi & Remy 1636, .5L, pottery, etched, c.1900, inlaid lid, $175.

c. Marzi & Remy 1617, .5L, pottery, etched, c.1900, inlaid lid, $200.

d. Marzi & Remy 1619, 1.0L, pottery, etched, c.1900, inlaid lid, $300.

e. Marzi & Remy 1620, 1.0L, pottery, etched, c.1900, inlaid lid, $325.

f. Marzi & Remy 1644, .5L, pottery, etched, hand-painted scene, c.1900, pewter lid, $175.

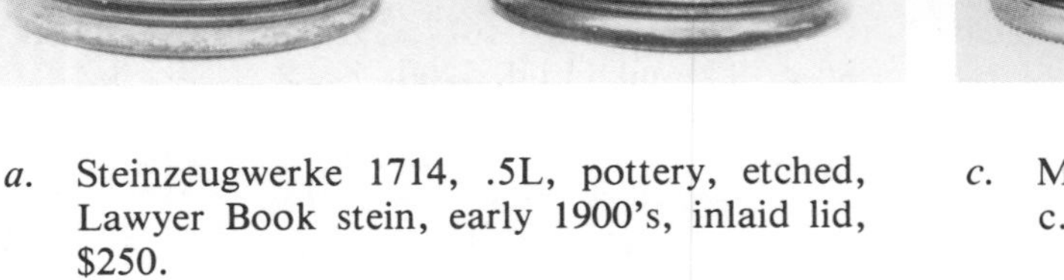

a. Steinzeugwerke 1714, .5L, pottery, etched, Lawyer Book stein, early 1900's, inlaid lid, $250.

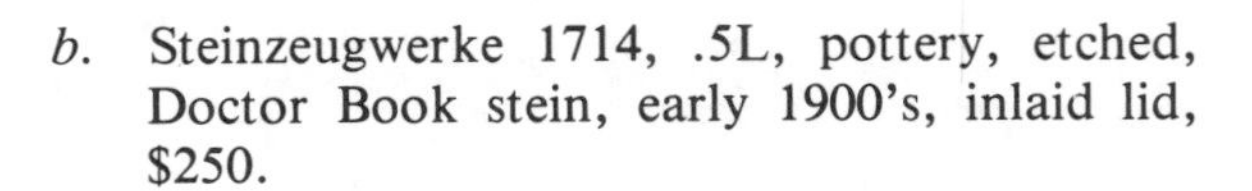

b. Steinzeugwerke 1714, .5L, pottery, etched, Doctor Book stein, early 1900's, inlaid lid, $250.

c. Marzi & Remy 1688, .5L, pottery, etched, c.1900, inlaid lid, $300.

d. Marzi & Remy 1629, 1.0L, pottery, etched, c.1900, inlaid lid, $300.

e. Marzi & Remy 1621, .5L, pottery, etched, c.1900, inlaid lid, $300.

f. Marzi & Remy 1614, .5L, pottery, etched, c.1900, inlaid lid, $275.

g. Marzi & Remy 1622, .5L, pottery, etched, c.1900, inlaid lid, $300.

h. Marzi & Remy 1767, .5L, pottery, etched, c.1900, inlaid lid, $300.

a. Marzi & Remy 972, .5L, pottery, etched, c.1900, inlaid lid, $250.

b. Marzi & Remy 6044, .5L, pottery, etched, *Souvenir of Florida* (St. Augustine), c.1900, inlaid lid, $225.

c. Steinzeugwerke 1757, .5L, pottery, etched, early 1900's, inlaid lid, $175.

d. Steinzeugwerke 1720, .5L, pottery, etched, early 1900's, inlaid lid, $175.

e. Marzi & Remy 1613, .5L, pottery, etched, c.1900, inlaid lid, $275.

f. Marzi & Remy 1618, 1.0L, pottery, etched, c.1900, inlaid lid, $300.

g. Marzi & Remy 1637, .5L, pottery, etched, c.1900, inlaid lid, $300.

h. Pottery 1453, .5L, etched, bicycles, c.1900, inlaid lid, $400.

a. J.W. Remy 962, 2.0L, pottery, etched, c.1900, inlaid lid, $325.

b. J.W. Remy 847, 2.0L, pottery, etched, c.1900, inlaid lid, $300.

c. Pottery, 1.5L, etched, c.1900, inlaid lid, $175.

d. Marzi & Remy 1682, 3.0L, pottery, etched, c.1900, inlaid lid, $450.

e. Marzi & Remy 1518, 1.5L, pottery, etched, c.1900, inlaid lid, $375.

a. A.J. Thewalt 391, 3.0L, pottery, etched, c.1900, pewter lid, $275.

b. Merkelbach & Wick 3002, 2.0L, pottery, etched, c.1900, inlaid lid, $250.

c. Matthias Girmscheid 947, 3.0L, pottery, etched, c. 1900, pewter lid, $250.

d. Marzi & Remy 1681, 3.0L, pottery, etched, c.1900, inlaid lid, $425.

e. Gerz 1235, 2.0L, pottery, etched, c.1900, pewter lid, $325.

f. Matthias Girmscheid, 4.0L, pottery, etched, c.1900, pewter lid, $400.

a. J.W. Remy 1218, .5L, pottery, etched, c.1900, inlaid lid, $175.

b. J.W. Remy 1221, .5L, pottery, etched, c.1900, inlaid lid, $175.

c. Pottery 1220, .5L, etched, mkd. *TP,* c.1900, inlaid lid, $175.

d. J.W. Remy 1340, .5L, pottery, etched, *Heidelberg,* c.1900, inlaid lid, $175.

e. J.W. Remy 829, .5L, pottery, etched, c.1900, inlaid lid, $175.

f. J.W. Remy 884, .5L, pottery, etched, c.1900, inlaid lid, $150.

g. J.W. Remy 1471, .3L, pottery, etched, c.1900, inlaid lid, $125.

a. J.W. Remy 907, .4L, pottery, etched, c.1900, inlaid lid, $150.

b. J.W. Remy 1291, .5L, pottery, etched, c.1900, inlaid lid, $150.

c. J.W. Remy 1294, .5L, pottery, etched, c.1900, inlaid lid, $150.

d. J.W. Remy 1334, .4L, pottery, etched, c.1900, inlaid lid, $150.

e. J.W. Remy 1227, .5L, pottery, etched, c.1900, inlaid lid, $175.

f. Pottery 1227, .5L, etched, mkd. *TP,* same mold as preceding stein, c.1900, inlaid lid, $175.

g. Pottery 1411, 1.0L, etched, mkd. *TP,* c.1900, inlaid lid, $250.

h. J.W. Remy 1409, .5L, pottery, etched, c.1900, inlaid lid, $225.

a. J.W. Remy 883, .4L, pottery, etched, c.1900, inlaid lid, $150.

b. J.W. Remy 1292, .5L, pottery, etched, c.1900, inlaid lid, $150.

c. J.W. Remy 1394, .5L, pottery, etched, c.1900, inlaid lid, $250.

d. J.W. Remy 1393, .5L, pottery, etched, c.1900, inlaid lid, $250.

e. J.W. Remy 954, .5L, pottery, etched, c.1900, inlaid lid, $225.

f. J.W. Remy 1222, 1.0L, pottery, etched, c.1900, inlaid lid, $200.

g. Matthias Girmscheid 843, .5L, pottery, etched, c.1900, pewter lid, $150.

a. A.J. Thewalt 441, .125L, pottery, etched, c.1900, inlaid lid, $100.

b. A.J. Thewalt 474, .5L, pottery, etched, c.1900, inlaid lid, $150.

c. Merkelback & Wick 3002B, 1.0L, pottery, etched, c.1900, pewter lid, $225.

d. Merkelbach & Wick 1175A, .5L, pottery, etched, c.1900, pewter lid, $200.

e. Pottery 1755, .5L, etched, c.1900, inlaid lid, $175.

f. Pottery 1138, .4L, etched, c.1900, inlaid lid, $175.

g. Pottery 334, .5L, etched, c.1900, inlaid lid, $175.

h. Pottery 327, .5L, etched, c.1900, inlaid lid, $175.

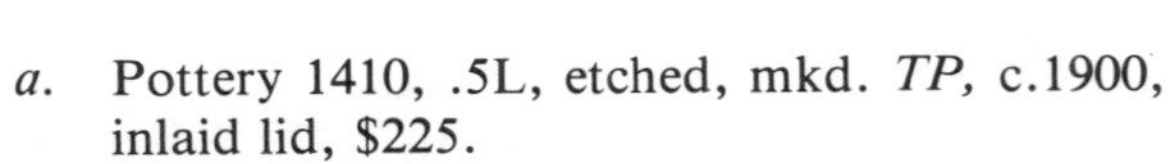
a. Pottery 1410, .5L, etched, mkd. *TP,* c.1900, inlaid lid, $225.

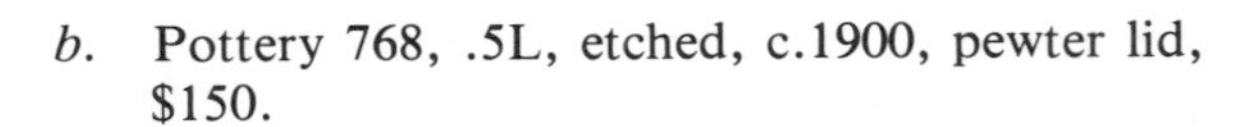
b. Pottery 768, .5L, etched, c.1900, pewter lid, $150.

c. Pottery 1296, 1.0L, etched, mkd. *TP,* c.1900, pewter lid, $175.

d. Pottery 1208, .5L, etched, mkd. *TP,* c.1900, inlaid lid, $175.

e. Pottery 617, .5L, etched, c.1900, pewter lid, $150.

f. Pottery 1551, .5L, etched, c.1900, pewter lid, $150.

g. Pottery 1555, .5L, etched, c.1900, pewter lid, $150.

h. Pottery 1553, .5L, etched, c.1900, pewter lid, $150.

a. Pottery 1512, .5L, etched, duck run over by car, c.1910, inlaid lid, $275.

b. Pottery 1581, .5L, etched, c.1900, inlaid lid, $175.

c. Pottery 1084A, .5L, etched, c.1900, pewter lid, $150.

d. Pottery, .4L, etched, c.1900, pewter lid, $125.

e. Matthias Girmscheid 926, .3L, pottery, etched, c.1900, pottery lid, $125.

f. Matthias Girmscheid 1088, 1.0L, pottery, etched, c.1900, pottery lid, $175.

g. Matthias Girmscheid 1085, .5L, pottery, etched, c.1900, pottery lid, $150.

h. Matthias Girmscheid 938, 1.0L, pottery, etched, c.1900, pewter lid, $150.

a. Pottery 1013, .5L, etched, c.1900, inlaid lid, $125.

b. Pottery 986, .5L, etched, c.1900, pewter lid, $100.

c. Gerz 1217, .5L, pottery, etched, c.1900, inlaid lid, $125.

d. Pottery 849, 1.0L, etched, c.1900, pewter lid, $175.

e. Pottery 1256, .5L, etched, c.1900, inlaid lid, $150.

f. Pottery 741, 1.0L, etched, c.1900, inlaid lid, $200.

g. Pottery 155, .5L, etched, c.1900, pewter lid, $225.

h. Pottery, .5L, etched, c.1900, inlaid lid, $200.

a. Steinzeugwerke 1664, 1.0L, pottery, etched, c.1920, inlaid lid, $200.

b. Steinzeugwerke 1611, 1.5L, pottery, etched, c.1920, inlaid lid, $225.

c. Steinzeugwerke 1851, 1.0L, pottery, etched, c.1920, inlaid lid, $200.

d. Steinzeugwerke 1719, .5L, pottery, etched, c.1920, inlaid lid, $175.

e. Pottery 1612, 2.0L, etched, c.1900, inlaid lid, $400.

f. J.W. Remy 848, 3.0L, pottery, etched, c.1900, inlaid lid, $375.

a. HR 429, .5L, pottery, etched, c.1900, pewter lid, $400.

b. HR 439, .5L, pottery, etched, c.1900, pewter lid, $425.

c. HR 417, .5L, pottery, etched, Lohengrin, c.1900, pewter lid, $425.

d. HR 418, .5L, pottery, etched, Lohengrin, c.1900, pewter lid, $425.

e. HR 441, .5L, pottery, etched, c.1900, pewter lid, $375.

f. HR 444, .5L, pottery, etched, c.1900, inlaid lid, $400.

g. HR 443, .5L, pottery, etched, c.1900, pewter lid, $375.

h. HR 161, .5L, pottery, etched, c.1900, pewter lid, $375.

a. HR 427, .5L, pottery, etched, c.1900, pewter lid, $375.

b. HR 411, .5L, pottery, etched, c.1900, pewter lid, $325.

c. HR 437, .5L, pottery, etched, c.1900, pewter lid, $350.

d. HR 494, .5L, pottery, etched, c.1900, pewter lid, $375.

e. HR 175, .5L, pottery, etched, c.1900, pewter lid, $350.

f. HR 489, .5L, pottery, etched, c.1900, pewter lid, $375.

g. HR 428, .5L, pottery, etched, c.1900, pewter lid, $350.

h. HR 413, .5L, pottery, etched, c.1900, pewter lid, $375.

a. HR 1001, .5L, pottery, etched, c.1900, pewter lid, $475.

b. HR 1002, .5L, pottery, etched, c.1900, pewter lid, $475.

c. HR 1004, .5L, pottery, etched, c.1900, pewter lid, $425.

d. HR 446, .5L, pottery, etched, c.1900, pewter lid, $325.

e. HR 520, .5L, pottery, etched, c.1900, pewter lid, $375.

f. HR 1005, .5L, pottery, etched, c.1900, pewter lid, $400.

g. HR 166, .5L, pottery, etched, c.1900, pewter lid, $500.

h. HR 438, .5L, pottery, etched, c.1900, pewter lid, $500.

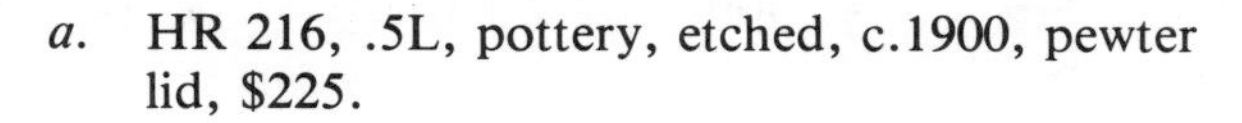

a. HR 216, .5L, pottery, etched, c.1900, pewter lid, $225.

b. HR 431, 1.0L, pottery, etched, c.1900, pewter lid, $400.

c. HR 514, 1.0L, pottery, etched, c.1900, pewter lid, $425.

d. HR 424, .5L, pottery, etched, Heidelberg, c.1900, pewter lid, $350.

e. HR 531, .5L, pottery, etched, *Nurnberg,* c.1900, pewter lid, $350.

f. HR 522, .5L, pottery, etched, c.1900, pewter lid, $375.

g. HR 476, .5L, pottery, etched, c.1900, pewter lid, $325.

a. HR 442, .5L, pottery, etched, c.1900, pewter lid, $450.

b. HR 419, .5L, pottery, etched, c.1900, pewter lid, $375.

c. HR 415, .5L, pottery, etched, c.1900, pewter lid, $400.

d. HR 416, .5L, pottery, etched, c.1900, pewter lid, $375.

e. HR 421, .5L, pottery, etched, c.1900, pewter lid, $400.

f. HR 436, .5L, pottery, etched, c.1900, pewter lid, $400.

g. HR 426, .5L, pottery, etched, c.1900, pewter lid, $400.

h. HR 405, .5L, pottery, etched, c.1900, inlaid lid, $425.

a. HR 510, .5L, pottery, etched, c.1900, inlaid lid, $475.

b. HR 162, .5L, stoneware, etched, c.1900, pewter lid, $175.

c. HR 156, .5L, pottery, etched, c.1900, pewter lid, $225.

d. HR 167, .5L, pottery, etched, c.1900, pewter lid, $175.

e. HR 528, .5L, pottery, etched, c.1900, pewter lid, $425.

f. HR 408, .5L, pottery, etched, c.1900, pewter lid, $375.

g. HR 482, .5L, pottery, etched, c.1900, pewter lid, $225.

a. HR 434, 2.0L, pottery, etched, c.1900, pewter lid, $500.

b. HR 433, 2.0L, pottery, etched, c.1900, pewter lid, $550.

c. HR 435, 2.0L, pottery, etched, c.1900, pewter lid, $550.

11. Other Pottery and Stoneware

This Section covers the post-1850 ceramic steins that are not etched (Section 10) or made by Mettlach (Section 9). Most of this Section's steins are *relief* types, but there are also some steins that have been *transfer decorated* or *hand-painted* onto smooth bodies. There is not as much information available on these steins as one might suspect. The production techniques are known, but the histories of the principal manufacturers is *usually* only superficially known. For the exceptional manufacturer for which there are good records and other information, it is generally because original stein catalogs from that company have been discovered. Often these have been reproduced, and Section 15 lists these excellent resources for those collectors particularly interested in these steins.

11.1 History

The earliest steins to come into the category of this Section are a direct consequence of the tastes of the Historicism, or neo-Renaissance, period. They are a revival of the 1500's Siegburg style: undecorated, gray stoneware with relief scenes. However, *unlike* the Siegburgs: the relief scenes are usually *genre* (realistic everyday themes), they are squat half-liters, and the lids have brightly decorated porcelain inlays. The clay is the white-to-grayish clay, or so-called *Rhenish* clay, found from Hohr-Grenzhausen to Cologne - but the manufacturer(s) of these steins is not known.

It is worth noting that personal steins were (and in some areas still are) kept at the neighborhood tavern. Regular customers thus had a fresh draught of beer served to them almost as soon as they arrived. Oil paintings from the period show these customers' steins stored along a high shelf, *upside-down* with the lid open and *over the edge* of the shelf. This practice makes it clear why so much attention was paid to the decoration of the porcelain inlays, and why they often depict portraits, occupations, or some other important remembrance or preference with which the stein's owner wished to be associated.

In the early 1860's Reinhold Hanke turned his attention to the resurrection of the "lost" art of producing fine, *cobalt glazed,* stoneware steins. Hanke worked hard to make the mass-production methods of his day work as best as possible to copy the Renaissance styles. This meant that *molds* must be used, but Hanke insisted that these molds be of outstanding craftsmanship. The shapes of these steins ranged from small cylindricals to large jugs, just as were common in the 1500's and 1600's. Decorations were also in the Renaissance style, but on toward the 1890's they changed to genre scenes, which continued to be produced into the 1900's by the Hanke firm.

The inside of a brewery in the early 1600's.

In 1869 Peter Dumler began working for Hanke; his specialty was making copies of the Renaissance stoneware designs. In 1883 he left that firm and joined with an in-law to begin a new stoneware manufacturer: Dumler & Breiden, which is still in operation.

Unfortunately, it is not possible here to relate the stories of all of the stein factories. There are records that, at one time, in the Hohr-Grenzhausen region *alone,* there were more than 600 potteries. Most of the pre-World War I stein makers began their businesses in the short time between Hanke's and Dumler's. Some of these include: Simon Peter Gerz in 1862, Merkelbach & Wick in 1872, and Marzi & Remi in 1879. A couple of firms, J.W. Remy (1830) and Reinhold-Merkelbach (1849), were started earlier, but did not produce steins until after Hanke. Other firms were relative latecomers, such as A.J. Thewalt in 1893, Eckhardt & Engler in 1898, and H.R. (possibly Hauber & Reuther). All of these companies, with the probable exception of H.R., were located in Hohr-Grenzhausen or nearby.

The 1880's were apparently tough times for stein makers, at least relief-decorated stein makers. Dumler wrote in his notebooks, 'after running like a dog' through the streets of Cologne trying to sell steins, that he 'didn't want to see another piece of stoneware.' But great numbers of steins were being made, and it wasn't until about 1909 that economic conditions slowed the stein industry to a near stop.

After World War I business in relief, hand-painted, and transfer-decorated steins rebounded, perhaps better than any other stein type. And the same rebound occurred after World War II. In fact, it rebounded so much, that beginning in the 1950's, hand-painted relief steins had begun a dominance of the stein market that they still hold today.

A stein-like covered pitcher on the table in a very early woodcut by W. Map of King Arthur, 1488.

11.2 Production

Pottery *(Steingut)* has a porous structure; stoneware *(Steinzeug)* is solid. Sometimes, with the same variety of colors of clay and glazes used on each, the easiest way to tell them apart is to notice that pottery will be substantially lighter than stoneware.

The recipe for pottery can vary from a rather ordinary clay, to a complex and expensive mixture of clay, quartz, feldspar, kaolin (fine white clay), and whiting (chalk). Pottery is usually fired at a lower temperature than stoneware, but occasionally will be fired at about the same temperature, 1200°C (2100°F).

Because of the porous structure of pottery it is important for it to be *glazed* so that it will be waterproof. It is possible to find some *lead-glazed* pottery steins that were being made up to the 1870's. Thereafter, however, only the *glass-based* glazes were being used, to protect against the possible health impacts of lead.

The making of *stoneware* is described in Section 3, and the common ways of using pottery and stoneware to make steins has been explained in Section 2, so these will not be repeated here; this just leaves the subject of *decorations.*

The relief steins were almost always decorated by hand. The steins with smooth surfaces could have been decorated in several ways. Especially on steins c.1900 and before, hand-painted designs are quite common. Occasionally, especially on these older steins or on regimentals, a metal-plate engraving was used to *print* a decal, which was then transferred to the stein and then touched-up, or colored in, by hand. A few of the decals were *silk-screened,* but the detail on these was not as precise as could be gotten from engraved plates, especially those that were prepared by photographic reductions. Most modern steins are decorated entirely with decals using no hand work. It is not very difficult to determine which decorating technique has been used. Hand-painted areas of steins can be recognized as having a feel that is not as *smooth* as decal, or transfer, decorated areas.

11.3 Collecting

These relief, hand-painted, and transfer-decorated steins are the styles of steins most frequently seen for sale. Their tremendous variety opens up many avenues for collecting strategies. Some *topical* specialties on which some collectors concentrate are steins decorated with: a Munich Child, scenes from Defregger paintings, playing cards, frogs, dwarfs, eagles and military themes, designs by Franz Ringer, occupationals (covered in Section 12), hunting, sports, and many others. Other than specializing on certain types of *decorations,* there are several other ways collectors find a thematic, or *cohesive,* element to pursue, such as through the collection of steins with: music box steins, ornate/heavy pewter lids, specific factories, inlaid lids, very deep relief, pottery figural lids, early gray relief stoneware, and so on.

When put together in a display these fine steins seem to greatly enhance each others' attractiveness. It cannot be for much longer that these old, higher quality steins will often be available for a fraction of the cost of new steins!

a. Pottery 348, .25L, relief, c.1900, pewter lid, $30.

b. Pottery 500, .25L, relief, c.1900, pewter lid, $40.

c. Reinhold Merkelbach 675, .25L, pottery, relief, c.1900, pewter lid, $50.

d. Pottery 82/431, .4L, relief, c.1900, pewter lid, $40.

e. Pottery 814, .4L, relief, c.1900, inlaid lid, $60.

f. Pottery 68, .5L, relief, c.1900, pewter lid, $125.

g. Pottery 67, .5L, relief, c.1900, pewter lid, $100.

h. Dumler & Breiden 547, 1.0L, pottery, relief, c.1900, pewter lid, $125.

i. Dumler & Breiden 682, 1.0L, pottery, relief, c.1900, pewter lid, $90.

a. Reinhold Merkelbach 1193, .5L, pottery, relief, c.1900, pewter lid, $150.

b. Merkelbach & Wick, .5L, pottery, hand-painted, c.1900, pewter lid, $90.

c. Marzi & Remy 57, .5L, pottery, relief, c.1900, pewter lid, $60.

d. Dumler & Breiden 548, .5L, pottery, relief, c.1900, pewter lid, $60.

e. Pottery 1762A, 1.0L, relief, c.1900, inlaid lid, $80.

f. Pottery 212, .5L, relief, c.1900, pewter lid, $65.

g. Pottery 406, 1.0L, relief, c.1900, pewter lid, $60.

h. Dumler & Breiden 550, .5L, pottery relief, c.1900, pewter lid, $80.

a. Steinzeugwerke 1272, .5L, pottery, relief, early 1900's, inlaid lid, $175.

b. Steinzeugwerke 1272, .5L, pottery, relief, early 1900's, pewter lid, $100.

c. Pottery 368, .5L, relief, c.1900, inlaid lid, $150.

d. Gerz 1109, .5L, relief, c.1900, pewter lid, $125.

e. Pottery 1232, .5L, relief, c.1900, pewter lid, $125.

f. Pottery 34, .5L, relief, c.1900, pewter lid, $60.

g. Pottery 874, .5L, relief, c.1900, pewter lid, $70.

h. Merkelbach & Wick, .5L, pottery, relief, c.1900, pewter lid, $60.

a. Rosskopf & Gerz 570, .5L, pottery, relief, hand-painted, c.1900, pewter lid, $80.

b. Dorfner Brothers, 1.0L, pottery, transfer, c.1900, pewter lid, $70.

c. Dorfner Brothers, 1.0L, pottery, transfer, c.1900, pewter lid, $100.

d. Dorfner Brothers, .5L, pottery, transfer, c.1900, pewter lid, $60.

e. Holocaust stein, .5L, pottery, relief, c.1900, inlaid lid, $250.

f. Marzi & Remy 1543, .5L, pottery, relief, c.1900, pewter lid, $90.

g. Merkelbach & Wick, 1.0L, pottery, transfer, c.1900, silver on copper lid, $100.

h. L.B. & C., .5L, stoneware, transfer, c.1900, inlaid lid, $100.

a. Stoneware, 1.0L, relief, c.1900, pewter lid, $80.

b. Reinhold Merkelbach 33, 1.0L, stoneware, relief, c.1900, pewter lid, $80.

c. Stoneware, 1.0L, relief, c.1900, pewter lid, $70.

d. Reinhold Hanke 320, 1.0L, stoneware, relief, c.1900, pewter lid, $90.

e. Reinhold Hanke 563, .5L, pottery, mold 1090, transfer, c.1900, pewter lid, $90.

f. Reinhold Hanke 565, .5L, pottery, mold 1090, transfer, c.1900, pewter lid, $90.

g. Rosskopf & Gerz 780, 1.0L, stoneware, relief, etched, c.1900, pewter lid, $125.

h. Rosskopf & Gerz 647, 1.0L, stoneware, relief, c.1900, pewter lid, $150.

a. Reinhold Merkelbach 349, .5L, stoneware, relief, c.1900, pewter lid, $70.

b. Marzi & Remy 248, .5L, stoneware, relief, c.1900, pewter lid, $70.

c. Gerz 27, .5L, stoneware, relief, c.1900, pewter lid, $100.

d. Reinhold Hanke 1150, .5L, stoneware, relief, *Christoph Columbus,* c.1900, inlaid lid, $200.

e. Marzi & Remy 2323, .5L, stoneware, relief, c.1900, pewter lid, $125.

f. Marzi & Remy 1802, .5L, stoneware, relief, c.1900, pewter lid, $125.

g. Marzi & Remy 1800, .5L, stoneware, relief, c.1900, pewter lid, $125.

h. Marzi & Remy 1848, .4L, stoneware, relief, c.1900, pewter lid, $110.

a. Stoneware 956, .5L, relief, c.1900, pewter lid, $25.

b. Stoneware, .5L, relief, c.1900, pewter lid, $35.

c. Stoneware, .25L, relief, c.1900, pewter lid, $20.

d. Stoneware 879, .5L, relief, c.1900, pewter lid, $25.

e. Merkelbach & Wick, 1.0L, stoneware, hand-painted, c.1900, pewter lid, $125.

f. Stoneware, 1.0L, transfer, Wartburg, c.1900, pewter lid, $125.

g. Merkelbach & Wick 2092, .5L, pottery, relief, college fraternity, c.1900, pewter lid, $90.

h. Marzi & Remy 1825, .5L, stoneware, relief, Gambrinus, c.1900, pewter lid, $125.

a. Stoneware, .5L, relief, c.1850, inlaid porcelain lid, $70.

b. Stoneware, .5L, relief, c.1850, inlaid porcelain lid, $70.

c. Stoneware, .5L, relief, c.1850, inlaid porcelain lid, $70.

d. Stoneware, .5L, relief, c.1850, inlaid porcelain lid, $70.

e. Stoneware 340, 1.5L, relief, c.1900, pewter lid, $100.

f. Gerz 1015C, 1.0L, stoneware, relief, c.1900, inlaid lid, $100.

g. Stoneware, 1.0L, relief, c.1900, pewter lid, $60.

h. Gerz 660B, .5L, stoneware, relief, c.1900, pewter lid, $100.

a. Rosskopf & Gerz, .5L, stoneware, transfer, *Nurnberg,* c.1900, pewter lid, $70.

b. Stoneware 1828, .5L, transfer, *Liedertafel Dachau,* c.1900, pewter lid, $60.

c. A.J. Thewalt 1483, .5L, stoneware, transfer design by Franz Ringer, c.1900, pewter lid, $80.

d. Stoneware, .5L, transfer design by Franz Ringer, *XI Deutsches Turnfest 1908, Frankfurt A.M.,* pewter lid, $100.

e. Merkelbach & Wick, 1.0L, stoneware, transfer design by Franz Ringer, c.1900, pewter lid, $90.

f. Stoneware, 1.0L, transfer, c.1900, pewter lid, $100.

g. Stoneware, 1.0L, transfer, *Redenfelden,* dtd. 1921, pewter lid, $100.

h. Stoneware, 1.0L, transfer, c.1900, pewter lid, $80.

a. Reinhold Merkelbach 5153, .5L, stoneware, transfer design by Franz Ringer, c.1900, pewter lid, $100.

b. Reinhold Merkelbach 5153, .5L, stoneware, transfer design by Franz Ringer, c.1900, pewter lid, $100.

c. Stoneware, .5L, transfer, c.1900, pewter lid, $60.

d. Stoneware 1492, .5L, relief, c.1900, pewter lid, $120.

e. Marzi & Remy 5, 1.0L, stoneware, transfer, c.1900, pewter lid, $90.

f. Merkelbach & Wick, 1.0L, stoneware, transfer, c.1900, pewter lid, $80.

g. Stoneware, 1.0L, transfer, brewery, c.1900, pewter lid, $120.

h. Reinhold Merkelbach 1741, 1.0L, stoneware, hand-painted, c.1900, pewter lid, $80.

a. Steinzeugwerke 1769, .5L, pottery, relief, c.1900, inlaid lid, $150.

b. Pottery, .5L, relief, *Greetings General Gas Light Company, Atlanta, GA., 1912,* pewter lid, $100.

c. Saargemund 2668, 1.0L, stoneware, relief, c.1900, pewter lid, $350.

a. Pottery 653, 2.5L, relief, c.1900, pewter lid, $200.

b. Pottery 1066, 1.5L, relief, c.1900, pottery lid, $200.

c. Pottery 1008, 2.5L, relief, c.1900, pottery lid, $175.

d. Pottery 156, 2.5L, relief, c.1900, pottery lid, $175.

Opposite:

d. Pottery, .5L, relief, Saarguemines, c.1900, pottery lid, $150.

e. Steinzeugwerke 1401, .5L, pottery, relief, early 1900's, pewter lid, $100.

f. Steinzeugwerke 1279, .5L, pottery, relief, composers, early 1900's, inlaid lid, $150.

g. Steinzeugwerke 1278, .5L, pottery, relief, composers, early 1900's, inlaid lid, $150.

a. Pottery 18, .5L, relief, c.1900, pewter lid, $70.

b. Pottery 8 and 66, 1.0L, hand-painted, c.1900, pewter lid, $100.

c. Pottery, .5L, hand-painted, c.1900, pewter lid, $90.

d. Reinhold Hanke 562, .5L, mold 1090, transfer, c.1900, pewter lid, $90.

e. Pottery 156, 2.0L, relief, c.1900, pottery lid, $175.

f. D.R.G.M. 606, 3.0L, relief, c.1900, pewter lid, $250.

g. D.R.G.M. 41, 2.0L, relief, c.1900, pewter lid, $200.

a. Marzi & Remy 377, .5L, pottery, relief, c.1900, pewter lid, $80.

b. Pottery, .5L, relief, c.1900, pewter lid, $50.

c. Pottery, .5L, relief, c.1900, pewter lid, $90.

d. Dumler & Breiden, .5L, pottery, relief, c.1900, pewter lid, $90.

e. Reinhold Hanke, 3.0L, pottery, transfer, c.1900, pewter lid, $150.

f. Gerz 660, 4.0L, pottery, relief, c.1900, pewter lid, $200.

g. Pottery 456, 3.0L, relief, c.1900, pewter lid, $150.

a. HR 459, .5L, pottery, relief, c.1900, pewter lid, $250.

b. HR 458, .5L, pottery, relief, c.1900, pewter lid, $125.

c. HR 454, 1.0L, pottery, relief, c.1900, pewter lid, $175.

d. HR 452, 1.0L, pottery, relief, c.1900, pewter lid, $175.

e. HR 451, .5L, pottery, relief, c.1900, pewter lid, $150.

f. HR 455, .5L, pottery, relief, c.1900, pewter lid, $150.

g. HR 457, .5L, pottery, relief, full color, c.1900, pewter lid, $175.

h. HR 453, .5L, pottery, relief, full color, c.1900, pewter lid, $175.

12. Occupationals

It's understandable that many stein purchasers of previous centuries, when choosing a *theme* for the decoration of their personal stein, decided on their *occupation*. In fact, that was such a common theme that there are those who specialize only in the collection of these so-called *occupational* steins.

There is a *predictable* pattern to the occupations that are most depicted on steins. Merchants, tradesmen, public servants, and professionals are the most common categories, with occupations such as: tailors, butchers, bakers, brewers, shoemakers, blacksmiths, locksmiths, teamsters, machinists, dairy workers, farmers, carpenters, firemen, postmen, and soldiers; and toward the end of the 1800's: doctors and lawyers.

Rarely depicted occupations can perhaps be explained using *three* reasons. 1. There may have been too little money for a stein or too little pride in some occupations, for example, servants, grave diggers, or street crews. 2. *Prudence* may have played a role in making some *occupationals* scarce, such as teachers, clergy, or judges. 3. Finally, some occupations have obviously just been very scarce: goldsmiths, street car operators, or circus performers.

The representation of the occupation is usually obvious, even to the untrained modern observer. The decoration on the body, lid, and/or thumblift usually shows the worker in *action* or in *uniform,* or the *products* or *tools* of his occupation. Some tools that may at first viewing be difficult to recognize are often the "bucket, stirrer, and scoop in a barrel" of the brewer or the "scissors and divider" of the tailor. *Oxheads* and *pretzels* are occasionally used rather casually as symbols of butchers and bakers, respectively. Steins in the form of books or sets of books are often *professional* occupationals and can be identified by examining the *titles* of the books.

When a famous craftsman is depicted, the stein may easily be missed as being an occupational. The most common examples are the poet Hans Sachs, a *shoemaker,* and the Hapsburg double-headed eagle, which was the symbol of the first *printer,* Johann Gutenberg.

Occupational steins can be found from all eras and all materials (with the possible exception of ivory), from 1600's incised stoneware to 1800's glass to 1900's porcelain. Occupational stein collectors, however, rarely seek *diversity* of eras and materials, unless it happens to be in their own occupation. The most commonly collected occupationals are those from around 1900 that have steepled pewter lids and porcelain or stoneware bodies, as are shown in the remainder of this Section.

a. Coach driver, .5L, porcelain, lithophane, c.1900, pewter lid, $275.

b. Dairy farmer, .5L, porcelain, lithophane, c.1900, pewter lid, $250.

c. Construction carpenter, .5L, porcelain, lithophane, c.1900, pewter lid, $225.

d. Butcher, .5L, porcelain, lithophane, dtd. 1909, pewter lid, $250.

e. Miner, .5L, porcelain, lithophane, c.1900, pewter lid, $325.

f. Wagon driver (beer barrels), .5L, porcelain, lithophane, c.1900, pewter lid, $275.

g. Construction carpenter, .5L, porcelain, lithophane, c.1900, pewter lid, $250.

h. Farmer, .5L, porcelain, lithophane, c.1900, pewter lid, $225.

a. Butcher, .5L, porcelain, lithophane, c.1900, pewter lid, $250.

b. Farrier (graduate of veterinary college), .5L, porcelain, lithophane, dtd. 1903, prism lid, $375.

c. Miller, .5L, porcelain, lithophane, c.1900, pewter lid, $250.

d. Cheese maker, .5L, porcelain, lithophane, c.1900, pewter lid, $275.

e. Newspaper deliverer, 1.0L, porcelain, lithophane, dtd. 1906, pewter lid, $400.

f. Blacksmith, .5L, porcelain, lithophane, dtd. 1910, pewter lid, $250.

g. Brewmaster, .5L, porcelain, lithophane, c.1900, pewter lid, $250.

h. Cheese maker, .5L, porcelain, lithophane, c.1900, pewter lid, $275.

a. Farmer, .5L, porcelain, lithophane, c.1900, pewter lid, $250.

b. Electrician, .5L, porcelain, lithophane, c.1900, pewter lid, $325.

c. Cooper (barrel maker), .5L, porcelain, lithophane, c.1900, pewter lid, $250.

d. Horse trader, .5L, porcelain, lithophane, c.1900, pewter lid, $300.

e. Postman, 1.0L, stoneware, dtd. 1913, pewter lid, $375.

f. Eisenbahner, 1.0L, stoneware, c.1900, pewter lid, $350.

g. Carpenter, .5L, stoneware, dtd. 1914, pewter lid, $300.

h. Locksmith, .5L, porcelain, lithophane, c.1900, pewter lid, $225.

13. Regimentals

Steins have served as souvenirs of military service ever since the 1600's. Regimental, or perhaps more accurately *Reservist,* steins have had some resurgence of popularity since 1950. These modern era souvenirs very often have no lid, and thus are *mugs,* and have simple decal-transfered decorations that make them less interesting to most collectors. The regimental steins that have generated the most interest, outside of a few scattered between the 1860's and the 1940's, have been the great number of steins made as souvenirs of service in the German Imperial Armies in the period from 1890 to 1918. These are the steins briefly described and pictured in this Section; some excellent reference books exist in this specialty, and they are listed in Section 15.

13.1 History of Regimentals

With an upsurge of nationalism, pride in the success of the Franco-Prussian War, and a young, popular Emperor, Kaiser Wilhelm II, Germany began an expansion of its military system in 1888.

Military service was obligatory for men 17 to 45 years old, the primary exceptions were criminals or others without civil rights. The tour of active duty was three years for cavalry and navy and two years for others, except one year for certain professionals. Upon completion of their active duty these men became *reservists.* It is the *reservists,* and not the professionals, who ordered souvenirs, such as steins, pipes, flasks, beakers, cups, swords, and many other items.

All reservists reported to their units in October and all "graduated" with the same "class" in a September. The cost of regimental steins, deducted automatically from wages, was very high, for example about two or three times the cost of a Mettlach stein. But pride in their "class" and pride in their unit was enormous, and in cases where it has been recorded, *all* the reservists ordered steins.

There were several branches of the Armies: infantry, cavalry, artillery, *Pionier* (engineering), *Jager* (hunter or rifleman), and the military train. There were also technical service units such as railway *(Eisenbahn),* telegraph, aviation, and airship *(Luftschiffer).* Volunteers from all of these units were provided for the colonial troops *(Schutztruppen).* The Navy was separate from the Armies, but had all the same types of souvenirs.

13.2 Production

Regimental steins were usually produced in porcelain, occasionally they were of pottery or stoneware, or, rarely, glass or pewter. A few *character* regimentals exist, skulls, sailors, or soldiers, but most of the steins have *vertical* sides, a built up base, and raised frieze bands above and below the main decorations.

The decorations were hand-painted on early porcelain and pottery regimentals. The other porcelain pieces were primarily *transfer* decorated, that is, the designs were printed or silk screened onto a decal that was put on the body, touched up and augmented, then fired.

These decorations generally depicted typical training scenes, portraits, or, rarely, combat scenes. The glazes on these steins included great varieties of *color* and *brilliance* that were made with formulas that have mostly been lost and cannot be duplicated.

Rosters can be found, usually near the handle, on most steins except the early regimentals. Where rosters are not included on later steins it is speculated that these were ordered on an individual basis, following discharge.

The *pewterwork* on most regimental steins is both elaborate and meaningful. Some of the varieties of lids include: steeples = usually early or small unit; fuses = field or foot artillery; prisms over scenes = usually Southern German; flat relief = usually Bavarian or Saxony; crowns = rarely used on some Bavarian units; helmets = occasional infantry or artillery; busbies = Hussar units; screw-off lids = mostly Southern; and the most common, the finial-type lid = most kinds of units.

The *finials* also are informative: field guns = artillery; locomotives = *Eisenbahn;* machine guns = machine gun companies; tschako = *Jager;* horse and rider = most often are cavalry but could be other types; eagles = mostly Prussian; and seated or standing soldiers which could be for almost any type of unit.

Different types of *thumblifts* tend to be more indicative of the *region* of the unit, but occasionally they represent different *types* of units. Examples include: eagle = Prussian; lion = Bavarian or Hessen; griffin = Baden; wren = Ulm; St. Barbara = artillery; St. Hubertus = *Jager;* and engineering implements = *Pionier.*

Villeroy and Boch of Mettlach produced many regimental steins, for a great number of different units. They all have print-under-glaze, PUG, decoration, usually of several soldiers in a single scene. The lids are flat domes, as were used on most of the Mettlach PUG steins.

13.3 Collecting Regimentals

The collecting strategy of most regimental collectors is to seek the beautiful, the unusual, and the *rare.* Some of the *predictably* rarer regimentals include those: issued before 1890 or during wartime; issued to French, Austrian, Italian, or Hungarian armies; in sizes other than .5L and 1.0L; and, of course, those for small or specialty units. Unfortunately, there is also a great deal of *unpredictable* rarity in regimental steins, such as larger units for which no steins have been "found." An understanding of regimentals thus requires some study of collections and prices - the following picture section will provide a very good start.

Reproductions of regimentals have been manufactured at least since the 1950's. Reproductions have generally been made of porcelain with finial-type lids. They can usually be identified by examining the historical accuracy of the information, decoration, and lid, but this knowledge may be beyond that which has been accumulated by the casual collector. So here are some production clues to the identification of reproductions.

Original regimentals almost never had *tapered* bodies; reproductions frequently do. Originals often were touched up by hand; reproductions usually have perfectly *smooth* decorations. Some reproductions have flimsy *stamped* lids, rather than carefully cast, as have the originals. Reproductions often have an *uncrowned* rampant lion for a thumblift. And finally, lithophanes of nudes, dancing girls, or girls in suggestive poses, definitely are reproductions; originals usually had lithophanes of a soldier and girl, home scenes, nature and outdoor scenes, busts of King Ludwig or Kaiser Wilhelm II, and naval scenes.

The Military Glossary that follows provides the meanings of many of the foreign words and abbreviations used in the following picture captions. For the most part the segments of the caption listed in *italics* have come directly from the stein; only a few obvious errors or important inconsistencies have been changed. Because many of the military names originated with Napolean, the unit names on the steins are a difficult combination of French, German and Germanized-French words. Hopefully this confusion will be outweighed by the convenience of having these unit names listed as they actually appear.

Military Glossary

Abteilung, Abtl., Abt.: detachment
Armierungs: armament
Artillerie: artillery
Backerie: bakery unit
Bataillon, Batl.: battalion
Batterie, Battr., Batt.: artillery battery
Bayr.: Bavarian
Bespannungs: draft horse
Betriebs: railway traffic
Bezirkskommando: district headquarters
Chevaulegers: light horse
Comp.: company
Dragoner: dragoon
Eisenbahn: railway
Eskadron, Eskr., Esk.: squadron
Fahrer: driver
Feld: field
Fusilier: fusilier
Fuss: foot
Garde: guard
Garnisons: garrison
Grenadier: grenadier
Grossherzog: grand duke
Handwerker: tailor or shoemaker
Herzog: duke
Husaren: hussar
Infanterie: infantry
Jager: yeager
Jager zu Pferde: mounted yeager
Kaiser: emporer
Kaiserin: empress
Kanonier: gunner
Kompagnie, Komp.: company
Kraftfahr: motor vehicle unit
Kurassier: cuirassier
Lazarett: hospital
Leib: life or personal
Luftschiffer: airshipper
Maschinengewehr: machine gun
Militarbacker: military baker
Nr.: number
Pferde: horse
Pionier: engineer or technician
Regiment, Regt.: regiment
Reiter: rider
Reservist: soldier who served minimum service time
Schutze: sharpshooter
Schweres: heavy
S.M.S.: ship
Train: supply
Ulanen: lancer
Versuchs: experimental or testing
Verkehrstruppen: technical troops

It was the German success in the Franco-Prussian War of 1870-1 that boosted nationalism and resulted in the proud reservist system; *above* Jagers and Infantry in action by the Eisenbahn at Bethincourt, *below* the artillery at Gravelotte.

Gläser an, hoch lebe der
Reservist Mente
Res. H. Heuser.
die Gläser an, hoch lebe der
Prosit Reserve
die Gläser an, hoch lebe der
Musketier Koch

Gläser an hoch lebe der
Res. Georg
68
die Gläser an, hoch lebe der
79
die Gläser an, hoch lebe der
Prosit Reserve
Reservist Espich

Opposite:

a. *Garde Grenadier-Regt. Nr. 1, Berlin, 1907-1909,* .5L, pottery, $500.

b. *Garde Grenadier-Regt. Nr. 2, Charlottenburg, 1904-1906,* .5L, porcelain, $475.

c. *Infanterie-Regt. Nr. 92, Braunschweig, 1904-1906,* .5L, pottery, $475.

d. *Infanterie-Regt. Nr. 117, Mainz, 1909-1911* and *Kriegsministerium* (War Ministry in Berlin), .5L, porcelain, $650.

a. *Infanterie-Regt. Nr. 40, Rastatt, 1909-1911,* .5L, porcelain, $350.

b. *Infanterie-Regt. Nr. 167, Kassel, 1906-1908,* .5L, porcelain, $325.

c. *Infanterie-Regt. Nr. 170, Offenburg, 1904-1906,* .5L, porcelain, $350.

d. *Infanterie-Regt. Nr. 174, Forbach, 1911-1913,* .5L, porcelain, $325.

Opposite:

e. *Bayr. 18. Infanterie-Regt., Landau, 1901-1903,* 1.0L, pottery, $475.

f. *Infanterie-Regt. Nr. 68, Koblenz, 1905-1907,* .5L, pottery, $375.

g. *Infanterie-Regt. Nr. 79, Hildesheim, 1903-1905,* .5L, pottery, Gibralter banner, inscription for Gibralter campaign, $475.

h. *Infanterie-Regt. Nr. 91, Oldenburg, 1904-1906,* .5L, pottery, unusual lid with owner's photo under glass, $375.

Opposite:

a. *Infanterie-Regt. Nr. 110, Mannheim, 1910-1912,* .5L, porcelain, 1911 King's Prize, $425.

b. *Infanterie-Regt. Nr. 113, Freiburg, 1908-1910,* .5L, porcelain, $350.

c. *Infanterie-Regt. Nr. 119, Stuttgart, 1912-1914,* .5L, porcelain, lid unscrews to reveal prism, finial unscrews, $525.

d. *Infanterie-Regt. Nr. 121, Ludwigsburg, 1906-1906,* .5L, porcelain, $325.

a. *Infanterie-Regt. Nr. 101, Dresden, 1904-1906,* .5L, porcelain, $325.

b. *Infanterie-Regt. Nr. 103, Bautzen, 1908-1910,* .5L, porcelain, $350.

c. *Infanterie-Regt. Nr. 105, Strassburg, 1903-1905,* .5L, porcelain, $350.

d. *Infanterie-Regt. Nr. 134, Plauen, 1910-1912,* .5L, porcelain, $375.

Opposite:

e. *Infanterie-Regt. Nr. 149, Schneidemuhl, 1911-1913,* .5L, pottery, $425.

f. *Infanterie-Regt. Nr. 82, Gottingen, 1903-1905,* .5L, pottery, $375.

g. *Infanterie-Regt. Nr. 28, Ehrenbreitstein, 1904-1906,* .5L, pottery, $350.

h. *Schutzen-Fusilier-Regt. Nr. 108, Dresden, 1902-1904,* .5L, pottery, appearance of Jager stein, $800.

Opposite:

a. *Bayr. Infanterie-Leib-Regt., Munchen, 1912-1914,* .5L, porcelain, 100 year commemorative, lid unscrews to reveal prism, $600.

b. *Bayr. 4. Infanterie-Regt., Metz, 1905-1907,* .5L, porcelain, 200 year commemorative, $400.

c. *Bayr. 4. Infanterie-Regt., Metz, 1904-1906,* .5L, porcelain, 200 year commemorative, $400.

d. *Bayr. 12. Infanterie-Regt., Neu-Ulm, 1912-1914,* .5L, stoneware, 100 year commemorative, lid unscrews to reveal portrait of Prinz Arnulf, $575.

a. *Bayr. Infanterie-Leib-Regt., Munchen, 1909-1911,* .5L, porcelain, 1909 King's Prize, $475.

b. *Bayr. 13. Infanterie-Regt., Ingolstadt, 1904-1906,* .5L, stoneware, 100 year commemorative, unusual lid, $500.

c. *Bayr. 21.* and *23. Infanterie-Regts., Eichstatt* and *Germersheim, 1912-1914,* .5L, porcelain, finial unscrews to reveal owner's photo, $575.

d. *Infanterie-Regt. Nr. 111, Rastatt, 1906-1907,* and *Infanterie Schiess Schule* (Marksmanship School), *Spandau-Ruhleben, 1907-1908,* .5L, porcelain, $675.

Opposite:

e. *Bayr. 2. Infanterie-Regt., Munchen, 1912-1914,* .5L, porcelain, lid unscrews to reveal prism, $575.

f. *Bayr. 5. Infanterie-Regt., Bamberg, 1909-1911,* .5L, porcelain, King's Prize, $425.

g. *Bayr. 13, Infanterie-Regt., Ingolstadt, 1910-1912,* .5L, porcelain, unusual lid, $700.

h. *Bayr. 16. Infanterie-Regt., Landshut, 1909-1911,* .5L, porcelain, owner's photo on front, $475.

RESERVE HAT RUH
1814
1914
10 Comp.
In Treue fest!
Gefreiter Georg Müller

RESERVE HAT RUH
Johann Schaberl
ERINNERUNG AN M. DIENSTZEIT
5
13
Karl Boscher
Max Riembök

a. *Infanterie-Regt. Nr. 88, Mainz, 1897-1899,* .5L, porcelain, thumblift is bust of Wilhelm II, $475.

b. *Infanterie-Regt. Nr. 112, Mulhausen, 1906-1907,* and *Infanterie Schiess Schule* (Marksmanship School), *Spandau,* 1907-1908, .5L, porcelain, $650.

c. *Bayr. 15. Infanterie-Regt., Neuburg, 1904-1906,* .5L, porcelain, very unusual lid, thumblift is large soldier shooting through wall, $650.

d. *Bayr. 13. Infanterie-Regt., Eichstatt, 1911-1913,* .5L, porcelain, named to *Pferdewarter,* has two side scenes grooming horses, prism lid, $550.

e. *Garde-Regt. Zu Fuss, Leib Cp., Potsdam, 1901-1903,* .5L, porcelain, miter helmet finial, .5L, porcelain, $1400.

f. *Bayr. Infanterie-Leib-Regt., Munchen, 1909-1911,* .5L, porcelain, pewter crown lid covers glass dome, under glass dome are guard house, soldier, and officer on horse, $950.

a. *Jager-Bataillon Nr. 11, Marburg, 1905-1907,* .5L, glass, $800.

b. *Jager-Bataillon Nr. 8, Schlettstadt, 1905-1907,* .5L, pottery, $900.

c. *Jager-Bataillon Nr. 9, Ratzenburg, 1910-1912,* .5L, pottery, $1200.

a. *Garde-Schutzen-Bataillon, Gr. Lichterfelde, 1909-1911,* .5L, pottery, $900.

b. *Jager-Bataillon Nr. 4, Bitsch, 1903-1905,* .5L, porcelain, $850.

c. *Jager-Bataillon Nr. 10, Bitsch, 1906-1908,* .5L, porcelain, $850.

d. *Bayr. 2. Jager-Bataillon, Aschaffenburg, 1906-1909,* carved horn on lid, tschako finial, $850.

a. *Bayr. 2. Jager-Bataillon, Aschaffenburg, 1908-1910,* .5L, pottery, King's Prize, tschako finial, $900.

b. *Jager-Bataillon Nr. 4, Naumburg, 1903-1905,* .5L, porcelain, $900.

c. *Jager-Bataillon Nr. 12, Freiberg, 1905-1907,* .5L, porcelain, King's Prize, tschako finial, $900.

d. *Jager-Bataillon Nr. 13, Dresden, 1909-1910,* .5L, stoneware, King's Prize, one year volunteer, tschako finial, $875.

Opposite:

e. *Garde-Jager-Bataillon, Potsdam, 1904-1906,* .5L, pottery, $900.

f. *Garde-Schutzen-Bataillon, Gr. Lichterfelde, 1903-1905,* .5L, porcelain, tschako finial, $1000.

g. *Jager-Bataillon Nr. 11, Marburg, 1901-1903,* .5L, porcelain, $850.

h. *Bayr. 2. Jager-Bataillon, Aschaffenburg, 1899-1901,* .5L, porcelain, 1899 Shooting Prize, roster has names of volunteers who went to China for Boxer Rebellion, $850.

a. *Bayr. 1. Jager-Bataillon, Straubing, 1898-1900,* .5L, porcelain, $650.

b. *Bayr. 2. Jager-Bataillon, Aschaffenburg, 1900-1902,* .5L, porcelain, $750.

c. *Bayr. 2. Jager-Bataillon, Aschaffenburg, 1902-1904,* .5L, porcelain, $800.

d. *Jager-Bataillon Nr. 8, Schlettstadt, 1899-1901,* .5L, porcelain, $850.

a. *Bayr. 1. Maschinengewehr-Abteilung des 1. Armee Korps, Augsburg, 1904-1906,* .5L, porcelain, tschako finial, $950.

b. *Maschinengewehr Comp., Bayr. 7. Infanterie-Regt., Bayreuth, 1909-1911,* .5L, porcelain, prism lid, $800.

c. *Maschinengewehr Comp. Bayr. 22. Infanterie-Regt., Zweibrucken, 1912-1914,* .5L, porcelain, $1050.

d. *Maschinengewehr Comp., Infanterie-Regt. Nr. 118, Worms, 1912-1914,* .5L, pottery, $1100.

Opposite:

e. *Maschinengewehr Comp., Infanterie-Regt. Nr. 125, Stuttgart-Comstatt, 1912-1914,* .5L, porcelain, lid unscrews to reveal prism, finial unscrews to reveal glass jewel, $1200.

f. *Maschinengewehr Comp., Bayr. 4. Infanterie-Regt., Metz, 1910-1912,* machine gun and crew finial on unusual lid, $1600.

g. *Maschinengewehr-Abteilung Nr. 4,* and *Nr. 9, Colmar, 1904-1906,* owner also served in Southwest Africa, .5L, porcelain, prism lid, $1500.

h. *Maschinengewehr-Abteilung Nr. 19, Leipzig, 1906-1907,* named to one year volunteer *Unteroffizier,* .5L, porcelain, $1300.

a. *Garde-Maschinengewehr-Abteilung Nr. 2, Gross-Lichterfelde, 1907-1909,* .5L, porcelain, $1500.

b. *Maschinengewehr-Abteilung Nr. 3, Bitsch und Strassburg, 1905-1907,* .5L, pottery, $1300.

c. *Maschinengewehr Comp., Infanterie-Regt. Nr. 106, Leipzig, 1909-1911,* .5L, porcelain, named to *Waffenmeister,* $1100.

d. *Maschinengewehr Comp., Bayr. 3, Infanterie-Regt., Augsburg, 1908-1910,* .5L, stoneware, $1000.

Opposite:

e. *Maschinengewehr Comp., Bayr. 20. Infanterie-Regt., Kempten, 1912-1914,* .5L, stoneware, $600.

f. *Maschinengewehr Comp., Infanterie-Regt. Nr. 83, Cassel, 1912-1914,* .5L, porcelain, machine gun with crew finial, $1300.

g. *Maschinengewehr Comp., Infanterie-Regt. Nr. 29, Trier, 1912-1914,* 1.0L, pottery, machine gun with crew finial, $1500.

h. *Maschinengewehr Comp., Bayr. 11, Infanterie-Regt., Regensburg, 1910-1912,* .5L, porcelain, prism lid, $800.

a. *Maschinengewehr Comp., Infanterie-Regt. Nr. 111, Rastatt, 1912-1914,* .5L, porcelain, $1100.

b. *Maschinengewehr Comp., Infanterie-Regt. Nr. 111, Rastatt, 1909-1911,* .5L, porcelain, $1050.

c. *Maschinengewehr Comp., Infanterie-Regt. Nr. 121, Ludwigsburg, 1910-1912,* .5L, porcelain, $1050.

d. *Maschinengewehr Comp., Infanterie-Regt. Nr. 119, Stuttgart, 1911-1913,* .5L, porcelain, $1050.

a. *Garde-Fuss-Artillerie-Regt., Spandau, 1903-1905,* .5L, porcelain, one large scene wraps around entire stein, $650.

b. *3. Garde-Feld.-Artillerie-Regt., Berlin, 1904-1906,* .5L, porcelain, $500.

c. *Feld.-Artillerie-Regt. Nr. 70,* and *Schiess-Schule, Juterbog, 1906-1908,* .5L, porcelain, $550.

d. *Feld.-Artillerie-Regt. Nr. 29, Ludwigsburg, 1905-1907,* .5L, porcelain, $400.

a. *Bayr. 2 Feld.-Artillerie-Regt., Wurzburg, 1901-1903,* .5L, porcelain, porcelain inlaid lid, $700.

b. *Feld.-Artillerie-Regt. Nr. 15, Morchingen, 1911-1913,* .5L, porcelain, $475.

c. *Feld.-Artillerie-Regt. Nr. 26, Verden, 1907-1909,* .5L, porcelain, $500.

d. *Feld.-Artillerie-Regt. Nr. 63, Mainz, 1910-1912,* .5L, porcelain, $500.

Opposite:

e. *Bayr. 1 Fuss-Artillerie-Regt., Bespannungs-Abtl., 1 Fahr, Batt., Neu-Ulm, 1908-1910,* .5L, porcelain, $700.

f. *Fuss-Artillerie-Regt. Nr. 2, Emden-Borkum, 1911-1913,* .5L, porcelain, $550.

g. *Feld.-Artillerie-Regt. Nr. 55, Naumburg, 1911-1913,* .5L, porcelain, $475.

h. *Feld.-Artillerie-Regt. Nr. 9, Itzehue, 1903-1905,* .5L, porcelain, porcelain inlaid lid, $850.

Opposite:

a. *Garde-Feld.-Artillerie-Regt. Reitende-Batterie, Berlin, 1906-1909,* .5L, porcelain, $625.

b. *Garde-Fuss-Artillerie-Regt., Spandau, 1906-1908,* .5L, porcelain, $675.

c. *Fuss-Artillerie-Regt. Nr. 8, Bespannungs-Abtl., Metz, 1904-1906,* .5L, porcelain, $700.

d. *Bayr. Feld.-Artillerie-Regt. Nr. 8, Nurnberg, 1910-1912,* and *Oberfeuerverlasschule, Munchen, 1912,* .5L, stoneware, pewter crown lid covers glass dome, under glass dome is cannon and crew, $1200.

a. *Feld.-Artillerie-Regt. Nr. 10, Hannover, 1902-1904,* .5L, pottery, $450.

b. *Feld.-Artillerie-Regt. Nr. 10, Hannover, 1902-1905,* .5L, pottery, $500.

c. *Feld.-Artillerie-Regt. Nr. 34, Metz, 1910-1912,* 1.0L, pottery, horse and rider thumblift, $550.

d. *Feld.-Artillerie-Regt. Nr. 10, Hannover, 1911-1912,* and *Feld.-Artillerie-Regt. Nr. 80, Hagenau, 1912-1913,* 1.0L, pottery, horse and rider thumblift, $550.

Opposite:

e. *2. Garde-Feld.-Artillerie-Regt., Potsdam, 1912-1914,* .5L, pottery, $625.

f. *4. Garde-Feld.-Artillerie-Regt., Potsdam, 1912-1914,* and *Schiess-Schule, Juterbog,* .5L, pottery, horse and rider thumblift, $650.

g. *Feld.-Artillerie-Regt. Nr. 63, Mainz, 1908-1910, Haubitz Battr.,* .5L, pottery, horse and rider thumblift, $550.

h. *Feld.-Artillerie-Regt. Nr. 27, Mainz, 1912-1914,* 1.0L, pottery, $575.

Reservist
Art. Rgt. 1. Comp.
Fußart. Rgt.
Erinnerung an meine
Obergefr. Spiess
Kanonier Gürtler

Ref. Gefr. Pütz
Es rasseln Geschütze
Es wiehern die Pferde
Gefreiter Baumeister
Gläser an, hoch lebe
treu gedient

Gläser an, hoch lebe der
Reserv. Egenolf

a. Bayr. 2. Pionier-Bataillon, Speyer, 1901-1903, .5L, porcelain, $575.

b. Pionier-Bataillon, Nr. 11, Mainz, 1899-1901, .5L, porcelain, $600.

c. Pionier-Bataillon Nr. 14, Kehl, 1902-1904, .5L, porcelain, $600.

d. Pionier-Bataillon Nr. 22, Riesa, 1902-1904, .5L, porcelain, $650.

a. *Garde-Pionier-Bataillon, Berlin, 1905-1907,* .5L, porcelain, $850.

b. *Pionier-Bataillon Nr. 20, Metz, 1907-1909,* .5L, porcelain, $700.

c. *Bayr. 1. Pionier-Bataillon, Ingolstadt, 1909-1911,* .5L, stoneware, side scene of Pioniers surveying flood damage of *June 17, 1901,* $700.

d. *Bayr. 2. Pionier-Bataillon,* and *Bayr. 4. Pionier-Bataillon, Ingolstadt, 1911-1913,* .5L, porcelain, lid unscrews to reveal prism, $850.

Opposite:

e. *Pionier-Bataillon Nr. 9, Harburg, 1912-1913* and *Militartubar Akademie, Berlin, 1913-1914,* .5L, pottery, $1100.

f. *Pionier-Bataillon Nr. 25, Mainz-Kastel, 1909-1911,* .5L, pottery, $750.

g. *Pionier-Bataillon Nr. 14, Kehl, 1904-1906,* .5L, porcelain, $700.

h. *Pionier-Bataillon Nr. 21, Mainz-Kastel, 1909-1911,* .5L, porcelain, $700.

a. *Pionier-Bataillon Nr. 3, Spandau, 1907-1909,* .5L, porcelain, $750.

b. *Pionier-Bataillon Nr. 4, Magdeburg, 1910-1912,* .5L, porcelain, finial unscrews, $800.

c. *Pionier-Bataillon Nr. 20, Metz, 1908-1910,* .5L, porcelain, $700.

d. *Pionier-Bataillon Nr. 21, Mainz-Kastel, 1908-1910,* .5L, porcelain, $800.

Opposite:

e. *Bayr. 1. Pionier-Bataillon, Ingolstadt, 1909-1911,* .5L, porcelain, finial unscrews, $700.

f. *Pionier-Bataillon Nr. 7, Koln-Riehl, 1909-1911,* .5L, pottery, $750.

g. *Pionier-Bataillon Nr. 11, Hannover-Munden, 1910-1912,* .5L, porcelain, $750.

h. *Pionier-Bataillon Nr. 16, Metz, 1906-1908,* .5L, porcelain, $700.

a. *Bayr. 2. Pionier-Bataillon, Speyer, 1904-1906,* .5L, porcelain, prism lid, $600.

b. *Bayr. 3. Pionier-Bataillon, Munchen, 1904-1906,* .5L, porcelain, prism lid, $575.

c. *Pionier-Bataillon Nr. 12, Dresden, 1909-1911,* .5L, porcelain, $600.

d. *Pionier-Bataillon Nr. 24, Koln-Riehl, 1911-1912,* and *Pionier Versuchs Kompagnie, Berlin, 1912-1913,* .5L, porcelain, $1400.

a. *Pionier Versuchskompagnie, Berlin, 1906-1908,* .5L, porcelain, $1500.

b. *Pionier-Bataillon Nr. 13, Ulm, 1911-1913, Scheinwerferzug,* .5L, porcelain, $1000.

c. *Armerungs-Batallion Nr. 14, 1916-1918,* .5L, porcelain, $1800.

d. *Bayr. 3. Pionier-Bataillon, Ingolstadt, 1912-1914, Scheinwerferzug,* .5L, porcelain, side scene depicts Pioniers using search lights, prism lid, $1200.

e. *Pionier-Bataillon Nr. 9, Harburg, 1909-1911,* .5L, porcelain, $700.

f. *Pionier-Bataillon Nr. 9, Harburg, 1911-1913,* 1.0L, pottery, $900.

a. *Eisenbahn Regt. Nr. 3, 1 Comp., Hanau, 1912-1914*, .5L, porcelain, $800.

b. *Bayr. Eisenbahn-Batl., 2 Comp., Munchen, 1911-1913*, .5L, stoneware, $750.

c. *Bayr. Eisenbahn-Batl., 2 Comp., Munchen, 1908-1910*, .5L, stoneware, $1000.

d. *Eisenbahn Regt. Nr. 2, 3 Comp., Berlin-Schoneberg, 1904-1906*, .5L, porcelain, $700.

e. *Versuchs-Abteilung der Verkehrstruppen (Versuchs-Komp.), Berlin-Schoneberg, 1907-1909*, .5L, stoneware, $1700.

a. *Eisenbahn-Regt. Nr. 3, 4 Comp., Berlin, 1903-1905,* .5L, pottery, $900.

b. *Eisenbahn-Regt. Nr. 2, 2 Comp., Berlin-Schoneberg, 1903-1905,* .5L, pottery, $775.

c. *Eisenbahn-Regt. Nr. 1, 3 Comp., Berlin, 1899-1901,* .5L, pottery, $750.

d. *Eisenbahn-Regt. Nr. 2, 3 Comp., Berlin, 1905-1907,* .5L, pottery, $1000.

a. *Eisenbahn Regt. Nr. 1, 8 Comp., Berlin, 1910-1912,* .5L, porcelain, $1000.

b. *Eisenbahn Regt. Nr. 2, 7 Comp., Berlin, 1904-1906,* .5L, porcelain, $800.

c. *Eisenbahn Regt. Nr. 3, 3 Comp., Hanau A.M., 1911-1913,* .5L, pottery, $1200.

d. *Bayr. Eisenbahn-Batl., 1 Comp., Munchen, 1902-1904,* .5L, porcelain, $775.

Opposite:

e. *Eisenbahn-Regt. Nr. 3, 8 Comp., Berlin-Schoneberg, 1908-1910,* .5L, pottery, $1150.

f. *Eisenbahn-Regt. Nr. 3, 4 Comp., Hanau, 1910-1912,* .5L, pottery, $1300.

g. *Betriebs Abteilung Eisenbahn-Brigade, Schoneberg-Berlin, 1900-1902,* .5L, pottery, $1200.

h. *Eisenbahn-Regt. Nr. 3, 2 Comp., Hanau, 1910-1912,* .5L, porcelain, $1100.

a. *Telegraphen-Batl. Nr. 1, Berlin, 1906-1908,* .5L, porcelain, $1150.

b. *Telegraphen-Batl. Nr. 2, Frankfurt, 1905-1907,* .5L, porcelain, $1250.

c. *Telegraphen-Batl. Nr. 3, Coblenz, 1899-1901,* .5L, porcelain, $1100.

d. *Telegraphen-Batl. Nr. 5, 4 (Funker) Comp., 1911-1913,* .5L, porcelain, $1450.

a. *Telegraphen-Batl. Nr. 4, Funker Abteilung, Karlsruhe, 1911-1913,* .5L, stoneware, $650.

b. *1. Komp. Telegraphen Detachement, Munchen, 1908-1910,* .5L, stoneware, $700.

c. *Bayr. 2. Telegraphen-Batl., 2 (Funker) Comp., Munchen, 1912-1914,* .5L, porcelain, lid unscrews to reveal scene of Munchen in pewter, $1600.

Opposite:

e. *Bayr. 10. Infanterie-Regt.,* and *Festungstelegraphen, Ingolstadt, 1912-1914,* .5L, porcelain, $1600.

f. *Telegraphen-Batl. Nr. 3, Coblenz, 1900-1902,* .5L, pottery, $1000.

g. *Telegraphen-Batl. Nr. 3, Coblenz, 1905-1907,* .5L, pottery, $1250.

h. *Telegraphen-Batl. Nr. 4, Karlsruhe, 1907-1909,* .5L, porcelain, $1200.

Kavallerie, auf dem
die Cavallerie auf dem Posten
Reservist Michel
die Kavallerie, auf dem

Regt. (2. schweres Rgt.)
Reiter Rgt. (1. Schweres Rgt.)
Hoch Reserve
die Cavallerie, auf dem
die Cavallerie auf dem

Opposite:

a. *Garde-Kurassier-Regt., Berlin, 1900-1903,* .5L, pottery, $1000.

b. *Kurassier-Regt. Nr. 2, Pasewalk, 1911-1914,* 1.0L, pottery, $1400.

c. *Kurassier-Regt. Nr. 4, Munster, 1909-1912,* .5L, pottery, $1100.

d. *Kurassier-Regt. Nr. 5, Riesenburg, 1909-1912,* 1.0L, pottery, $1300.

a. *Saxon Garde-Reiter-Regt., Dresden, 1910-1913,* .5L, porcelain, $1500.

b. *Leib Garde Ihrer Magestat der Kaiserin, Potsdam, 1899-1902,* .5L, porcelain, $2200.

c. *Regiment der Gardes du Corps, Potsdam, 1911-1914,* .5L, pottery, $1300.

d. *Garde-Kurassier-Regt., Berlin, 1897-1900,* .5L, pottery, $1000.

Opposite:

e. *Saxon Karabinier-Regt., Borna, 1908-1911,* .5L, porcelain, $1400.

f. *Saxon Garde-Reiter-Regt., Dresden, 1909-1912,* .5L, pottery, $1500.

g. *Kurassier-Regt. Nr. 4, Munster, 1906-1909,* .5L, pottery, $1100.

h. *Kurassier-Regt. Nr. 5, Riesenburg, 1896-1899,* .5L, pottery, $1100.

a. *Regiment der Gardes du Corps, Potsdam, 1899-1902,* .5L, porcelain, $1100.

b. *Garde-Kurassier-Regt., Berlin, 1910-1913,* .5L, pottery, $1100.

c. *Kurassier-Regt. Nr. 8, Coln-Deutz, 1913,* gift to *Gefreiter* on Christmas 1913 from recruits in his session, .5L, porcelain, $1100.

d. *Kurassier-Regt. Nr. 8, Deutz, 1900,* .5L pottery, $1000.

a. *Husaren-Regt. Nr. 7, Bonn, 1908-1910,* .5L, pottery, $900.

b. *Husaren-Regt. Nr. 9, Strassburg, 1909-1912,* .5L, pottery, $950.

c. *Husaren-Regt. Nr. 11, Krefeld, 1908-1911,* .5L, pottery, $1000.

d. *Husaren-Regt. Nr. 16, Schleswig, 1904-1907,* .5L, pottery, $900.

Opposite:

e. *Leib-Garde-Husaren-Regt., Leib Esk., Potsdam, 1904-1907,* .5L, pottery, $1100.

f. *2. Leib-Husaren-Regt., Posen* and *Danzig-Langfuhr, 1896-1899,* .5L, porcelain, $1200.

g. *Husaren-Regt. Nr. 3, Rathenow, 1908-1911,* .5L, pottery, $900.

h. *Husaren-Regt. Nr. 4, Ohlau, 1910-1913,* .5L, porcelain, $1000.

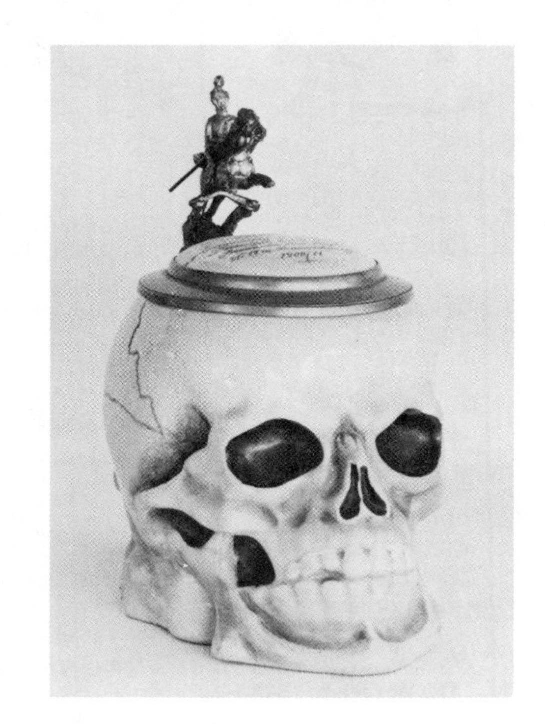

e. *Husaren-Regt. Nr. 17, Braunschweig, 1908-1911,* .5L, pottery skull, $1800.

Opposite:

a. *Husaren-Regt. Nr. 14, Kassel, 1910-1913,* .5L, porcelain, $900.

b. *Husaren-Regt. Nr. 18, Grossenhain, 1909-1912,* .5L, porcelain, $1000.

c. *Husaren-Regt. Nr. 19, Grimma, 1904-1907,* .5L, porcelain, $950.

d. *Husaren-Regt. Nr. 20, Bautzen, 1910-1913,* .5L, porcelain, two Ulanen-Regt. Nr. 17 side scenes (former unit), $1100.

a. *Leib-Garde-Husaren-Regt., Leib, Esk., Potsdam, 1912-1915,* .5L, porcelain, $1200.

b. *Husaren-Regt. Nr. 13, Diedenhofen, 1910-1913,* .5L, pottery, $900.

c. *Husaren-Regt. Nr. 17, Braunschweig, 1908-1911,* .5L, porcelain, $1000.

d. *Husaren-Regt. Nr. 19, Grimma, 1911-1914,* .5L, porcelain, lid unscrews to reveal glass jewel, $1100.

Opposite:

e. *Husaren-Regt. Nr. 8, Paderborn, 1900-1903,* .5L, porcelain, $850.

f. *Husaren-Regt. Nr. 12, Torgau, 1906-1909,* .5L, porcelain, $750.

g. *Husaren-Regt. Nr. 13, Mainz, 1900-1903,* .5L, porcelain, $750.

h. *Husaren-Regt. Nr. 15, Wandsbeck, 1904-1907,* .5L, porcelain, $900.

Reservist Schuchardt
Gefreiter Lutze
Sieg oder Tod

Reservist Linke

Res. Moll.
Parole Heimat
Parole Heimat

Garde Ulan Regt. Berlin 1905

Opposite:

a. *Ulanen-Regt. Nr. 5, Dusseldorf, 1906-1909,* .5L, pottery, $750.

b. *Ulanen-Regt. Nr. 7, Saarbrucken, 1904-1907,* .5L, pottery, $750.

c. *Ulanen-Regt. Nr. 11, Saarburg, 1902-1905,* .5L, pottery, $775.

d. *Ulanen-Regt. Nr. 15, Saarburg, 1906-1909,* .5L, pottery, $775.

a. *Ulanen-Regt. Nr. 6, Hanau, 1905-1908,* .5L, pottery, $800.

b. *Ulanen-Regt. Nr. 14, St. Arold, 1905-1908,* .5L, porcelain, $1000.

c. *Ulanen-Regt. Nr. 21, Chemnitz, 1905-1908,* .5L, porcelain, $900.

d. *Bayr. 2, Ulanen-Regt., Ansbach, 1912-1915,* .5L, porcelain, $700.

Opposite:

e. *1. Garde-Ulanen-Regt., Potsdam, 1909-1912,* 1.0L, pottery, $1200.

f. *2. Garde-Ulanen-Regt., Berlin, 1905-1908,* .5L, pottery, $1000.

g. *3. Garde-Ulanen-Regt., Potsdam,* undated, .5L, porcelain, $900.

h. *Ulanen-Regt. Nr. 1, Militsch, 1901-1904,* .5L, porcelain, $1000.

Opposite:

a. *Ulanen-Regt. Nr. 20, Ludwigsburg, 1910-1913,* .5L, porcelain $775.

b. *Ulanen-Regt. Nr. 21, Chemnitz, 1908-1911,* .5L, porcelain, $900.

c. *Bayr. 1, Ulanen-Regt., Bamberg, 1903-1906,* .5L, porcelain, $650.

d. *Bayr. 2. Ulanen-Regt., Ansbach, 1911-1914,* .5L, porcelain, lid unscrews to reveal relief pewter scene, $750.

a. *Ulanen-Regt. Nr. 3, Furstenwalde, 1907-1910,* .5L, porcelain, $750.

b. *Ulanen-Regt. Nr. 13, Hannover, 1907-1910,* .5L, porcelain, $800.

c. *Ulanen-Regt. Nr. 17, Oschatz, 1903-1906,* .5L, porcelain, $850.

d. *Ulanen-Regt. Nr. 18, Leipzig, 1902-1905,* .5L, porcelain, $850.

Opposite:

e. *Ulanen-Regt. Nr. 12, Insterburg* and *Kavallerie Telegraphenschule, 1907-1911,* .5L, porcelain, $1300.

f. *Garde-Ulanen-Regt., Potsdam, 1906-1909,* .5L, porcelain, $1100.

g. *Ulanen-Regt. Nr. 19, Ulm, 1911-1914,* .5L, porcelain, $750.

h. *Bayr. 1. Ulanen-Regt., Bamberg, 1907-1910,* .5L, porcelain, $700.

Gefreiter Haug.
Ulan Rechenberger

Kavallerie, auf dem Posten
Reservist Schälicke.

die Kavallerie, auf dem
die Kavallerie, auf dem
(2. Württ.) Nr. 26, 3. Esk. Stuttg

die Cavallerie auf dem Posten
Reservist Clever
Magdeburg. Drag. Regt. Nr. 6. Mainz
Res. Gfr. Schneider.
die Cavallerie auf dem Posten
Reservist Kopfmann
Drag. Regt. No 21. in Schwetzingen
Drag. Regt. Prinz Karl Nr. 22 Mülhausen

Opposite:

a. *Ulanen-Regt. Nr. 3, Furstenwalde, 1911-1914 Kommando in Hannover, 1914,* .5L, porcelain, $1200.

b. *Dragoner-Regt. Nr. 5, Hofgeismar, 1910-1913,* .5L, pottery, $850.

c. *Dragoner-Regt. Nr. 16, Luneburg, 1907-1910,* .5L, pottery, $800.

d. *Dragoner-Regt. Nr. 26, Stuttgart-Cannstatt, 1911-1914,* .5L, porcelain, lid unscrews in two places to reveal prism, $800.

a. *Dragoner-Regt. Nr. 9, Metz, 1902-1905,* .5L, pottery, $775.

b. *Dragoner-Regt. Nr. 23, Darmstadt, 1907-1910,* .5L, porcelain, $800.

c. *1. Garde-Dragoner-Regt., Berlin, 1903-1906,* .5L, pottery, $1300.

d. *2. Garde-Dragoner-Regt., Berlin, 1909-1912,* .5L, pottery, $1400.

Opposite:

e. *Dragoner-Regt. Nr. 6, Mainz, 1907-1910,* .5L, porcelain, $700.

f. *Dragoner-Regt. Nr. 9, Metz, 1906-1909,* .5L, porcelain, $700.

g. *Dragoner-Regt. Nr. 21, Schwetzingen, 1910-1913,* .5L, porcelain, $700.

h. *Dragoner-Regt. Nr. 22, Mulhausen, 1904-1907,* .5L, porcelain, $750.

a. *Dragoner-Regt. Nr. 15, Hagenau, 1907-1910,* .5L, pottery, $850.

b. *Dragoner-Regt. Nr. 7, Saarbrucken, 1904-1907,* .5L, pottery, $800.

c. *Dragoner-Regt. Nr. 13, Metz, 1904-1908,* .5L, porcelain, $725.

d. *Dragoner-Regt. Nr. 15, Hagenau, 1910-1913,* .5L, porcelain, $750.

a. *Jager-Regt. zu Pferde, Nr. 3, Colmar, 1908-1911,* 1.0L, porcelain, $1250.

b. *Jager-Regt. zu Pferde, Nr. 4, Graudenz, 1909-1912,* .5L, pottery, $1350.

c. *Jager-Regt. zu Pferde, Nr. 7, Trier, 1913-1914* and *Ulanen-Regt. Nr. 13, Hannover, 1911-1913,* .5L, pottery, $1350.

d. *Jager-Regt. zu Pferde, Nr. 13, Saarlouis* and *Dragoner-Regt. Nr. 22, Mulhausen, 1911-1914,* .5L, porcelain, $1200.

Opposite:

e. *Garnison Lazarett, Train-Batl. Nr. 25, Darmstadt, 1899-1901,* .5L, porcelain, one one side has medical scene, $1250.

f. *Garde-Train-Batl.* and *Kavallerie Telegraphenschule, Berlin, 1908-1910,* .5L, porcelain, $1300.

g. *Bayr. 1. Train-Batl., Munchen, 1909-1910,* .5L, porcelain, pewter crown lid covers glass dome, under glass dome is horse & rider, $1000.

Opposite:

a. *Jager-Regt. zu Pferde, Nr. 8, Trier, 1913-1915,* and *Husaren-Regt. Nr. 14, Cassel, 1912-1913,* .5L, pottery, $1400.

b. *Jager-Regt. zu Pferde, Nr. 2, Langensalza, 1911-1914,* .5L, porcelain, $1100.

c. *Jager-Regt. zu Pferde, VI, Posen, 1901-1904,* .5L, porcelain, $1100.

d. *Eskadron Jager zu Pferde, XII Arme Corps, Dresden, 1899-1902,* .5L, porcelain, $1250.

a. *Garde Eskadron Jager zu Pferde, Potsdam, 1900-1903,* .5L, porcelain, $1350.

b. *Meldereiter Detachement XI Arme Corps, Langensalza, 1900-1903,* .5L, porcelain, $1050.

c. *Jager-Regt. zu Pferde, Nr. 5, Mulhausen* and *Husaren-Regt. Nr. 3, Rathanow, 1906-1909,* .5L, porcelain, $1200.

d. *Jager-Regt. zu Pferde, Nr. 11, Tarnowitz, 1913-1915,* and *Husaren-Regt. Nr. 12, Torgau, 1912-1913,* .5L, pottery, $1250.

Opposite:

e. *Garde Eskadron Jager zu Pferde, Potsdam, 1904-1905,* and *Jager-Regt. zu Pferde, Nr. 2, Langensalza, 1905-1907,* .5L, porcelain, $1400.

f. *3. Esk. Comp. Jager-Regt. zu Pferde, Posen, 1902-1905,* .5L, porcelain, $1200.

g. *Jager-Regt. zu Pferde, Nr. 12, Oschatz, 1904-1905* and *Ulanen-Regt. Nr. 21, Chemnitz, 1905-1907,* .5L, porcelain, $1200.

h. *Eskadron Jager zu Pferde, I Bayr. Armeekorps, Munchen, 1902-1905,* .5L, stoneware, $1200.

Kaiser Wilhelm II.
MEINE DIENS

a. *Bayr. 2 Chevaulegers-Regt., Dillingen-Regensburg, 1908-1911,* .5L, porcelain, finial unscrews to reveal photo locket, $700.

b. *Bayr. 3 Chevaulegers-Regt., Dieuze, 1909-1912,* .5L, porcelain, $700.

c. *Bayr. 5 Chevaulegers-Regt., Saargemund, 1909-1912,* .5L, porcelain, $650.

d. *Bayr. 8 Chevaulegers-Regt. Dillingen, 1911-1914,* .5L, porcelain, lid unscrews to reveal prism, finial unscrews to reveal photo locket, $800.

e. *Bayr. 1 Schweres Reiter-Regt., Munchen, 1916-1919,* .5L, porcelain, $700.

f. *Bayr. 1 Schweres Reiter-Regt., Munchen, 1910-1913,* .5L, porcelain, finial unscrews to reveal photo of owner, $750.

a. *Kaiserlichen Schutztruppe Deutsch Sud West Afrika, 1904-1906, Feldzug,* .5L, porcelain, $2300.

b. *Bayr. 3. Feld Artl.-Regt., 5 Batt., Munchen, 1894-1896, 2. Haubitz Batl., China, 1900-1901,* .5L, porcelain, $2200.

c. *Bespannungs Abteilung d. Kgl. Bayr. Versuchstruppen, Munchen, 1908-1910,* .5L, stoneware, pewter crown lid covers glass dome, $1800.

d. *Bespannungs Abteilung d. Kgl. Bayr. Verkehrstruppen, Munchen, 1910-1912,* .5L, porcelain, $1600.

a. *Bayr. 19. Infanterie-Regt., Erlangen, 1906-1908,* named to *Sanitatsgefreiter,* .5L, porcelain, one side has medical scene, $1100.

b. *Bayr. 1. Infanterie-Regt., Munchen, 1904,* named to *Militarkrankenwarter,* .5L, porcelain, two medical scenes in side panels, $1250.

c. *Bayr. 1. Schweres Reiter-Regt., Munchen, 1908-1911,* named to *Fahnenschmied,* .5L, porcelain, $1000.

d. *Bayr. Kreigsbeleidungsamt I Armeecorps, 1914,* named to *Okonomiehandwerker,* .5L, porcelain, $1100.

a. *97. Lehrgang der Heeres Lehrschmiede, Munchen,* undated, approximately 1905, .5L, porcelain, $800.

b. *Infanterie-Regt. Nr. 181, Chemnitz, 1911-1912,* named to *Krankentrager,* .5L, porcelain, $700.

c. *Garnisons Lazarett, III Armeecorps, Erlangen, 1912-1914,* .5L, porcelain, medical scenes in side panels and under prism, $1250.

d. *Garnisons Lazarett, Regensburg, 1912-1914,* .5L, porcelain, medical scenes on side panels, lid unscrews to reveal prism with medical scene, $1400.

Opposite:

e. *Garnisons Lazarett, Bamberg, 1912-1914,* .5L, porcelain, $1000.

f. *Bayr. 13. Infanterie-Regt., Ingolstadt, 1904-1906,* named to *Sanitatsgefreiter,* .5L, stoneware, one side has medical scene, $1100.

g. *Bayr. 15. Infanterie-Regt., Neuburg, 1900-1902,* named to *Sanitatsgefreiter,* .5L, porcelain, two medical scenes in side panels, $1150.

h. *Garnisons Lazarett, III Armeekorps, Ingolstadt, 1906-1908,* named to *Sanitatsgefreiter,* .5L, porcelain, two medical scenes in side panels, $1200.

a. *Bayr. Bekleidungsamt I Armeecorps, Munchen, 1906-1908,* .5L, porcelain, $1000.

b. *Bekleidungsamt VI Armeecorps, Breslau, 1900-1902,* .5L, porcelain, $1100.

c. *Bekleidungsamt XI Armeecorps, Handwerker Abtl., Cassel, 1901-1903,* .5L, porcelain, $1000.

d. *Bezirkskomando, Heidelberg, 1912-1914,* .5L, pottery, $1500.

Opposite:

e. *Bekleidungsamt XIII Armeecorps, Ludwigsburg, 1894-1896,* .5L, porcelain, $800.

f. *Infanterie-Regt. Nr. 134, Plauen, 1906,* and *Militar Backer Abteilung des 2 Armeecorps Nr. 19, Riesa,* .5L, porcelain, $1100.

g. *Militarbackerie, Ulm, 1907-1909,* .5L, porcelain, $1000.

h. *Militar Backer Abteilung, Darmstadt, 1895-1897,* .5L, porcelain, $800.

a. *Bayr. Kraftfahrer Ersatz Abtlg., Munchen, 1914-1918,* .5L, porcelain, $2100.

b. *Bayr. 20, Infanterie-Regt., Radfahr Detach., Munchen, 1899,* .5L, porcelain, $2200.

c. *Infanterie-Regt. Nr. 145, Kraftfahrer-Abteilung, Metz, 1910-1912,* .5L, porcelain, $2400.

d. *Bayr. 10. Infanterie-Regt. Ingolstadt* and *Bezirkskomando, Dilligen,* undated, .5L, porcelain, $1200.

a. Luftschiffer u. Kraftfahr Bataillon, Munchen-Kraftfahr Komp. Reserve, 1912-1914, .5L, stoneware, $1800.

b. Luftschiffer Batl., 2 Comp., Berlin, 1901-1903, .5L, pottery, $2200.

c. Armierungs Bn., Bayr. III Armeekorp, 4 Komp, Ingolstadt, 1914-1915, .5L, porcelain, $1700.

d. Kgl. Luftschiffer, 1893-1895, Mettlach, 406, .5L, $1900.

a. *Luftschiffer Abteilung, Munchen, 1904-1906,* .5L, stoneware, $2200.

b. *Luftschiffer Abteilung, Munchen, 1901-1903,* .5L, stoneware, $2200.

c. *Luftschiffer Abteilung, Munchen, 1906-1908,* .5L, stoneware, $2300.

a. *S.M.S. Drache, 1908-1911,* .5L, porcelain, $900.

b. *S.M.S. Wettin, 1905-1908,* .5L, porcelain, $875.

c. *S.M.S. Kaiser Wilhelm der Grosse,* undated, .5L, porcelain, $975.

d. *S.M.S. Niobe, 1905-1908,* .5L, porcelain, $975.

a. *S.M.S. Oldenburg* and *S.M.S. Schlesien, 1910-1913,* 1.0L, pottery, $1300.

b. *S.M.S. Pommern, 1912-1915,* 1.0L, pottery, $1350.

c. *S.M.S. Helgoland, 1912-1915,* 1.0L, pottery lid unscrews to reveal porcelain with scene of Helgoland, $1400.

d. *S.M.S. Frederich Karl, 1910-1913,* 1.0L, pottery, $1300.

Opposite:

e. *S.M.S. Westfalen, 1911-1914,* 1.0L, pottery, $1250.

f. *S.M.S. Hessen* and *S.M.S. Nassau, 1908-1911,* 1.0L, pottery, $1150.

g. *S.M.S. Hamburg, 1906-1909,* 1.0L, pottery, $1100.

h. *II See Bataillon, Wilhelmshaven, 1907-1910,* .5L, pottery, $1600.

Opposite:

a. *S.M.S. Hohenzollern, 1907-1910,* 1.0L, pottery, $1200.

b. *S.M.S. Kaiser Barbarossa, 1905-1908,* .5L, pottery, $875.

c. *S.M.S. Braunschweig, 1906-1908,* .5L, pottery, $875.

d. *S.M.S. Pfeil, 1906-1909,* .5L, pottery, unusual front scene, $1100.

a. *S.M.S. Schleswig Holstein, 1910-1913,* 1.0L, pottery, $1200.

b. *S.M.S. Nassau, 1909-1912,* 1.0L, pottery, $1200.

c. *S.M.S. Kaiser Karl der Grosse, 1908-1909* and *S.M.S. Braunschweig, 1909-1911,* 1.0L, pottery, $1150.

d. *S.M.S. Rheinland, 1909-1912,* 1.0L, pottery, $1100.

Opposite:

e. *Maschinengewehr Zug, II See Bataillon, Wilhelmshaven, 1911-1914,* .5L, porcelain, $1600.

f. *S.M.S. Gneisenau, 1909-1912,* 1.0L, pottery, Neptune pottery lid, $1600.

g. *S.M.S. Vineta, 1910-1913,* 1.0L, pottery, $1300.

h. *S.M.S. Bremen, 1909-1912,* 1.0L, pottery, side scene with U.S. flag, lid unscrews to reveal relief pewter scene, $1500.

Reservist Waller.
Dienstzeit an Bord S.M.S. Kaiser
RESERVE HAT RUH
Reservist Wenzel.

Reservist Reinert.
See Bataillon Wilhelmshafen
Reservist Wirriges.
RESERVE HAT RUH
Res. Parusel
Reservist Willy Fikermann.

a. *S.M.S. Kaiser Friedrich III, 1901-1904,* .5L, pottery, $750.

b. *Telegraphen Zug, II See Bataillon, Wilhelmshaven, 1910-1913,* .5L, porcelain, $1500.

c. *5. Matrosen Artillerie Abteilung, Helgoland, 1911-1914,* .5L, porcelain, lid unscrews to reveal porcelain with scene of Helgoland, $1700.

d. *Matrosen Artillerie, Tsingtau, 1910-1913,* 1.0L, pottery, $1800.

e. *S.M.S. Stuttgart, 1909-1912,* 1.0L, porcelain, $1600.

f. *S.M.S. Preussen, 1910-1913,* 1.0L, pottery, character, $2000.

14. Characters

A *character* stein is a stein with a shape designed to represent an object, person, or an animal. So, like occupationals and regimentals it is a *style* category as opposed to the *materials* categories described in the earlier Sections.

14.1 History and Production

Although figural vessels date back to several centuries before the Greeks, true character steins had to await the development of the hinged lid, in the early 1500's. And, in fact, there *are* stoneware character steins that date from about that period, generally in the form of owls or seated bears, but they are quite rare.

Just why there are so few character steins that pre-date the late 1800's can only be speculated. One theory is that the odd shapes were too whimsical or weird to be socially acceptable in earlier times. The other popular theory is that there was just too much effort required to produce these "statuettes" before the advent, in the late 1800's, of molds that could more easily accommodate such shapes - such as the slip molds described in Subsection 2.3.

Some of the character steins that appeared around the 1850's were dull-finished bisque porcelain pieces that were made in slip molds. Among the most common are various varieties of skulls, used by medical students, secret societies, and some fraternities, among others. Many have been identified as made by *E. Bohne Soehne* of the Thuringen region, a factory that started in 1854. This factory, along with a couple in *Plaue* are believed to be responsible for much of the initial manufacture of character steins.

Beginning in the 1870's several other factories that produced character steins were *founded,* but they probably did not actually begin *production* of character steins until the 1880's. Some of these include Merkelbach & Wick, Dumler & Breiden, Reinhold-Merkelbach, Simon Peter Gerz, and Marzi & Remi. The Villeroy & Boch factory at Mettlach began producing character steins in about 1892. Marks of these factories are shown at the end of Section 2.

The commonly seen *hash* or *cross-hatch* mark is still something of a mystery. It is known to have been used by the Porzellanmanufaktur Plaue, but seems to have been utilized by others as well. It was apparently similar to the "C within a circle" mark that is used presently, as a *copyright protection.* Indeed it often is accompanied by *MUSTERSCHUTZ* which has that same meaning. The cross-hatch is most often seen in green, *MUSTERSCHUTZ* in blue.

That Plaue factory has long been associated with *lithophane* manufacture, which deserves a word here. Lithophanes are the panels, occasionally found in the bottom of porcelain steins, that show a picture when put up to a source of light. The darker or lighter areas are accomplished with thicker or thinner areas of porcelain.

Lithophanes were designed by first putting a layer of translucent bee's wax on a pane of glass with a light underneath. The wax was carved until the desired scene was completed, then the wax was used to make the plaster mold for the base of the stein. Rarely, steins can be found where colored glazes have been used to tint the outside of the lithophane, which then shows a subtilely colored scene when viewed.

While many character steins are made of porcelain there are also other important materials. Next to porcelain the most common is stoneware, often also slip molded, but occasionally stoneware steins are seen that were pressed into molds. These stoneware steins were mostly decorated with blue or purple saltglazes, or a kind of blackish combination. Brown and green saltglazes were also known in the late 1800's, and are sometimes seen on stoneware character steins. There are a number of character steins that can exist in both the porcelain or stoneware forms, perhaps they were made from the same mold.

Various kinds of pottery, earthenware, and pewter round out the character stein materials that are occasionally encountered.

Many of the *porcelain* character steins can be found with more than one distinct coloring pattern. The most common example is a tan and brown stein that is frequently known to exist in a full color version and in blues. The blue and white versions are often noticeably thinner and may have been produced with a slightly different porcelain recipe. Some of these are so delicate it is easy to imagine that they were intended only as decorative items.

14.2 Collecting Characters

Unlike many occupational steins, individual character steins were often produced in such numbers that a collector can often seek out and find a particular stein. This effects collecting strategies.

For one thing it makes *condition* more important on the *common* steins. When versions are known to be available in better condition, the price often has to be discounted more in order to make a transaction.

In addition, with several of the same stein available, a market price establishes itself for *specific* character steins. And it is not a market that lends itself to any kind of formulas. *Rarity* is probably the most important determinant of this market price, but rarity can not be identified by looking at a character stein. Even the absurd looking steins, like the radishes, can be relatively common.

Aesthetic appeal, although it can be judged by looking at a stein, is not always a good indicator of high market price. In fact, it sometimes seems that the most attractive character steins are often relatively common, and thus lower in price.

With no generalities or formulas available, all that can be done is to make the picture-price portion of this Section as large as possible, without making it disproportionate to its relative importance as an area of stein collecting.

Some unusually shaped steins from an E.J. Sullivan illustration.

a. Gentleman Fox, .5L, porcelain, mkd. *MUSTERSCHUTZ,* tan, brown, green, c.1900, $2000.

b. Gentleman Dog, .5L, porcelain, mkd. *MUSTERSCHUTZ,* tan, brown, green, c.1900, $2000.

c. Gentleman Rabbit, .5L, porcelain, mkd. *MUSTERSCHUTZ,* tan, brown, green, c.1900, $2000.

d. Stag, .5L, porcelain, mkd. *MUSTERSCHUTZ,* tan, brown, c.1900, $2800.

e. Gentleman Boar, .5L, porcelain, mkd. *MUSTERSCHUTZ,* gray, black, green, c.1900, $2600; tan, brown, $2000.

f. Owl, .5L, porcelain, mkd. *MUSTERSCHUTZ,* tan, white, yellow, gold, c.1900, $1000.

g. Gentleman Rooster, .5L, porcelain, mkd. *MUSTERSCHUTZ,* red, brown, tan, c.1900, $1700.

a. Fish, .5L, pottery, mkd. *1152 Reinhold Merkelbach,* tan, black, c.1900, $300.

b. Frog, .5L, pottery, mkd. *27,* by Dumler & Breiden, tan, red, dressed as a Roman Field Commander, c.1900, $350.

c. Frog, .5L, porcelain, unmarked, white, green, c.1900, $850.

d. Eagle, .5L, pottery, mkd. *M. Sch. & Co. Ulm MUSTERSCHUTZ,* tan, brown, c.1900, $300; stoneware, saltglaze, .5L, $325; .3L, $300.

e. Frog, .5L, porcelain, mkd. *MUSTERSCHUTZ,* white, green, c.1900, $1000.

f. Fish, .5L, porcelain, mkd. *MUSTERSCHUTZ,* white, gray, black, c.1900, $850.

g. Alligator, .5L, porcelain, mkd. *MUSTERSCHUTZ,* white, green, tan, c.1900; 1.0L, $1100; .5L, $900.

h. Wrap Around Alligator, .5L, porcelain, bisque glaze, probably by E. Bohne Soehne, bluish white, green, c.1900, $700; .25L, $475.

a. Frog, .5L, porcelain, unmarked, white, green, music box base, c.1900, $950.

b. Berlin Bear, .5L, porcelain, mkd. *MUSTERSCHUTZ,* tan, c.1900, $800.

c. Drunken Monkey, .5L, porcelain, mkd. *MUSTERSCHUTZ,* tan, c.1900, $500; blue, white, $750.

d. Cat with Hangover, .5L, porcelain, mkd. *MUSTERSCHUTZ,* tan, c.1900, $600; blue, white, $800.

e. Frog Dueler, .5L, porcelain, unmarked, white, tan, c.1900, $800.

f. Rabbit Hunter, .5L, porcelain, mkd. with hash marks, white, tan, probably 1920's, $500.

g. Rabbit Hunter, .5L, porcelain, mkd. *R.P.M.,* green, tan, c.1950, $325.

h. Fox, .5L, porcelain, unmarked, white, black, brown, lithophane, c.1900, $325.

a. Lion, .5L, porcelain, mkd. *MUSTERSCHUTZ,* tan, c.1900, $1500.

b. Bison, .3L, porcelain, bisque glaze, probably by E. Bohne Soehne, black, bluish white, c.1900; .5L, $1200; .3L, $800.

c. Bison, .3L, porcelain, bisque glaze, probably by E. Bohne Soehne, black, bluish white, c.1900, $500.

d. Elephant, .5L, porcelain, mkd. *MUSTERSCHUTZ,* grays, c.1900, $900; tan, brown, $900.

e. Elephant, .5L, pottery, mkd. *1447,* by Steinzeugwerke, gray, black, early 1900's, $300.

f. Donkey, .5L, pottery, mkd. *1454,* by Steinzeugwerke, gray, early 1900's, $300.

g. Rhinoceros, .5L, pottery, mkd. *1451,* by Steinzeugwerke, black, early, 1900's, $300.

a. Pig, .5L, pottery, mkd. *1770,* tan, c.1900, $225.

b. Pig, .5L, pottery, mkd. *1260,* by Steinzeugwerke, pink, early 1900's, $225.

c. Smoking Pig, .5L, porcelain, mkd. *MUSTERSCHUTZ,* white, tan, pink, c.1900, $400; .3L, $350; blue, white, .5L, $600.

d. Singing Pig, .5L, porcelain, mkd. *MUSTERSCHUTZ,* white, tan, pink, c.1900, $400; .3L, $350; blue, white, .5L, $600.

e. Pig, .5L, pottery, mkd. *1116, Reinhold Merkelbach,* tan, c.1900, $300.

f. Pig, .5L, pottery, mkd. *1116, Reinhold Merkelbach,* tan, c.1900, $300.

g. Pig, .5L, pottery, mkd. *1116, Reinhold Merkelbach,* tan, c.1900, $300.

h. Seated Ram, .5L, porcelain, mkd. *MUSTERSCHUTZ,* tan, c.1900, $550.

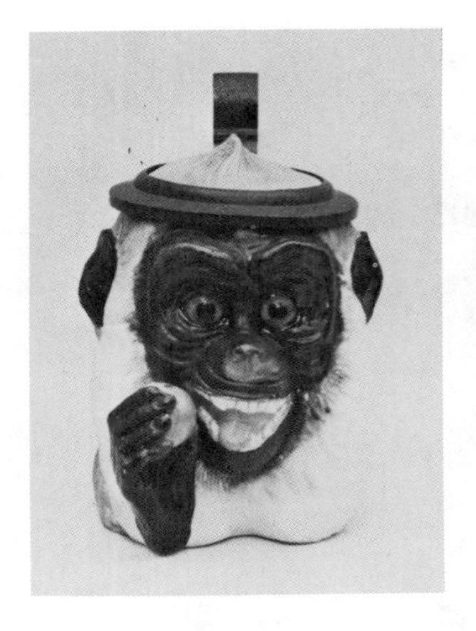

a. Monkey, .3L, porcelain, bisque glaze, probably by E. Bohne Soehne, white, black, gray, c.1900, $1000.

b. Ram, .5L, porcelain, mkd. MUSTERSCHUTZ, tan, c.1900, $1000.

c. Fox, .5L, stoneware, unmarked, blue saltglaze, c.1900, $250.

d. Bear, .5L, pottery, mkd. *731, Reinhold Merkelbach,* brown, c.1900, $300.

e. Monkey, .5L, stoneware, unmarked, blue saltglaze, c.1900, $275.

f. Fox, .5L, stoneware, unmarked, blue saltglaze, c.1900, $250.

g. Pig, .5L, pottery, mkd. *698 D.R.G.M.,* tan, pink, c.1900, $275.

a. Monkey, .5L, pottery, mkd. *858 D.R.G.M.,* brown, c.1900, $250.

b. Monkey, .5L, pottery, mkd. *817 D.R.G.M.,* brown, c.1900, $250.

c. Monkey, .5L, pottery, mkd. *1261,* by Steinzeugwerke, brown, tan, early 1900's, $225.

d. Monkey, .5L, pottery, mkd. *694,* tan, brown, blue, c.1900, $325.

e. Monkey, .5L, pottery, mkd. *421 Eckhardt & Engler KG,* brown, 1920's, $225.

f. Monkey, 1.0L, pottery, mkd. *1286,* by Steinzeugwerke, tan, brown, early 1900's, $300.

g. Monkey, .5L, pottery, mkd. *1261,* by Steinzeugwerke, tan, brown, early 1900's, $275.

h. Military Monkey, .5L, pottery, unmarked, by J.W. Remy, brown, black, gold, c.1900, $350.

a. Owl, .5L, pottery, mkd. *147,* by Reinhold Merkelbach, brown, tan, c.1900, $275.

b. Owl, .5L, pottery, mkd. *740,* brown, tan, c.1900, $275.

c. Owl, .5L, pottery, mkd. *Merkelbach & Wick,* tan, brown, c.1900, $300.

d. Owl, .5L, pottery, mkd. *147,* probably by Reinhold Merkelbach, brown, tan, c.1900, $300.

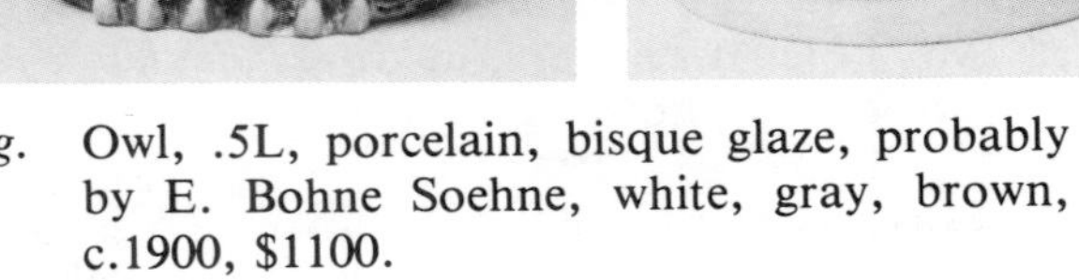

e. Owl, .5L, stoneware, mkd. *HR 64,* blue and purple saltglazes, c.1900, $350.

f. Owl, .5L, pottery, mkd. *444 Gerz,* tan, brown, c.1900, $325.

g. Owl, .5L, porcelain, bisque glaze, probably by E. Bohne Soehne, white, gray, brown, c.1900, $1100.

h. Owl, 2.9L, pottery, mkd. *584,* tan, brown, c.1900, $450.

a. Poodle, .5L, pottery, mkd. *1452,* probably by Steinzeugwerke, tan, brown, early 1900's, $375.

b. Cat, .5L, pottery, mkd. *511,* tan, brown, c.1900, $300.

c. Cat, .5L, pottery, mkd. *701 D.R.G.M.,* tan, yellow, brown, c.1900, $325.

d. Monkey, .5L, pottery, mkd. *1444,* tan, brown, c.1900, $275.

e. Ram, .5L, pottery, mkd. *700 D.R.G.M.,* brown, tan, black, c.1900, $250.

f. Ram, .5L, stoneware, mkd. *Merkelbach & Wick,* blue saltglaze, c.1900, $275.

g. Bulldog, .5L, pottery, mkd. *1440,* probably by Steinzeugwerke, tan, brown, early 1900's, $250.

a. Cat, .5L, pottery, unmarked, probably by Reinhold Merkelbach, brown, gray, black, c.1900, $325.

b. Cat, .5L, pottery, mkd. *576 Reinhold Merkelbach,* brown, gray, black, c.1900, $375.

c. Cat, .5L, pottery, mkd. *Merkelbach & Wick,* tan, black, c.1900, $250.

d. Cat, .5L, pottery, mkd. *767,* by J.W. Remy, tan, brown, black, c.1900, $275.

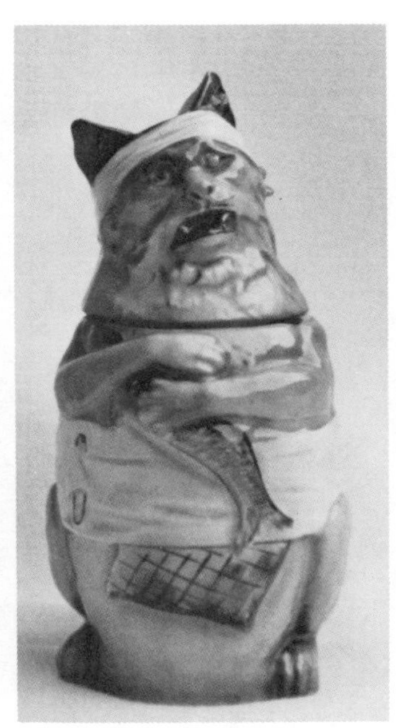

e. Cat, .5L, porcelain, mkd. *MUSTERSCHUTZ,* white, black, gray, c.1900, $850.

f. Cat, .1L, stoneware, mkd. *Simon Peter Gerz,* blue saltglaze, c.1900, $150.

g. Cat, .5L, pottery, mkd. *364 Kleinlein & Cie,* tan, black, c.1900, $275.

h. Cat, .5L, porcelain, unmarked, white, gray, c.1900, $800.

a. Clown, .5L, porcelain, mkd. *MUSTERSCHUTZ,* white, pink, red, c.1900, $2000.

b. Clown, .5L, porcelain, unmarked, white, red, lithophane, c.1900, $800.

c. Indian Chief, .5L, porcelain, bisque glaze, mkd. *E. Bohne Soehne,* white, black, tan, c.1900, $750; .25L, $475.

d. Alpine Man, .5L, porcelain, unmarked, green, black, pink, c.1900, $700.

e. Heidelberg Student, .5L, porcelain, mkd. *MUSTERSCHUTZ,* tan, white, brown, c.1900, $1200.

f. Pixie, .5L, porcelain, mkd. *MUSTERSCHUTZ,* tan, white, brown, c.1900, $850.

g. Pixie, .5L, porcelain, mkd. *MUSTERSCHUTZ,* tan, white, brown, music box base, c.1900, $950.

a. Bismarck, .5L, porcelain, mkd. *MUSTERSCHUTZ,* tan, brown, c.1900, $550; .3L, $440; .5L, mkd. *MUSTERSCHUTZ,* full color, $2500; .5L, heavy porcelain, mkd. with hash marks, full color, c.1925, $200.

b. Wilhelm II, .5L, porcelain, mkd. *MUSTERSCHUTZ,* tan, brown, c.1900, $1600; full color, $2500.

c. Wilhelm II, .5L, porcelain, mkd. *MUSTERSCHUTZ,* tan, brown, c.1900, $1000.

d. Von Moltke, .5L, porcelain, mkd. *MUSTERSCHUTZ,* tan, brown, c.1900, $950.

e. Chinese-German Soldier, .5L, porcelain, mkd. *MUSTERSCHUTZ,* tan, brown, c.1900, $1600.

f. Bismarck in Retirement, .5L, porcelain, mkd. *MUSTERSCHUTZ,* tan, brown, c.1900, $950.

a. Wilhelm I, .5L, porcelain, mkd. *MUSTERSCHUTZ,* tan, brown, c.1900, $1000.

b. Soldier, .5L, porcelain, mkd. *MUSTERSCHUTZ,* tan, brown, c.1900, $1000.

c. Uncle Sam, .5L, porcelain, mkd. *MUSTERSCHUTZ,* tan, brown, c.1900, $1700; full color, $3000.

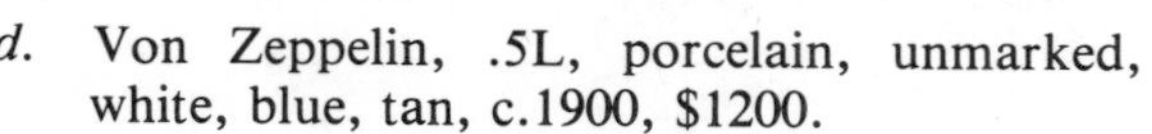

d. Von Zeppelin, .5L, porcelain, unmarked, white, blue, tan, c.1900, $1200.

e. Soldier, .5L, porcelain, unmarked, blue, red, tan, c.1900, $1100.

f. King Ludwig II, .5L, porcelain, bisque glaze, unmarked, tan, brown, c.1900, $2000.

a. Frederich III, .5L, porcelain, mkd. *MUSTERSCHUTZ,* tan, brown, c.1900, $2000.

b. Soldier, .5L, porcelain, mkd. *MUSTERSCHUTZ,* tan, brown, c.1900, $1200.

c. Father Jahn, .5L, porcelain, mkd. *MUSTERSCHUTZ,* tan, brown, c.1900, $1100.

d. English Sailor, .125L, porcelain, unmarked, white, blue, black, c.1900, $500.

e. Chinaman, .5L, porcelain, mkd. *MUSTERSCHUTZ,* tan, brown, c.1900, $750.

f. Judge, .5L, porcelain, mkd. *MUSTERSCHUTZ,* tan, brown, c.1900, $700.

a. Father Jahn, 1.0L, porcelain, mkd. *MUSTERSCHUTZ,* blue, white, c.1900, $1500; tan, brown, $1300.

b. Father Jahn, .5L, porcelain, mkd. *MUSTERSCHUTZ,* tan, white, brown, c.1900, $1100.

c. Masquerade Lady, .5L, porcelain, mkd. *MUSTERSCHUTZ,* tan, white, brown, c.1900, $1600.

d. Monk, .5L, porcelain, bisque glaze, mkd. *E. Bohne Soehne,* orange, tan, c.1900, $850; .25L, $600.

e. Hops Lady, .5L, porcelain, mkd. *MUSTERSCHUTZ,* tan, green, brown, c.1900, $700.

f. Caroline, .5L, porcelain, mkd. *MUSTERSCHUTZ,* tan, brown, $650.

g. Karoline, .5L, porcelain, mkd. *MUSTERSCHUTZ,* tan, brown, $1500.

a. Uncomfortable Burger, .5L, pottery, mkd. *1426,* tan, brown, pink, c.1900, pewter lid, $175.

b. Man with Pipe, .5L, pottery, mkd. *1459,* by Steinzeugwerke, tan, brown, white, early 1900's, pewter lid, $175.

c. Man with Pipe, .5L, pottery, mkd. unmarked, tan, pink, brown, c.1900, pewter lid, $150.

d. Student, .5L, pottery, mkd. *Eckhardt & Engler KG,* tan, brown, pink, c.1925, $225; mkd. *426,* by Rosskopf & Gerz, c.1900, $275.

e. Happy Radish, .3L, porcelain, mkd. *MUSTERSCHUTZ,* tan, brown, green, c.1900; .5L, $375; .3L, $325; blue, white, .5L, $550; .3L, $500.

f. Sad Radish, .5L, porcelain, mkd. *MUSTERSCHUTZ,* tan, brown, green, c.1900, $375; .3L, $325; blue, white, .5L, $550; .3L, $500.

g. Sad Radish, 3.0L, porcelain, mkd. *MUSTERSCHUTZ,* tan, brown, green, c.1900, $950.

h. Bismarck Radish, .5L, porcelain, mkd. *MUSTERSCHUTZ,* tan, brown, green, c.1900, $475; .25L, $400.

a. Sea Captain, .5L, stoneware, mkd. *L B & C,* blue saltglaze, c.1900, $475.

b. Bismarck, .5L, stoneware, unmarked, probably by Whites Pottery, blue saltglaze, c.1900, $375.

c. Swiss Soldier, .5L, stoneware, mkd. *L B & C,* blue saltglaze, c.1900, $475.

d. Duelist, 1.0L, pottery, mkd. *2885 Saareguemines,* tan, brown, pink, c.1900, pewter lid, $225.

e. Drunken Man, .5L, pottery, mkd. *17 Eckhardt & Engler KG,* tan, brown, pink, c.1925, pewter lid, $150.

f. Smirking Man, .5L, pottery, mkd. *693 D.R.G.M.,* tan, brown, pink, c.1900, $225.

a. Black Boy, .5L, porcelain, unmarked, white, black, brown, c.1900, $850.

b. Mephisto, .5L, porcelain, mkd. *MUSTERSCHUTZ,* red, black, tan, brown, c.1900, $1800.

c. Devil, .5L, porcelain, bisque glaze, mkd. *E. Bohne Soehne,* red, white, black, c.1900, $700; .25L, $475.

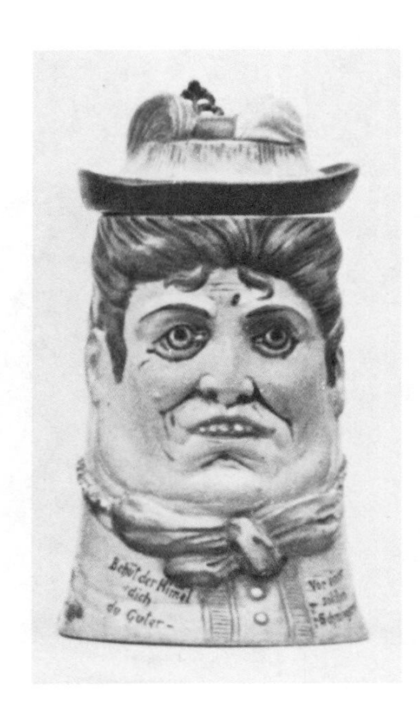

d. Caroline, .5L, pottery, mkd. *753,* tan, brown, pink, c.1900, $300.

e. Hops Lady, .5L, pottery, mkd. *1424,* tan, brown, pink, c.1900, pewter lid, $150.

f. Woman, .5L, pottery, mkd. *429,* tan, brown, yellow, c.1900, $325.

a. Skull, .5L, porcelain, bisque glaze, mkd. *E. Bohne Soehne,* tan, white, brown, c.1900; .625L, $550; .5L, $475; .4L, $400; .3L, $375; .25L, $375.

b. Skull & Devil, .25L, porcelain, bisque glaze, mkd. *E. Bohne Soehne,* tan, black, c.1900, $475.

c. Skull, .5L, porcelain, bisque glaze, unmarked, tan, white, black, red, devil handle, c.1900, pewter lid, $550.

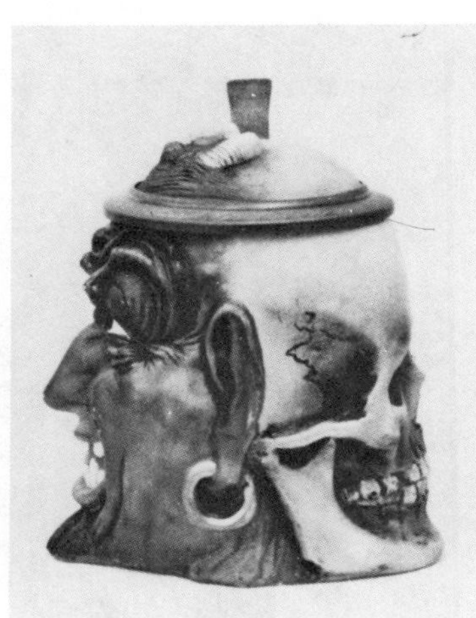

d. Skull, .25L, porcelain, bisque glaze, unmarked, tan, black, c.1900; .5L, $350; .3L, $300.

e. Skull, .25L, porcelain, bisque glaze, unmarked, tan, black, c.1900, $325.

f. Skull, .4L, porcelain, bisque glaze, tan, black, c.1900, $400.

g. Skull & Devil, .5L, porcelain, bisque glaze, mkd. *E. Bohne Soehne,* tan, black, red, c.1900, $625.

a. Man in the Moon, .4L, porcelain, mkd. *E. Bohne Soehne,* tan, c.1900, $950.

b. Chinaman, .5L, porcelain, mkd. *J. REINEMANN MUNCHEN,* yellow, red, black, lithophane, c.1900, pewter lid, $550.

c. Devil, .5L, stoneware, mkd. *Merkelbach & Wick,* purple saltglaze, c.1900, $250.

d. Radish, .5L, porcelain, mkd. *E. Bohne Soehne,* gray, green, c.1900, $500.

e. Radish, .5L, pottery, mkd. *1225,* yellow, green, brown, c.1900, $225.

f. Happy Radish, .5L, porcelain, unmarked, white, pink, green, c.1900, $450.

g. Happy Radish, .5L, porcelain, unmarked, tan, green, lithophane, c.1900, $800.

a. Cavalier, .5L, stoneware, mkd. *Merkelbach & Wick,* blue and purple saltglazes, c.1900, $275.

b. Robust Man, .5L, stoneware, unmarked, blue saltglaze, c.1900, $275.

c. Man, .5L, stoneware, mkd. *804,* blue and purple saltglazes, c.1900, $300.

d. Fireman, .5L, stoneware, unmarked, blue saltglaze, c.1900, $325.

e. Rich Man, .5L, stoneware, unmarked, probably Reinhold Merkelbach, blue and purple saltglazes, c.1900, $350.

f. Robust Man, .5L, stoneware, unmarked, blue and purple saltglazes, c.1900, $250.

g. Rich Man, .5L, pottery, mkd. *Merkelbach & Wick,* tan, green, c.1900, $275.

h. Rich Man, .5L, pottery, mkd. *8669,* tan, brown, c.1900, $250; mkd. *722,* by Marzi & Remy, $275.

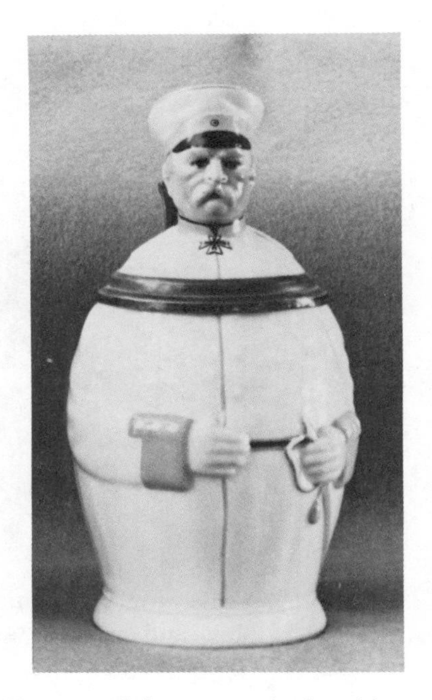

a. Frederick III, .5L, pottery, mkd. *Merkelbach & Wick,* tan, brown, blue, c.1900, $400.

b. Frederick III, .5L, pottery, mkd. *T W 20,* tan, blue, c.1900, $475.

c. Bismarck, .5L, porcelain, unmarked, white, black, pink, lithophane, c.1900, $850.

d. Wilhelm I, .5L, stoneware, mkd. *Merkelbach & Wick,* blue and purple saltglazes, c.1900, $450.

e. Rich Man, .5L, pottery, mkd. *175 A.J. Thewalt,* tan, brown, black, red, c.1900, $300.

f. Bearded Man, .5L, pottery, mkd. *697 D.R.G.M.,* tan, brown, black, c.1900, $275.

g. Black Boy, .5L, pottery, mkd. *737,* black, tan, red, c.1900, $400.

a. Gooseman of Nurnberg, .5L, porcelain, white, red, brown, black, lithophane, c.1900, $500.

b. Miner, .5L, pottery, mkd. *1241,* tan, brown, black, c.1900, $350.

c. Bowler, .5L, pottery, mkd. *1226,* tan, brown, black, c.1900, $350.

d. Heidelberg Student, .5L, porcelain, mkd. with hash marks, black, tan, pink, gray, c.1925, $350.

e. Cavalier, .5L, pottery, mkd. *1439,* by Steinzeugwerke, tan, yellow, red, green, early 1900's, $250.

f. Cavalier, 1.0L, porcelain, mkd. *Bavaria,* tan, white, c.1900, $800.

g. Funnel Man, .5L, pottery, mkd. *622,* by Reinhold Hanke, tan, brown, c.1900, $300.

h. Clown, .5L, pottery, mkd. *987,* by Reinhold Hanke, tan, brown, c.1900, $300.

a. Smiling Chinaman, .5L, stoneware, unmarked, blue saltglaze, c.1900, $300.

b. Hunter, .5L, stoneware, unmarked, blue saltglaze, c.1900, $325.

c. Iron Maiden of Nurnberg, .5L, stoneware, mkd. *T W,* possibly Theodore Wieseler, purple saltglaze, c.1900, $350.

d. Miner, .5L, pottery, mkd. *736,* by Reinhold Merkelbach, tan, brown, black, c.1900, $375.

e. Von Moltke, .5L, pottery, unmarked, tan, brown, c.1900, $375.

f. Knight, .5L, stoneware, mkd. *746,* blue and purple saltglazes, c.1900, $400.

g. Dutch Girl, .5L, pottery, mkd. *685 Reinhold Merkelbach,* tan, brown, c.1900, $325.

h. Heidelberg Black Student, .5L, porcelain, unmarked, black, white, gray, lithophane, c.1900, $400.

a. Dutch Boy, .5L, porcelain, mkd. *MUSTERSCHUTZ,* brown, tan, orange, green, c.1900, $1000; blue, white, $750.

b. Dutch Girl, .5L, porcelain, mkd. *MUSTERSCHUTZ,* white, black, green, blue, c.1900, $1200; blue, white, $750.

c. Coffee Girl, .5L, porcelain, bisque glaze, unmarked, white, blue, lithophane, c.1900, $1300.

d. Round Man, .5L, stoneware, mkd. *J. Reinemann Munchen,* gray, blue, c.1900, $275.

e. Snowman, .5L, porcelain, mkd. *MUSTERSCHUTZ,* white, blue, c.1900, $950.

f. Landlord, .5L, porcelain, unmarked, tan, brown, white, c.1900, $800.

a. Sea Captain, .5L, porcelain, mkd. *MUSTERSCHUTZ,* tan, brown, c.1900, $900.

b. Alpine Man, .5L, porcelain, mkd. MUSTERSCHUTZ, tan, brown, white, c.1900, $1100.

c. Turkish Man, .5L, porcelain, mkd. *MUSTERSCHUTZ,* tan, brown, white, c.1900, $900.

d. Judge, 5L, porcelain, mkd. *MUSTERSCHUTZ,* tan, brown, white, porcelain jester thumblift, c.1900, $1100.

e. Barmaid, .5L, porcelain, mkd. *MUSTERSCHUTZ,* tan, brown, white, c.1900, $1500.

f. Tyrolean Schoolteacher, .5L, porcelain, bisque glaze, mkd. *M. Pauson Munchen,* green, brown, white, c.1900, $1000.

a. Monk, .5L, pottery, mkd. *1574,* by Steinzeugwerke, brown, black, early 1900's, $300.

b. Barmaid, .5L, pottery, mkd. *1571,* by Steinzeugwerke, brown, tan, blue, early 1900's, $300.

c. Minstrel Man, .5L, pottery, mkd. *1005 Geschutzt,* white, brown, tan, c.1900, $250.

d. Man, .5L, pottery, mkd. *1045 Geschutzt,* tan, brown, c.1900, $400.

e. Soldier, .5L, pottery, mkd. *1577,* by Steinzeugwerke, white, black, red, early 1900's, $350.

f. Woman, .5L, pottery, mkd. *1579,* by Steinzeugwerke, tan, blue, red, early 1900's, $350.

g. Woman with Baby, .5L, pottery, mkd. *1580,* by Steinzeugwerke, tan, brown, red, early 1900's, $350.

h. Fat Man, .5L, pottery, mkd. *1566,* by Steinzeugwerke, brown, yellow, gray, early 1900's, $300.

a. Chinaman, .5L, pottery, mkd. *Merkelbach & Wick,* tan, yellow, blue, c.1900, $375.

b. Cavalier, .5L, pottery, mkd. *Merkelbach & Wick,* tan, blue, brown, c.1900, $300.

c. Woodsman, .5L, pottery, mkd. *695 D.R.G.M.,* brown, green, c.1900, $250.

d. Gambrinus, .5L, pottery, mkd. *705 D.R.G.M.,* brown, tan, black, purple, c.1900, $275.

e. Gambrinus, .25L, pottery, *127 D.R.G.M.,* c.1900, $225.

f. Little Red Hiding Hood, .25L, pottery, mkd. *J. Reinemann Munchen,* tan, red, c.1900, $250.

g. Clown, .5L, pottery, mkd. *1570,* by Steinzeugwerke, tan, yellow, gray, c.1900, $300.

h. Man with Newspaper, .5L, pottery, mkd. *871,* by Reinhold Hanke, tan, brown, c.1900, $225.

i. Hobo, .5L, pottery, mkd. *723,* tan, brown, c.1900, $225.

a. Gooseman of Nurnberg, .5L, porcelain, bisque glaze, unmarked, tan, white, brown, orange, c.1900, $1300; .25L, $700.

b. Gooseman of Nurnberg, .5L, porcelain, unmarked, tan, white, brown, lithophane, c.1900, $800.

c. Gooseman of Nurnberg, .5L, porcelain, unmarked, green, bronze, c.1900, $850; .25L, $500.

d. Perkeo, .5L, porcelain, unmarked, green, white, c.1900, $800.

e. Rich Lady, .5L, pottery, mkd. *680,* blue, black, tan, c.1900, $350.

f. Top Hat, .5L, pottery, mkd. D.R.G.M., tan, brown, yellow, black, c.1900, $300.

g. Fireman, .5L, stoneware, marked *750,* blue and purple saltglazes, c.1900, $350.

h. Woman, .5L, pottery, mkd. *Merkelbach & Wick,* tan, brown, pink, c.1900. $275.

a. Lady with Bustle, .5L, pewter and wood, unmarked, c.1900, $1400.

b. Mephistopheles Tempting the Maiden, .5L, pewter, unmarked, c.1900, $2000.

c. Bavaria, 1.0L, pottery, unmarked, tan, brown, black, c.1900, $750.

a. Moneybags, .5L, porcelain, mkd. *403,* blue, black, green, c.1900, $450.

b. Mushroom Lady, .5L, porcelain, mkd. *MUSTERSCHUTZ,* white, orange, lavender, c.1900, $1500.

c. Radish Lady, .5L, porcelain, mkd. *MUSTERSCHUTZ,* white, green, blue, c.1900, $1800.

d. Newspaper Lady, .5L, porcelain, mkd. *MUSTERSCHUTZ,* blue, tan, brown, c.1900, $1800.

Opposite:

d. Woman, 2.0L, faience, unmarked, white, blue, purple, probably late 1800's, $750.

e. Man, 2.0L, faience, unmarked, white, blue, 1800's, $750.

f. Knight, 1.5L, stoneware, mkd. *133,* blue saltglaze, c.1900, $500.

a. Monk, .5L, pottery, mkd. *Merkelbach & Wick,* tan, brown, c.1900, $400.

b. Munich Child, .5L, pewter, unmarked, c.1900, $475.

c. Monk, .5L, pewter, unmarked, c.1900, $450.

d. Monk, .5L, stoneware, mkd. *112,* purple saltglaze, c.1900, $225.

e. Monk, .5L, pottery, mkd. *67,* tan, brown, c.1900, $225.

f. Monk, .5L, pottery, mkd. *8670,* black, brown, c.1900, $225.

g. Monk, .5L, porcelain, unmarked, red, white, pink, lithophane, c.1900, $250.

a. Munich Child, .5L, pottery, mkd. *314,* by Marzi & Remy, tan, black, c.1900, $300.

b. Munich Child, .5L, pottery, mkd. *323 Reinhold Merkelbach,* tan, black, c.1900, $300.

c. Nun, .5L, pottery, mkd. *462,* by Reinhold Hanke, tan, brown, black, c.1900, $225.

d. Munich Child, .5L, pottery, mkd. *Joseph M. Mayer Munchen,* tan, black, c.1900, $325.

e. Nun, .5L, porcelain, unmarked, black, white, lithophane, c.1900, $250.

f. Nun, .5L, stoneware, mkd. *194,* blue, saltglaze, c.1900, $225.

g. Nun, .5L, pottery, mkd. *462,* tan, brown, c.1900, $225.

h. Nun, .5L, pottery, mkd. *Merkelbach & Wick,* brown, c.1900, $250.

a. Munich Child, .5L, porcelain, unmarked, red, yellow, c.1900, $250; .25L, $175.

b. Munich Child, .5L, porcelain, unmarked, black, yellow, lithophane, c.1900, $300.

c. Munich Child, .5L, porcelain, bisque glaze, mkd. *Martin Pauson Munchen,* black, yellow, blue, lithophane, c.1900, $475.

d. Munich Child, .5L, porcelain, mkd. *Martin Pauson Munchen MUSTERSCHUTZ,* tan, brown, gray, lithophane, c.1900, $475.

e. Munich Child, .5L, pottery, mkd. *J. Reinemann Munchen,* black, tan, c.1900, $200; .3L, $150; .25L, $150; .125L, $125.

f. Munich Child, .5L, pottery, mkd. *F,* by Reinhold Merkelbach, black, tan, c.1900, $325.

g. Munich Child, .5L, porcelain, unmarked, black, tan, gold, c.1900, $425.

h. Munich Child, .5L, stoneware, mkd. *JRM,* by J. Reinemann Munchen, blue and purple saltglazes, c.1900, $400.

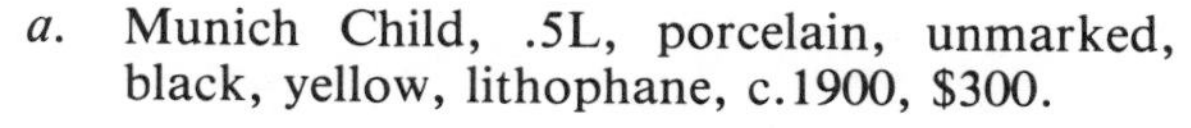

a. Munich Child, .5L, porcelain, unmarked, black, yellow, lithophane, c.1900, $300.

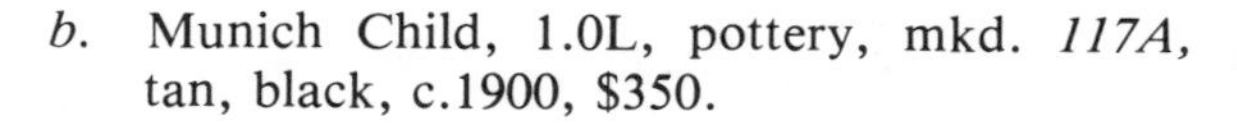

b. Munich Child, 1.0L, pottery, mkd. *117A,* tan, black, c.1900, $350.

c. Munich Child, 1.0L, stoneware, mkd. *1285,* gray, black, c.1900, porcelain lid, $375.

d. Munich Child, .1L, porcelain, unmarked, black, gray, yellow, c.1900, $250.

e. Munich Child, .25L, porcelain, mkd. *Joseph M. Mayer Munchen,* black, tan, gold, lithophane, c.1900; 1.0L, $500; .5L, $400; .25L, $325.

f. Munich Child, .5L, stoneware, mkd. *1585,* gray, black, c.1900, pottery lid, $300.

g. Munich Child, .5L, stoneware, unmarked, purple saltglaze, c.1900, $325.

h. Munich Child, .3L, pottery, mkd. *Joseph M. Mayer Munchen,* tan, black, c.1900, $350.

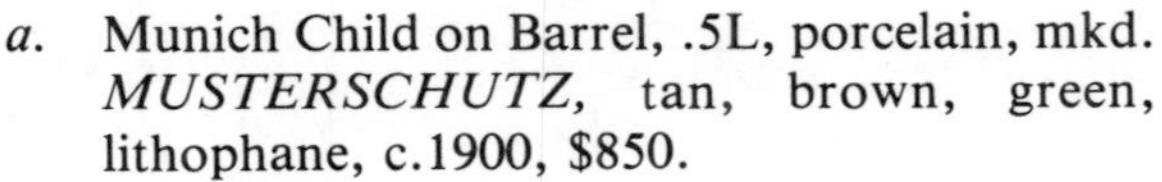

a. Munich Child on Barrel, .5L, porcelain, mkd. *MUSTERSCHUTZ,* tan, brown, green, lithophane, c.1900, $850.

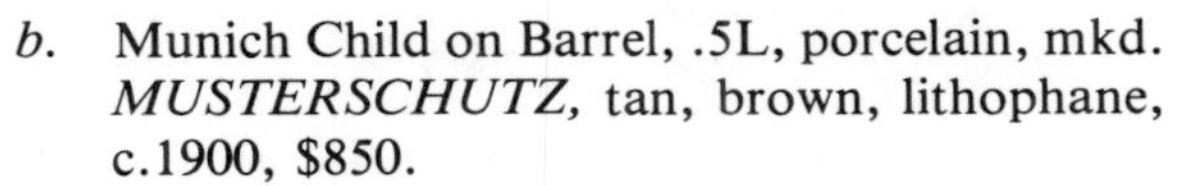

b. Munich Child on Barrel, .5L, porcelain, mkd. *MUSTERSCHUTZ,* tan, brown, lithophane, c.1900, $850.

c. Munich Child, .25L, stoneware, mkd. *J. Reinemann Munchen,* black, yellow, c.1900, $250.

d. Munich Child on Barrel, .5L, porcelain mkd. *Martin Pauson Munchen,* tan, black, lithophane, c.1900, $750.

e. Munich Child on Barrel, 1.0L, porcelain, mkd. *MUSTERSCHUTZ Martin Pauson Munchen,* tan, black, lithophane, c.1900, $900.

f. Perkeo on Barrel, .5L, porcelain, mkd. *MUSTERSCHUTZ,* tan, brown, lithophane, c.1900, $650.

a. Bowling Pin, .5L, porcelain, mkd. *MUSTERSCHUTZ,* tan, brown, lithophane, c.1900, $450.

b. Bowling Pin, .5L, pottery, mkd. *1140,* by Steinzeugwerke, tan, brown, early 1900's, $250.

c. Bowling Pin, .5L, pottery, mkd. *885,* by Reinhold Merkelbach, tan, brown, c.1900, $300.

d. Bowling Pin, 1.0L, pottery, mkd. *1266,* brown, green, c.1900, $275.

e. Bowling Pin, .5L, pottery, mkd. *1134,* by Steinzeugwerke, tan, brown, early 1900's, $150.

f. Bowling Pin, .5L, pottery, mkd. *885,* by Reinhold Merkelbach, tan, brown, c.1900, $300.

g. Bowling Pin, .5L, porcelain, unmarked, tan, brown, c.1900, $375.

a. Lawn Tennis, .5L, pottery, mkd. *1226,* probably by Steinzeugwerke, green, tan, early 1900's, $350.

b. Barbell, .5L, pottery, mkd. *1227,* probably by Steinzeugwerke, tan, green, early 1900's, $350.

c. Weight, .5L, pottery, mkd. *1251,* by Steinzeugwerke, black, tan, green, early 1900's, $350.

d. Football, .5L, porcelain, mkd. *T. Maddocks Sons Co., Trenton, N.J.,* orange, black, c.1900, $275.

e. Bowling Ball, .5L, porcelain, mkd. *MUSTERSCHUTZ,* tan, brown, black, c.1900, $350.

f. Soccer Ball, .5L, pottery mkd. *1106 Rochlitz Sporthaus Charlottenburg,* tan, gray, c. 1900, $350.

a. L.A.W. Bicycle, .5L, porcelain, mkd. *MUSTERSCHUTZ,* tan, brown, lithophane, c.1900, $375.

b. Bicycle, .5L, porcelain, mkd. *MUSTERSCHUTZ,* tan, brown, lithophane, c.1900, $400.

c. Pig in a Poke, .5L, porcelain, mkd. *5399,* gray, white, c.1900, $350.

d. Nurnberg Trichter, .5L, porcelain, mkd. *MUSTERSCHUTZ,* gray, black, orange, lithophane, c.1900, $550; .25L, $400.

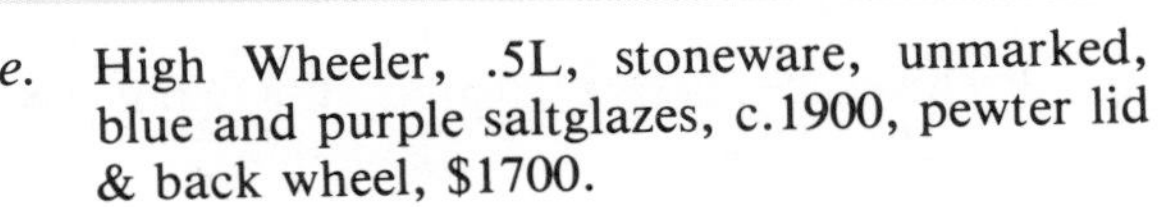

e. High Wheeler, .5L, stoneware, unmarked, blue and purple saltglazes, c.1900, pewter lid & back wheel, $1700.

f. Bowling Pin, 2.0L, pottery, unmarked, brown, tan, c.1900, $350.

g. Football, 2.0L, porcelain, mkd. *T. Maddocks Sons Co., Trenton, NJ,* orange, black, c.1900, $450.

a. Apple and Snake, .5L, porcelain, no marks, yellow, c.1900, $550.

b. Bearded Man, 1.0L, pewter, mkd. *B & G Imperial Zinn,* $350.

c. Pillow Flight, .5L, pewter, mkd. *F. Barte Munchen,* dtd. *1872,* $1000.

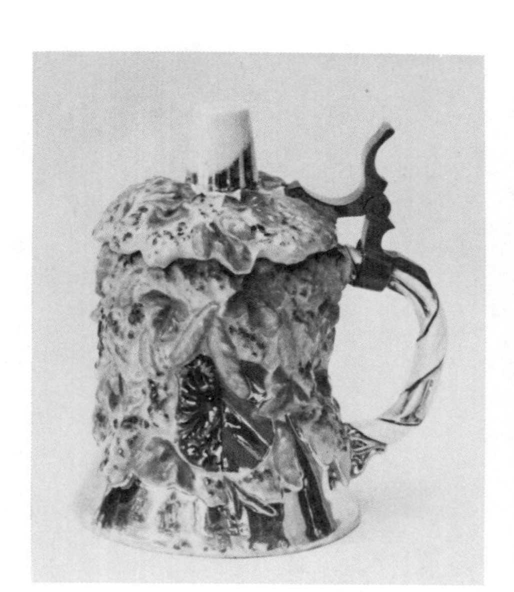

d. Trichter, .5L, porcelain, unmarked, white, gray, green, c.1900, $550.

e. Beehive, .5L, pottery, mkd. 1384, tan, red, c.1900, $250.

f. Bottle, .5L, stoneware, mkd. *L B & C,* blue saltglaze, c.1900, $300.

a. Mushroom, .5L, porcelain, mkd. *MUSTERSCHUTZ,* tan, brown, c.1900, $1500.

b. Horn and Boar, .5L, porcelain, mkd. *MUSTERSCHUTZ,* brown, white, c.1900, $800.

c. Horn and Bird, .25L, porcelain, mkd. *MUSTERSCHUTZ,* brown, white, c.1900, $500.

d. Taxpayer, .25L, porcelain, mkd. *2205,* brown, tan, c.1900, $475.

e. Berlin Barrel, .5L, porcelain, mkd. *MUSTERSCHUTZ,* tan, brown, c.1900, $600.

a. Salzburg Tower, .5L, pottery, mkd. *Gesetzl Geschutzt,* tan, black, c.1900, $325.

b. Tower, .5L, stoneware, unmarked, blue saltglaze, c.1900, pewter lid, $250.

c. Frauenkirche Tower, .5L, stoneware, mkd. *T W,* purple saltglaze, c.1900, pewter lid, $225.

d. Tower, .5L, pottery, mkd. *1541,* orange, brown, c.1900, $350.

e. Durerturm Tower, .5L, pottery, mkd. *1190 F & M N,* tan, brown, c.1900, pewter lid, $225.

f. Durerturm Tower, 1.0L, stoneware, mkd. *T W,* blue and purple saltglazes, c.1900, pewter lid, $275.

g. Durerturm Tower, .125L, stoneware, unmarked, blue and purple saltglazes, c.1900, pewter lid, $150.

h. Durerturm Tower, .5L, stoneware, mkd. *T W,* blue and purple saltglazes, c.1900, pewter lid, $200.

i. Durerturm Tower, .125L, pottery, mkd. *520 F & M N,* tan, brown, c.1900, $175.

a. Frauenkirche Tower, 1.0L, porcelain, mkd. *Martin Pauson Munchen,* red, white, green, lithophane, c.1900, $1100; .5L, $850.

b. Berlin City Hall, 1.0L, porcelain, unmarked, pink, white, black, c.1900, $1000.

c. Castle, 1.0L, pewter, unmarked, late 1800's, $850.

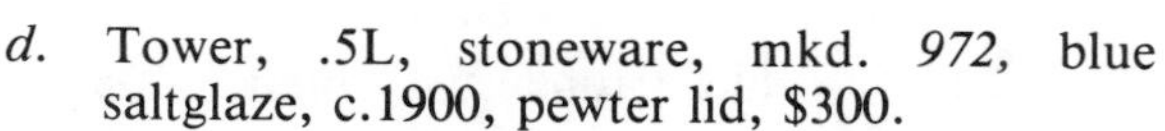

d. Tower, .5L, stoneware, mkd. *972,* blue saltglaze, c.1900, pewter lid, $300.

e. Durerturm Tower, .2L, pewter lid, mkd. *D.R.G.M.,* c.1900, $200.

f. Durerturm Tower, .1L, pewter lid, mkd. *D.R.G.M.,* c.1900, $180.

g. House, .5L, porcelain, mkd. *M. Pauson,* white, gray, red, green, dtd. 1895, $900.

a. Rook, .5L, stoneware, mkd. *J. Reinemann Munchen,* blue saltglaze, c.1900, $375.

b. Umbrella Men, .5L, porcelain, unmarked, pink, red, gray, music box base, c.1900, $1000.

c. Hot Air Balloon, .5L, pottery, mkd. *1232 Theodore Wieseler,* yellow, green, black, c.1910, $850; tan, brown, $650.

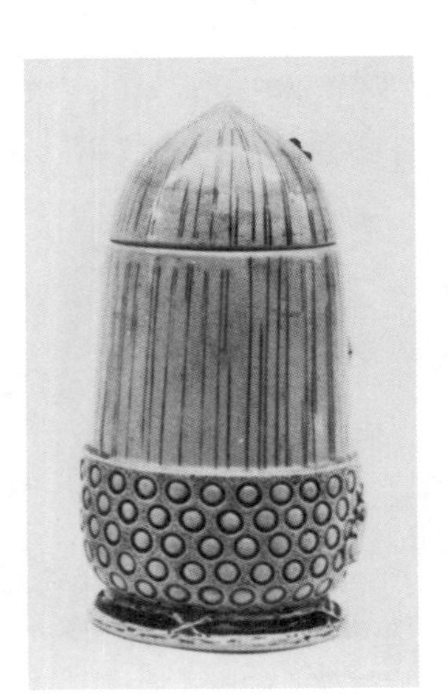

d. Acorn, .5L, pottery, mkd. *1235,* brown, green, yellow, c.1900, $225.

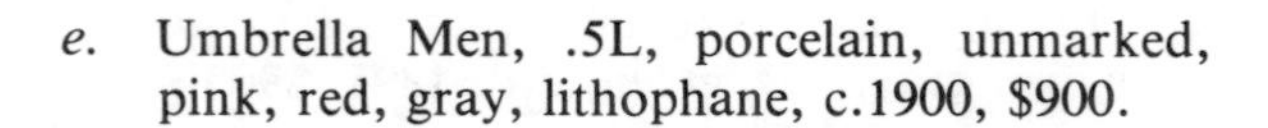

e. Umbrella Men, .5L, porcelain, unmarked, pink, red, gray, lithophane, c.1900, $900.

f. Zugspitze, .5L, stoneware, mkd. *Martin Pauson Munchen,* gray, black, green, c.1900, $650.

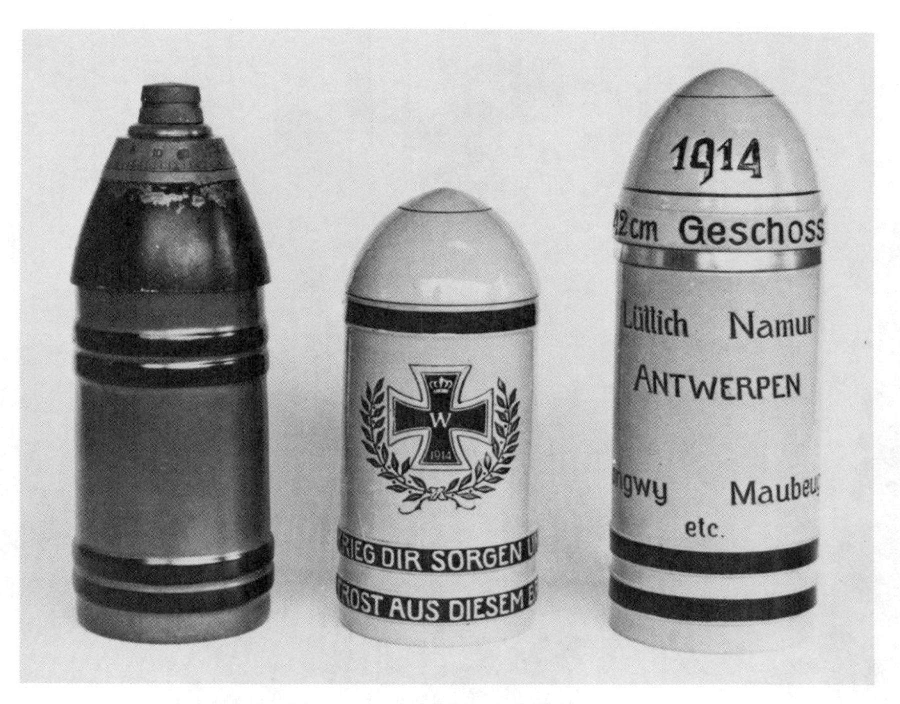

a. Artillery Shell, .5L, porcelain, unmarked, bronze, black, lithophane, c.1920, pewter lid, $225.

b. Artillery Shell, .5L, stoneware, mkd. *5309,* blue, black, after 1914, $225.

c. Artillery Shell, .5L, pottery, mkd. *441546 PA,* blue, black, after 1914, $225.

d. Artillery Shell, .5L, pottery, mkd. *617,* tan, brown, early 1900's, $300.

e. Navy Hat, .5L, porcelain, unmarked, blue, white, red, lithophane, c.1900, $450.

f. Acorn, .5L, porcelain, mkd. *Germany,* tan, blue, green, c.1900, $600.

g. Globe, .5L, pottery, mkd. *2368,* blue, brown, S./S. President Lincoln, c.1930, $350.

a. Munich Child, 2.5L, pottery, mkd. *789,* black, tan, c.1900, $600.

b. Fox, 2.0L, pottery, mkd. *D.R.G.M.,* yellow, tan, red, rust, c.1900, $850.

15. Bibliography and References

Journals

Der Gemutlichkeit, Stein Collectors International, *1,* September 1965, to *16,* June 1969.

Keramos, Villeroy & Boch Keramische Werke K.G., *1,* 1952, to *6,* 1978.

Mettlacher Turm, Mettlacher Steinzeugsammler E.V., *1,* 1977, to *10,* 1981.

Prosit, Stein Collectors International, *17,* September 1969, to *78,* December 1984.

General

Bernay, J. et. al., 1983. *Das Grosse Lexikon vom Bier und seinen Brauereien,* Scripta Verlag, Stuttgart.

Dexel, W., 1939. *Deutsches Handwerksgut - Eine Kultur - und Formengeschichte des Hausgerats,* Berlin.

Erling, F., et. al., 1978. *Bier-Trinkgefasse,* Limpert-Verlag, Bad Homburg.

Gruhl, J., 1982. "Queen of the Drinking Vessels," *Prosit, 70,* Stein Collectors International, p. 978-980, December.

Hansen, H.J., 1970. *Das pompose Zeitalter zwischen Biedermeier and Jugendstil,* Gerhard Stallung Verlag, Oldenburg.

Harrell, J.L., 1979. *Regimental Steins,* The Old Soldier Press, Frederick MD.

Kohlhausen, H., 1955. *Geschichte des deutschen Kunstwerks,* Munich.

Lowenstein, J.G., 1974. *A Stein Bibliography,* Princeton NJ.

Manusov, E., 1976. *Encyclopedia of Character Steins,* Wallace Homestead Book Co., Des Moines, Iowa.

Monson-Fitzjohn, G.J., 1927. *Drinking Vessels of Bygone Days,* London.

Munich, 1976. *125 Jahre Bayerischer Kunstgewerbeverein,* Munchner Stadtmuseum.

Oshkosh, 1969. *Antique Steins at the Paine Art Center.*

Schiedlausky, G., 1956. *Essen und Trinken,* Munchen.

Scholz, R., 1978. *Humpen und Kruge-Trinkgefasse 16.-20. Jahrhundert,* Keyser, Munchen.

Uhlig, O.O., 1982. *Bierkrug-Deckel,* Rosenheimer.

Wilson, R.D., 1982 "Misconceptions About Dates Implied By *Made in Germany* on Steins," *Stein Zeitung,* S.C.I. Erste Gruppe, Summer.

Glass

Dexel, T., 1977. *Gebrauchsglas,* Braunschweig.

Frankfurt a.M. Museums fur Kunsthandwerk, 1973. *Europaisches und aussereuropaisches Glas,* Frankfurt a.M.

Fuchs, F.L., 1956. *Die Glaskunst im Wandel der Jahrtausende,* Darmstadt.

Kalnein, W.G., 1978. *Das Wein Gefass,* Ariel Verlag, Frankfurt a.M.

Kampfer, F., 1966. *Viertausend Jahre Glas,* Dresden.

Klesse, B. and G. Reineking-von Bock, 1973. *Kunstgewerbemuseum der Stadt Koln: Glas,* Koln.

Lipp, F.C., 1974. *Bemalte Glaser,* Munchen.

Schade, G., 1968. *Deutsches Glas,* Leipzig.

Schlosser, J., 1977. *Das alte Glas,* Braunschweig.

Schmidt, R., 1922. *Das Glas,* Berlin/Leipzig.

von Saldern, A., 1965. *German Enameled Glass,* New York NY.

Unusual Materials

Brunner, H., 1964. *Altes Tafelsilber,* Munchen.

Doucet, F.W., 1973. *Silber,* Munchen.

Fritz, J.M., 1964. *Goldschmiedearbeiten des 14.-18. Jhrs. im Rhein,* in *Bonner Jahrbuch, 164,* pg. 407.

Neuwirth, W., 1978. *Markenlexikon fur Kunstgewerbe, Edle und unedle Metalle, vol. 1,* 1875-1900, Wien.

Philippovich, E.v., 1966. *Elfenbein,* Braunschweig.

Rohde, A., 1937. *Bernstein, ein deutscher Werkstoff,* Berlin.

Theuerkauff, C., 1967. *Elfenbeinarbeiten aus dem Barock,* Hamburg/Berlin.

Weinholz, G., undated. *Gefasse und Gerate aus Bernstein,* Staatliche Kunstsammlungen Dresden, Dresden.

Pewter

Dietz, A., 1903. *Das Frankfurter Zinngiessergewerbe und seine Blutezeit im 18. Jh.,* Historischen Museums in Frankfurt a.M., Frankfurt a.M.

Dolz, 1974. *Zinn,* Munchen.

Drier, F.-A., 1959. *Die mittelalterlichen Balusterzinnkannen Norddeutschlands,* in *Zeitschrift fur Kunstwissenschaft, 13,* pg. 27-50.

Haedeke, H.-U., 1973. *Zinn, Zentren der Zinngiesserkunst von der Antike bis zum Jugendstil,* Leipzig.

Hintze, E., 1928. *Die deutschen Zinngiesser und Ihre Marken,* 7 vols., Karl W. Hiersemann, Leipzig.

Mory, L., 1975. *Schones Zinn,* 5. Aufl., Munchen.

Ohm, A. and M. Bauer, 1977. *Steinzeug und Zinn,* Catalog of the Museums fur Kunsthandwerk, Frankfurt a.M.

Wagner, E., 1977. *Jugend-Zinn,* Munchen.

Wuhr, H., 1957. *Altes Zinn,* Darmstadt.

Faience and Porcelain

Bauer, M., 1977. *Europaische Fayencen,* Museum fur Kunsthandwerk, Frankfurt a.M.

Behse, A., 1955. *Deutsches Fayencemarken-Brevier,* Braunschweig.

Behse, A., 1965. *Porzellanmarken-Brevier,* Braunschweig.

Bosch, H., 1983. *German Faience Jugs and Tankards of the 17th and 18th Centuries,* Verlag Philipp von Zabern, Mainz a.R.

Danckert, L., 1954. *Handbuch des Europaischen Porzellans,* Munchen.

Dewiel, L., 1977. *Deutsche Fayencen,* Munchen.

Ducret, S., 1962. *Deutsches Porzellan und deutsche Fayencen,* Baden-Baden.

Ducret, S., 1972. *Meissner Porzellan bemalt in Augsburg,* Brunswick.

Fregnac, C., 1976. *Europaische Fayencen,* Fribourg.

Fuchs, E. and P. Heiland, 1925. *Die deutsche Fayence-Kultur,* Munchen.

Graesse, J.G. and E. Jaennicke, 1967. *Fuhrer fur Sammler von Porzellan und Fayence,* Brunswick.

Hofmann, F.H., 1932. *Das Porzellan der europaischen Manufakturen im 18. Jahrhundert,* Berlin.

Huseler, K., 1956-1958. *Deutsche Fayencen, Ein Handbuch der Fabriken, ihrer Meister und Werke,* 3 vols., Stuttgart.

Jedding, H., 1971. *Europaisches Porzellan,* vol. 1, Munchen.

Klein, A., 1975. *Deutsche Fayencen,* Braunschweig.

Pazaurek, G.E., 1925. *Deutsche Fayence- und Porzellan-Hausmaler,* 2 vols., Leipzig.

Riesebieter, O., 1921. *Die deutsche Fayencen des 17. und 18. Jahrhunderts,* Leipzig.

Schnorr von Carolsfeld, L., 1956. *Porzellan der europaischen Fabriken,* Braunschweig.

Schwarze, W., 1980. *Alte Deutsche Fayence-Kruge,* Schwarze Verlag, Wuppertal.

Stohr, A., 1920. *Deutsche Fayencen und deutsches Steingut,* Berlin.

Ceramic

Albrecht, R., 1909. *Die Topferkunst in Creussen,* Rothenburg o.T.

Amsterdam, 1977. *Villeroy & Boch 1748-1930, Two Centuries of Ceramic Products,* Rijksmuseum Amsterdam.

Arens, F., 1971. *Die ursprungliche Verwendung Gotischer Stein- und Tonmodel,* in *Mainzer Zeitschrift, 66,* pg. 106.

Borrmann, R., undated. *Moderne Keramik,* Leipzig.

Clarke, P.J., and J.O'Connor, 1977. "The Mettlach Occupationalists," *Prosit, 48,* Stein Collectors International, p. 408, June.

Cohausen, A. von, 1879. "Einige technische Bemerkungen uber die groberen Thonwaaren auf der Pariser Austellung 1879," in *Mittheilungen des Gewerbevereins fur Nassau.*

Cox, W.E., 1959. *The Book of Pottery and Porcelain,* New York, NY.

Dexel, W., 1958. *Keramik, Stoff und Form,* Braunschweig/Berlin.

Dexel, W., 1962. *Das Hausgerat Mitteleuropas; Wesen und Wandel der Formen in Zwei Jahrtausend,* Braunschweig/Berlin.

Eber, H., 1913. *Creussner Topferkunst,* Munchen.

Engelmeier, P., 1969. *Westerwalder Steinzeugkruge mit dem Monogram GR,* in *Keramos, 44,* Pgs. 3-11.

Falke, O.v., 1908. *Das rheinische Steinzeug,* 2 vols., Berlin.

Fischer, W., 1927. *Die Saltglasur,* Coburg.

Funcke, W.F., 1927. *Die Entwicklung des rheinischen Topfergewerbes seit dem 15, Jahrhundert,* Universitat Koln, Gladbach.

Graesse, J.G., 1974. *Fuhrer fur Sammler von Porzellan, Fayence, Steinzeug, Steingut, usw.,* Braunschweig.

Groschopf, G., 1937. *Die suddeutsche Hafnerkeramik,* in *Jahrbuch 1937 d. Bayerischen Landesvereins fur Heimatsschutz.*

Haedecke, H.-U., 1967. *Zur Soziologie der Topfer im Rheinland,* in *Keramos, 37,* pgs. 63-68.

Harrell, J.L., 1979. *Regimental Steins,* The Old Soldier Press, Frederick, Maryland.

Hillier, B., 1968. *Pottery and Porcelain 1700-1914, The Social History of Decorative Arts,* London.

Honey, W.B., 1949. *European Ceramic Art, 2 vols,* London.

Honey, W.B., 1952. *European Ceramic Art from the End of the Middle Ages to about 1815,* London.

Horschik, J., 1977. "Sachisches und Thuringisches Steinzeug," *9. Int. Hafnerei-Symposium,* Frechen.

Hughes, G.B., 1959. *Victorian Pottery and Porcelain,* London.

Jaennicke, F., 1978. *Deutsches Steinzeug.*

Jaennicke, F., 1900. *Geschichte der Keramik,* Leipzig.

Just R., 1960. "Creussen un sachsische Steinzeug mit Emailfarbenbemalung," in *Keramik-Freunde der Schweiz, 52,* pgs. 18-24, Zurich.

Klinge, E., 1977. *Creussner Steinzeug,* Neue Presse, Coburg.

Klinge, E., 1979. *Deutsches Steinzeug der Renaissance und Barockzeit,* Hetjens-Museum, Dusseldorf.

Kirsner, G., 1982. "Signatures on Etched Mettlach Steins: What Are They Worth?," *Stein Report,* June.

Kirsner, G., and J. Gruhl (ed.), 1983. *The Mettlach Book,* Seven Hills Books, Cincinnati OH.

Liebscher-Willert, 1955. *Technologie der Keramik,* Dresden.

Lowenstein, J.G., and P. Clarke, 1974. *English Translation 1899 Mettlach Catalogue with Supplement Steins,* Princeton, NJ.

Manusov, E., 1976. *Encyclopedia of Character Steins,* Wallace Homestead Book Co., Des Moines, Iowa.

Mettlach, 1937. *Dreitausend Jahre Topferkunst: Ein Rundgang durch das Keramische Museum von Villeroy & Boch.*

Ohm, A. and M. Bauer, 1977. *Steinzeug und Zinn,* Museum fur Kunsthandwerk, Frankfurt Besitz, Frankfurt a.M.

Pazaurek, 1927. *Steingut, Formgebung und Geschichte,* Stuttgart.

Pelka, O., 1924. *Keramik der Neuzeit,* Leipzig.

Reineking von Bock, G., 1970. *Steinzeug - Nachahmung, Nachbildung oder Falschung,* in *Keramos 49.*

Reineking von Bock, G., 1978. *Meister der deutschen Keramik 1900-1950,* Kunstgewerbemuseum Koln.

Reinheckel, G., 1978. *German and Austrian Ceramics,* Tokyo.

Rolfes, D., 1982. *Keramikmuseum Westerwald - Deutsche Sammlung fur historische und zeitgenossische Keramik,* Keramikmuseum Westerwald, Hohr-Grenzhausen.

Seng. A., 1983. *Dumler & Breiden - 100 Jahre Keramik,* Hohr-Grenzhausen.

Stieber, P., 1973. *Deutsches Hafnergeschirr,* in *Keysers Kunst- und Antiquitatenbuch III,* Munchen.

Stoehr, A., 1920. *Deutsche Fayencen und deutsches Steingut,* Berlin.

Strauss, K., 1925. *Die Topferkunst in Hessen,* in *Studien zur Deutschen Kunstgeschichte, vol. 228,* Strassburg.

Thieler, E.R., 1909. *Making Steins in an Old Monastery,* Brochure by E.R. Thieler Co.

Thieler, E.R., 1909. *Mettlach Wares Catalog.*

Thomas, T., 1976. "Mettlacher Steinzeug - Spiegel des Zeitgeschmacks," in *Keramos,* research newspaper Villeroy & Boch, p. 28-30.

Thomas, T., (ed.). 1978. *Keramos, 6,* Augsburger Druck- und Verlagshaus, Augsburg.

Thomas T., and A. Post, 1975. *Mettlacher Steinzeug 1885 - 1905,* Ammelounx, Hans J. Publisher, Wheeling IL.

von Moltheim, A.W., 1924. "Die deutsche Keramik der Renaissance in Nachbildung und Falschung," in *Belvedere Forum, 5,* pg. 37, Wien.

Wald, M., 1980. *HR Steins,* S.C.I. Publications, Kingston NJ.

Wilson, R.D., 1979. "Date Your Mettlach Steins," *Prosit, 57,* Stein Collectors International, p. 597-598, September.

Wilson, R.D., 1980. "Mettlach's Phanolith Fabrication," *Stein Zeitung,* S.C.I. Erste Gruppe, Spring.

Wilson, R.D., 1980. "Mettlach Size Number Code," *Stein Talk, 39,* S.C.I. Thirsty Knights Chapter, December.

Zobeltiz, H. von, 1899. "Villeroy & Boch," in *Velhagen und Klassing's Monatesheften XIII,* Bd. 1, p. 193-207.

Coopers at work making barrels, from a late 1500's engraving by J. Amman.

Appendix A
Price Adjustments for Condition

Many factors contribute to the value of a specific stein. But unlike some assets which have alternative productive uses, steins have a value only as something beautiful to collect or to accumulate for enjoyment or speculative purposes. For this reason the value of any antique stein is simply what one person will pay another in order to own it; dealers do not and could not collude to set prices.

The *prices,* or *values,* on all the steins shown throughout this book have been set at the *average* U.S. retail price of that stein in *reasonably good* condition. Deviations from these prices can occur for any number of reasons, reasons that are important to many collectors. This, then, is the information that is contained in this Appendix.

A.1 Normal Variations

The stein market is a relatively stable market, and prices of certain types of steins generally move up in an orderly fashion. Of course, even for identical steins in good condition, there can be expected to be *fluctuations* in the day-to-day transactions. What causes these fluctuations? Large variations can occur when the buyer or the seller, or both, do not have a good understanding, or reference, for the price of a type of stein. Occasionally a stein will come up at a small auction where there are no competing interests.

Aside from these variations due to abnormal circumstances, what could be considered *realistic* price variations? *Realistic* variations are those where the buyer and the seller know the market price of a stein, but have decided on a different price due to personal preferences, time constraints, or speculation. Take, for example, the realistic variations in prices of Mettlach steins. For steins under $200 such variations might be as much as ±20%. For somewhat more valuable steins the range decreases to about ±10%. And for Mettlach steins valued at over $500, realistic variations might be in the range of ±5% to ±10%.

The variations for other types of steins are not too different. Pewter, occupational, faience, early stoneware, and etched ceramic steins will have variations slightly greater than Mettlach's. Relief pottery, glass, porcelain, very rare steins, or steins of unusual materials will generally have somewhat greater fluctuations. Character and regimental steins could have realistic variations of about the same magnitude as the lower to middle price-ranged Mettlachs.

There are *real* costs and *time* costs involved in finding alternative sellers or buyers of the same stein, and in many respects this is the reason for these realistic fluctuations.

Stein prices in Germany are somewhat different from those in this book, some higher, some lower. Occasionally, the foreign prices may be different enough to cause substantial shipments of steins in or out of the United States. These temporary differences are mostly caused by currency fluctuations, and not by sudden changes of tastes or supplies.

A.2 Original Quality of Body

The *color* on steins is generally made using glazes or enamels that are quite resistant to fading. Thus, when there is a stein that has noticeably less attractive coloring, it is generally *not* due to original color variations, but to repairs or improper cleaning, such as with abrasives or caustic cleansers (vinegar, turpentine, or ammonia).

Although most transfer-decorated porcelains or stonewares *will* be affected by caustic cleansers, most other types of steins will not. In any event, if the aesthetic appeal of the stein is affected, the value will be affected proportionately.

Blotching or sloppy decorations can occasionally be seen, mostly on newer steins or saltglazed steins where too much salt was used in the firing. Of course, blotching near the handle or away from the detail on the front of the stein, will affect the price less than immediately noticeable imperfections.

Firing lines are primarily a concern with etched Mettlach steins, and are due to slightly different shrinkages of the dyed clays and the body clays. Reductions in price rarely exceed 5 or 10%, unless there is a heavy concentration of firing lines in an important part of the decoration.

Occasionally, transfer-decorated steins will show a tear, gap, or distortion in the decoration, or hand-painted steins will show some similar flaws, and these again must be evaluated with respect to the effect on the overall appearance of the stein. Price adjustments in excess of 15% are occasionally necessary in order to make a fair valuation.

A.3 Body Damage and Repairs

There is a *tremendous* variation in the price reduction that generally compensates for damage to a stein. There are a few generalities concerning these reductions that should be understood.

1. Damage is more tolerable, even acceptable, on very old steins. For example, cracks and chips would be the norm on c. 1600 stoneware steins, but cracks and chips on a 1983 Mettlach Collectors' Society stein would necessitate tremendous discounting in order to stimulate a sale.
2. The more visible the damage the more the effect on price. Chips or cracks on glass steins are more visible, and thus more important than those on stoneware. Damage to the "front" (opposite the handle) discounts the price more than damage to the back or to the inside.
3. Oddly, damage to more *fragile* steins reduces their value more than similar damage to steins made from *sturdier* materials. For example, chips and cracks to glass or porcelain cause greater price reductions than similar damage to ceramic or pewter steins.
4. Damage to *common* steins is more important than damage to one-of-a-kind steins. This is apparently due to the fact that whenever collectors know they can wait and get a better example they will wait, unless the discounts are significant.

Damage to Mettlach steins is often important because of this last point. A study was made for *The Mettlach Book* of the price reductions for damage, and these are roughly summarized here. Repaired chips of sizes up to 1" cause value reductions from 10% to 25%. Repaired, larger chips and broken pieces can cause reductions of 50% or more. Repaired hairline cracks reduce value from 15% to 30%.

The cost of high quality repairs can sometimes be greater than the finished product is worth, from $25 to $200 depending upon the extent of damage and detailed work involved. New handles or sections of a stein can cost $100 or more. Besides being aware that the repaired stein may not be worth the cost of repairs, there are other precautions of which to be aware. On older pieces, where damage is more acceptable, repairs are less acceptable. That is to say, leave very old steins unrepaired unless they can't be displayed with their damage unrepaired. It is also a fact that some parts, such as handles or inlays, are easier to *make* than to *repair*. So, insist that the original part be used in repairs unless it is missing or beyond all usefulness. Also, be aware that very few people are capable of making high quality repairs or replacement parts; stein dealers can help you find these people.

A.4 Original Mountings

The quality or type of the original lid can be an important factor in the price of a stein. And the prices for steins shown in this book are based upon the stein having the specific type of lid that is shown.

Mettlach steins almost always could originally be ordered with a choice of plain or fancy pewter lids, ceramic insert lids, or no lids. When they were ordered without lids they undoubtedly were sent to special pewterers (often in Munich) at additional expense to get spectacular pewter lids. The fancy pewter lids that Mettlach provided (possibly consigned locally rather than actually attached by Villeroy and Boch) were mostly more expensive than the ceramic inlaid lids. The original cost of lids, however, does not relate directly to current desirability. In fact, especially on the smaller-sized etched Mettlach steins, the inlaid lids are almost always the most desirable type of lid for today's collectors. Steins that have less desirable pewter lids will be worth about 10% to 35% less.

Other ceramic stein manufacturers either concentrated on using heavy pewter lids (such as H.R.) or generally used ceramic inlaid lids (J.W. Remy, Gerz, Marzi & Remy, and most others). There is usually little or no discount for such steins when they are found with a different type of high-quality lid.

There is, however, a *low-quality* pewter lid that will always be measurably less desirable. That lid has been made, since the early 1900's, out of a lighter weight pewter alloy that has been *stamped* into a shallower steepled lid. Its design is often not sharp and the shape is more conical, to accommodate the stamping process. With few exceptions, such as reproductions, those lids have been the only kind used since the 1930's.

Older steins are occasionally found with 'out-of-period' lids which after examination of the strapping around the middle (as described in Section 2) seem to be *original.* Examples would be steins from the 1600's with lids typical of the 1700's, or more commonly, steins from the 1700's with 1800's lids. It should be noted that there may well be 'old' replacements. In almost all European wars people were asked to turn in any metal that could be obtained. If the lid were replaced later, of course, they would be of a more modern type. It also seems likely that some lids were intentionally changed to become more 'stylish.' Although such steins might have more mystery or romance, collectors and museums are generally looking for *archetypical* steins without *confusing* appearances. Therefore, these steins often must be somewhat discounted in order to pass through the market.

The same is usually true of steins which have lids of materials that are not typical. For example, Mettlach steins with silver-plated, copper, or brass lids will generally be worth somewhere around 30% to 50% less. Upgraded materials, such as sterling for the usual pewter, will usually increase the value except if the lids seem suspicious or incongruous (such as silver on pewter or faceted glass on pottery.)

A.5 Damaged, Replaced, or Missing Mountings

Section 2 contains some important information about the mountings on steins, and about how to detect when a lid has been replaced. There is some additional information about the mountings, from the point of view of *pricing,* that is worth noting here.

A most common occurrence is to find a very nice stein, unfortunately without a lid. Also unfortunately, lids for steins were not made in a *set* of standard sizes. And it is surprising that "plus or minus an eighth of an inch" is often not good enough to insure the proper fitting of a replacement lid. Also, the tang and the shaft must be the appropriate length, or a difficult splicing must take place. Thus, particularly for older steins, a missing lid will make for a substantial price reduction. Badly damaged old steins, or unattractive c.1900 steins with nice lids, are often purchased and made into 'mugs' because the lid is perfect for some special piece that a collector has. Intentionally seeking such *matches* has some of the pleasures, as well as the displeasures, of gambling.

The picture sections of this book clearly show which types of steins generally have *footrings,* such as faience and some glass steins. When these are missing, of course, they have much less visual impact than do missing lids. So the price reduction is much less. Also, it would seem that with only a *diameter* with which to be concerned, it would be easier to find replacements. But there are precious few good footrings available, even from repairmen who are constantly trying to stock up on good lids. Therefore, do not *count* on being able to find a footring for a stein you may be considering for purchase.

Although pewter is easily damaged, with dings and tears, it is also relatively easily repaired. The following are some of the more common types of damage.

Hinges occasionally bind up. Often they can be cleaned with water (do not use oil). If that doesn't work, rather than force the hinge, have a repairman deal with it.

A tooth or ring missing from the hinge will have only a nominal influence on value, usually less than 5%.

Tears, dents, and missing thumblifts can be fixed for about $20 to $50, and, once fixed, should not reduce the value of the stein by more than about 10%.

The cost of repairs to the *strap* are also about in this range. Recall that repairs to the strap often signify that the lid has been replaced, which can mean a price reduction in the range from 10% to as much as 25% or 35%. If the lid is not appropriate to the stein, the reduction can be 25% to 50%.

Some collectors and museums feel it is essential to the proper care and display of pewter and silver to have them polished. Other collectors would rather see the dark patina, especially on pewter. *Unabrasive* polishing *should* have no effect on price, but be forewarned that a few collectors will shy away from such steins. On the other hand, "diseased" pewter, such as pewter that is pitted, powdered, or scaled, can reduce the value of a stein by 10%, or more if the pewter is heavily damaged.

An early symbol of the brewers.

Lad carrying a *hexagram,* the early symbol of the brewer, from a Ludwig Richter early 1800's drawing.

Appendix B
Important Information for Collectors

The Appendix of *The Mettlach Book* that contains miscellaneous information has been pointed to by many collectors as being very helpful. Thus some of that information is again discussed here.

B.1 Sources of Steins

The first important collections of steins seem to have been started in the middle 1800's by museums vying for examples of fine Renaissance art. Private collectors became an important force in stein collecting in the late 1800's, and some astonishingly high prices were paid in those times for the best examples of Renaissance steins.

Of course, long before this collecting of *antique* steins, there were many stein collections, of a sort. In kitchens and in taverns and inns, narrow shelves along the upper parts of the walls, so-called *plate rails,* held collections of steins. In homes, the *number* of steins was a measure of hospitality, in taverns it was a measure of prosperity, being the number of regular customers. To increase this *measure,* and probably for aesthetic reasons as well, there were often more steins displayed than were really necessary.

Such displays of steins have continued to be important decorations in both rustic and refined tavern, inn, and home settings. Such decorative tastes were brought to the United States by the early English settlers, the Pennsylvanian Dutch, and the many waves of European immigrants.

Great numbers of German stoneware steins were brought to Canada and the Northeastern United States in the 1700's. Important stoneware shipments were also made in the late 1800's, and led some U.S. manufacturers of that time to begin their own production of stoneware and porcelain steins. Mettlach and other German factories actively advertised their steins in the U.S. beginning in the late 1800's. Important quantities of steins also began flowing into the United States beginning in the 1940's. These came back with soldiers, tourists, and, beginning in the late 1950's, with antiques importers. With all of the political and economic turmoil in Europe, this U.S. supply of steins has become an important fraction of the world supply.

In both Europe and the U.S., the more desirable steins, once scattered throughout the countryside, have continued to become more concentrated in collections. Increasingly, the places to find good steins have become a small number of U.S. and German dealers, auctions, and fellow collectors upgrading or disposing of their collections.

If the intent of a collector is to buy a stein only occasionally and with little consideration for the type or characteristics of the stein, then canvasing the antique shops and antique shows should yield the desired results. However, should a specific objective be important, such as acquiring a nicely planned collection, it would be advantageous to develop contacts with the knowledgeable and trustworthy dealers and collectors.

B.2 Collection Strategies

In varying degrees, most collectors combine the *enjoyment* and *investment* aspects of stein collecting. First, consider the investment angle.

During the 1960's and early 1970's steins proved to be a very good investment, both in comparison to other antiques and to other investment possibilities. Their performace in the mid- and late- 1970's was not as strong, with some other antiques increasing in value far more rapidly. In the last two years, with the deflation of many of those antique values, however, steins have remained steady and thus have proved to be a relatively strong, if unspectacular, performer.

It is difficult to predict a precise future price trend, but based upon past performance it is likely that steins will be a fairly good investment on a long-term basis. A general and rapid appreciation in prices over any short period of time is unlikely, but there will always be a few spectacular performers. Those steins that were originally relatively expensive, are often quite beautiful and rare, and thus may offer potential for those also interested in the investment angles. Also, those steins that seem to a collector, who has looked over all the steins in this book, to be disproportionately lowly priced, are also likely to be the best investments.

Also with respect to the future, the relatively strong performance of steins over the past two years seems to indicate a very solid base. It is the *collectors* who have created the demands and prices for steins not the *investors.* This lack of investment money artifically forcing up the price of steins, beyond the price collectors would be willing to pay, has kept the prices firm even as other investment opportunities changed drastically. As economic conditions improve and money market rates become less attractive it seems likely that old and new collectors will plunge back into the bidding war with musuems and the resultant prices will continue upward.

Since steins come in many sizes and types, and cover a wide range of prices, different approaches to collecting are possible. Collections always contain certain elements of *similarity* and certain elements of *diversity.* Most often the *materials* are similar and the *decorations* are diverse.

Most collectors enjoy the quest of putting together sets or pairs, particularly of the scarcer or more aesthetically pleasing items. The artistic arrangement of a collection can also greatly enhance its appeal to the collector, and the use of plaques, bowls, and other items together with steins provides an additional dimension that ought to be considered.

A collection should contain what the individual collector likes, and not what seems to be in vogue, rare, or expensive. If you like a stein there will always be a proper place for it to be displayed in your collection.

B.3 Buying Steins

If steins are bought at prices near to those in this book, you will be receiving a fair value for your money. These are prices that other collectors are willing to pay for the same pieces. Of course this assumes that any defects that might exist have been detected and properly discounted.

Recognizing repaired defects has gotten to be increasingly difficult. In the last few years the techniques, materials, and experience developed by a few repairmen have resulted in some excellent repairs being performed on some steins. Many steins have been sold at auctions, by dealers, and by collectors, with repairs or damages that were not indicated to the buyer. Some sellers do not know of the repairs or do not feel obligated to point out repairs or damages to prospective buyers.

Learning how to detect repairs and damage, and to distinguish them from factory flaws, takes time, and the advice and coaching of experienced collectors or dealers. In the meantime, relying on the reputation of the individual dealer or collector from whom you make your purchases is essential.

Do not assume that an advertisement of steins for sale, even one carried in a respectable publication such as an antiques periodical, can be relied upon for accuracy. While most dealers and collectors are honest, a lack of knowledge by some, and a tendancy for the dishonest dealers to gravitate toward advertising, has left knowledgeable buyers with a cautious suspicion toward advertisements. Many advertisers *do deliver* what is promised, but be certain you can return the stein if you are not satisfied, and do not expect the publication to be of any help should a problem arise.

Auctions are a uniquely different way to buy. If you have a very good idea what you are doing, and you have time and patience, you might do very well. If you are not well informed or are not patient, watch out, you are the collector for whom they are waiting. Simple rules to remember for auction buyers are:

1) most auctioneers know very little or nothing about steins and even less about repairs;

2) auctions that sell *as is* (no description or condition), naturally tend to attract merchandise with defects that sellers would rather not describe;

3) many auctions are not truly auctions, until the price of the item being sold reaches a level above the price that the consignor (owner) is willing to accept, not all items at auction are *protected* this way but many are; and

4) if a buyer's premium exists, usually 10%, remember to add that to your total cost before you make your bids.

Should you decide to buy steins at an auction, try to arrive in plenty of time to thoroughly examine the steins at the preview. Take copious notes on conditions, qualities, and maximum bids you will make, even for items only remotely of interest to you. If possible try to frequent only those auctioneers who knowledgeably indicate damage and sell to the highest bidder without *protected* prices. Generally, only experience or colleagues will tell you which auctioneers these are.

B.4 Protecting Your Collection

First there are some common-sense procedures to follow so as to keep from damaging your own steins. Hot beverages should be kept out of steins, and no hot water washes or dishwashers should be used to clean steins -

just use luke warm water, mild soap, and a soft brush. Displaying steins in sunlit windows, or storing them in extremely hot or cold locations, can cause stress lines to develop in the bodies of the steins. Wrapping steins in newspaper and storing them in damp basements can discolor the pewter. When choosing a place to display steins try to find an area free from flying objects, swinging brooms, or vacuum cleaner handles. Instruct curious friends in the proper techniques for holding or examining steins; warn them especially not to flop closed the inlaid or heavy pewter lids.

Steins often break when transported. Wrap and box them carefully, then wrap and rebox the first box, and insure all packages that are sent.

Finally, valuable collections in homes should be fully covered by insurance policies; and to protect larger collections security systems should also be considered. Stein dealers can provide you with accurate insurance appraisals of your pieces for nominal fees. Do not advertise your home address, use a post office box or work through a dealer.

B.5 Selling

Steins have always had a fairly high degree of liquidity relative to other antiques. Collectors throughout the country are always looking for desirable items to add to their collections. Many antique dealers around the country are also quite anxious to own a nice stein or two, in order to dress up their inventory.

Still it is important to select the proper method, among the many available, for selling your stein or your collection. First there are several avenues open for selling a *small* number of steins with a fairly low total dollar value.

1) *Direct to a collector:* This is excellent idea, if you know a collector who wants the stein(s) that you want to sell.

2) *To a local antique dealer:* This is a fairly easy and appropriate method if a local dealer is willing to pay a fair price for your steins. Keep in mind he has to resell them at a profit. Depending on his location, he may be able to sell them quickly, or he may have to wait a long time before buyers come along. These factors will contribute to the price he can afford to pay. Many dealers would rather take expensive steins on consignment; if they sell, then you will get a percentage of the sale price.

3) *Through an auction:* Many auctioneers are anxious to have high quality steins to sell. Expect to pay about a 20% commission perhaps higher. If a buyer's premium is charged, consider that part of the commission, because the buyer will keep this in mind and bid lower. Rarely do steins sell at very high prices in an auction, generally they will bring less than the *retail* price.

4) *Advertise in an antiques publication:* Fairly good results can be achieved sometimes, but there is no guarantee the right person will see your advertisement, and most steins are difficult to describe accurately.

5) *Respond to an advertisement from a collector or a dealer in an antiques publication:* Responding to a *want* advertisement from a collector may result in a sale, but he will have to want the stein(s) you are selling in order to pay a fair price. A dealer who specializes in steins will generally pay a fair *wholesale* price. He will usually buy for resale at a fairly small margin because his turnover is probably more rapid than the average dealer, and he will know steins very well and thus will not have to make allowances to cover risks due to his ignorance.

Should you have a *large* collection to sell, realizing a high percentage of the retail price could be of significant importance. A ten percent difference in the total price could amount to a large sum of money. A number of things must be considered. Do you want to sell everything in one group, to one buyer? Do you want to sell immediately, or over a short or perhaps long period of time? Are you willing to work hard at selling your collection; communicating widely, wrapping packages, mailing the steins, and so on? To sell a large collection at *retail,* you would have to be prepared to undertake the expenses and do the work of being the dealer, advertiser, traveler, wrapper, and shipper. While this is possible, it is not practical for everyone. Some collectors have done this successfully, but most that have tried eventually became frustrated and impatient, and ultimately would have faired better with another approach.

A dealer specializing in steins, who is thus familiar with the market, can generally realize a retail price on a greater number of steins from a large collection, and with greater ease, than can a collector selling for the first time. Depending upon the *quality* of the collection, that is to say its desirability, diversification, and condition, a collector can expect to sell a collection to a stein dealer at a discount in the vicinity of 20 to 30% from the retail prices. This can, of course, be altered greatly depending upon the collection and general business factors.

Just as for the small collections, auctions offer a method for disposing a large collection. Auctions provide a *number* of options, but certain factors do not vary substantially. It will cost about 20%, frequently more, to sell a collection at auction. This commission is a percentage of the *selling* price, not the *retail* price. While some steins may sell at auction above a fair retail price, a *large* collection will not sell at auction, on average, above a fair retail price.

This should provide the seller with some way of calculating the range of prices that are likely to be realized in the sale of steins. Take these prices, adjust for commissions and buyer's premiums, and compare the results for the various methods of selling. Steins can represent a substantial investment of a seller's time and resources, and it will be well worthwhile for him to take the time to work enough of the mathematics to allow for a good bottom line comparison of these alternative ways of selling a collection.

A flagon-shaped stein in a 1484 woodcut illustrating pilgrims at the dinner table.

Glossary

Allegory, the representation of incidents, scenes, or characters in a way that evokes a dual interest, providing both aesthetic enjoyment and a deeper intellectual interpretation.

Apostlekrug, a stout-shaped stein with the Apostles in relief around its body.

Art nourveau, literally *modern style,* the bold and flat sinuous motifs abstractly based upon seaweed and other plant forms; this style was popular from 1895-1915 and was a rebellion against the derivative style of *historicism;* see ***periods.***

Baluster shape, bulbous in the middle with a thinned neck and pedestal base; a popular shape of early earthenware vessels.

Baroque, an ornate, florid, flamboyant style popular from 1600-1770; see ***periods.***

Beaker, a cup-like drinking vessel, sometimes with a handle but never with a lid; contrast with ***pokal.***

Biedermeier, a *peasant style* of folk art that was important from 1810-1850, a provincial, rustic, sturdy functionalism favored by the new middle class; see ***periods.***

Blockzinn, see ***pewter purities.***

Britannia metal, alloy of tin and antimony.

Cameo, a type of stein design with low relief made from a translucent, porcelain-like material that allows for contrasting background colors to show through the thinnest areas; compare with ***relief.***

Character stein, or ***figural stein,*** a stein with a shape designed to represent a person, animal, or object, often a personified object.

Chinoiseries, style of design popular in the 1700's depicting Chinese genre scenes and Chinese landscapes; see ***periods.***

Chip-carving, or ***Kerbschnitt,*** a pattern of vertical creases, sometimes hand cut, sometimes simulated with a mold.

Clay glaze, see ***glaze.***

Clay slip, or ***colored slip,*** see ***slip.***

Cold painting, a non-durable method of stein decoration that does not require firing, using varnishes or gold leaf.

Crack, an open break; compare with ***hairline.***

Double firing, the process of firing biscuit (unglazed) pottery, then glazing and decorating and refiring.

Earthenware, porous ceramic material, fired to only about 800°C (1500°F); sometimes made impervious to liquids with the addition of a lead glaze, as in hafnerware and folk pottery; see ***stoneware.***

Edelzinn, Engelmarke, and Englischzinn, see ***pewter purities.***

Engobe, see ***slip, colored.***

Engraved, use of abrasive material to cut lines, ornaments, or script into a hard surface.

Etched, a type of stein decoration with distinctive incised black outlining of uniformly colored design areas.

Faience, a porous earthenware, glazed with a white tin oxide (stanniferous) glaze; originally a porcelain substitute first made in Faenza, Italy.

Feinzinn, see ***pewter purities.***

Footring, a pewter collar around the base of some steins to protect them against chipping and wear; see ***pewter mountings.***

Four F, or ***4F,*** a symbol of the German gymnastic or athletic society; the Fs are flipped in a pattern that puts all their corners together making a cross shape; 4F stands for *Frisch, Fromm, Froh, Frei* meaning alert, devout, joyful, free.

Form number, or ***mold number,*** usually an incised number in the base of a stein used to identify the mold from which it was made, providing a catalog number.

Gambrinus, legendary king of Flanders who supposedly discovered beer; the subject of many stein decorations.

Glaze, a hard impervious coating fired onto ceramic materials, it can be clear or colored, transparent or opaque, matt or glossy; ***clay glazes*** are like ***slips*** and were used on very early ceramics, other glazes are all forms of glass made from powdered glass, feldspar, borax, salts, or metal oxides; ***lead glaze*** is found on hafnerware and folk pottery; ***leopard glaze*** is a strong brown speckled salt glaze found especially on Frechen wares; ***salt glazes*** are produced by pouring large quantities of salt into the furnace at its peak firing temperature, the sodium chloride reacts with water (hydrogen oxide) to produce a glassy coating (sodium oxide) and hydrochloric acid vapors; ***tin glaze,*** as commonly used on faience, is made from tin oxide.

Greenware, formed pottery that is air dried but unfired and thus still raw clay.

Hafnerware, lead glazed earthenwares, including steins, made by potters best known for their oven tiles.

Hairline, a closed break that sometimes shows as a thin black line in ceramic materials; contrast with ***crack.***

Hand painted, a type of ware that is either glazed and fired, or just cold painted, with some design.

Hausmalers, or ***studio painters,*** often resulted from houses being rebuilt after the Thirty Years War (in the middle 1600's) with artists' studios included; these artists decorated wares, mostly porcelain or faience, as independent craftsmen in their own home studios.

Historicism, the style of art that dominated the Continent from about 1840-1910; it sought a return to the Renaissance with powerful sculptural forms, complicated outlines and friezes, and deep reliefs or contrasting shadows; it originated with archeological findings of numerous awe-inspiring Renaissance artifacts, and in response, art schools began instructing pupils by having them copy the forms and ornaments of these artifacts; see ***periods.***

Incised, refers to lines impressed into the unfired ceramic material by means of a stamp, press, or mold; sometimes used synonymously with ***etched.***

Inlay, the name of a type of lid for steins that have an insert, usually ceramic, porcelain, or glass, set into the pewter or silver flange of the lid; or ***inlay*** can be a decorative technique where one material has been inlaid into another so as to help form the design, such as pewter inlaid wood; contrast with ***overlay.***

Ivory stoneware, or ***yellow stoneware,*** a fine light-colored clay fired as stoneware and used to make many steins from about 1850 to the present.

Kayser-Zinn, not a measure of the quality of the pewter, instead indicating manufacture by the J.P. Kayser Company in Krefeld-Bockum between the end of the 1800's and the beginning of the 1900's, many pieces being of the art nouveau style.

Krug, literally a jug, but often used to indicate a large, or master, stein.

Liter, or ***L,*** the metric measure of capacity, slightly more (1.057) than a quart.

Lithophane, an unglazed porcelain panel, found in the bottom of many porcelain steins, with a relief decoration that is visible when light passes through it; lithophane molds were taken from beeswax carvings made over lighted panels.

Luster, a metal oxide decoration fired onto a stein; including occasional platinum accents on early Mettlach steins, metal alkali sheens all over some glass steins, and many other types.

Mettlach, village next to the Saar River in West Germany where Villeroy & Boch has had one of their ceramics factories; commonly also used as the name of the steins from that factory.

Mosaic, a type of stein on which colored glazes are painted into protruding ridged sections of the stoneware or pottery.

Muffle-fired, a lower temperature third firing achieved by protecting the ceramic materials from the main heat of the kiln by placing them behind muffling fire bricks, or chamotte capsules; this made available an almost unlimited range of glaze colors.

Mug, a cup, usually cylindrical, with a handle; a ***lidded mug*** is a mug with a set-on lid (not hinged), often used in spas for mineral water; contrast with ***beaker*** and ***stein.***

Munich Child, Munich Maid, or ***Munich Monk,*** a common theme on steins, the symbol of the city of Munich, supposedly showing a monk's robe on the first child born in Munich after the 10th Century massacre.

Musterschutz, literally meaning *copyright protection,* but occasionally used almost as if it were a factory name for the factory that made many porcelain character steins and used no other marking (except sometimes a #).

Occupational stein, a stein with a decoration or shape that depicts or symbolizes an occupation, probably the occupation of the original owner of the stein.

Orivit, a pewter and silver alloy mostly used around 1900.

Overglaze, a special glass and flux mixture that provides a clear glossy coating for extra sheen and vividness on ceramic materials.

Overlay, filigree, or ***latticework,*** an ornamental openwork of intricate design, usually of pewter, applied to the outside of a stein.

Pate-sur-pate, marbelized porcelain, usually green and white.

Patina, an oxidation layer on metals, or often including an other evidences of long wear or age.

Periods, or ***styles,*** the names of different types of fashionable art, see ***Renaissance, Baroque, Rococo, Chinoiseries, Biedermeier, Historicism,*** and ***Art nouveau,*** as the most important styles for steins.

Pewter, a very workable metallic alloy containing as much as 90% tin, with the remainder made up of lead, copper, zinc, nickel, bismuth, or antimony; see the following two entries.

Pewter mountings, includes the *footring* and all the pewterwork that is used to attach the lid to the handle of a stein; the attaching pewterwork has a whole set of terminology that is important in describing damage and repairs; the ***strap*** encircles the handle and a, usually triangular, ***strap support*** runs somewhat down the outside of the handle; the ***shank*** goes from the strap to the ***hinge;*** a ***hinge pin*** will show on most steins made after about 1860; it will not show on earlier steins; an odd number of ***rings*** or ***teeth*** make up the hinge; the ***tang*** proceeds from the hinge to the ***lid rim;*** the ***thumblift*** can be over the hinge or fastened to the rim; if there is an ***inlay*** a pewter ***flange*** will hold it in place; the top of some all-pewter lids may contain an ornate pewter ***finial.***

Pewter purities, have been carefully marked since the Middle Ages when lead and other impurities were suspected of being health threats; ***Bergzinn, Blockzinn, Feinzinn,*** and ***Klar und Lauter Zinn*** are pewters that are quite pure and known to contain very small quantities of copper or brass (copper and tin alloy), often they had to have no recyled pewter; ***Engelmarke*** or ***Angel-marked*** is Feinzinn from the 1700's or 1800's marked with an angel and sword and scales (or trumpet and palm frond); ***Englisch Zinn*** or ***English Pewter*** is Feinzinn certified to also be lead-free; ***Rosenmarke*** or ***Rose-marked*** is a touchmark for Englisch Zinn; ***Probezinn*** contains lead but no more than 1/5 or a 4 tin to 1 lead ratio, ***Nurnberger Probe*** is 10 to 1, ***Kolnische Probe*** is 6 to 1, ***Frankfurter Probe*** is 4 to 1; ***Edelzinn*** is from the 1800's and contains too much lead to allow use as a utensil; ***Geringes Zinn, Mankgut,*** or ***Low Pewter*** may contain as much as 50% lead and is occasionally found in thumblifts or applied relief on steins; see also ***Britannia metal*** and ***Orivit.***

Pickelhaube, a spiked soldier's helmut, often with plumes.

Pokal, or ***brimmer,*** a large ceremonial handleless beaker with a separate set-on lid and usually having a pedestal base.

Porcelain, a vitrified fine white clay, quartz, and feldspar mixture that has a hard surface; hard porcelain is fired to about 1450°C(2650°F) while soft porcelain is fired to about 1200°C (2200°F); compare to ***stoneware*** and ***pottery.***

Porcellaine, another name for faience, which was originally intended as a porcelain substitute.

Pottery, or ***Steingut,*** a rather imprecise term for a usually light-colored porous ceramic with a hardness dependent upon the temperature of the firing, from 960°C (1800°F) to 1300°C (2350°F).

Print under glaze, PUG, transfer printed, or ***transfer decorated,*** the name for a process of decoration that takes hand-painted, silk-screened, or printed decals, transfers those decals to a smooth surface, then fires them in place.

Probe, a mark occasionally found on trial or test pieces; or ***Probe*** can also refer to the lead contents of the pewter, see ***pewter purities.***

Prunts, bosses, or ***Nuppen,*** glass drops, sometimes with an impressed design, found attached to the sides of glass vessels as a decoration.

Pug mill, a device somewhat like a blender, but very large, previously horse driven, used for refining and mixing clay recipes.

Regimental stein, reservist's stein, or ***military stein,*** a stein that was purchased as a souvenir of service in the military; most often refers to those purchased by reservists upon discharge from the Imperial German Armies in the years 1890 to 1914.

Relief, the name of a type of ware that has figures or designs of opaque material, usually tan or white, that stand out substantially from the smooth or textured background; contrast with ***cameo.***

Renaissance, the style of art, and the name of the time period from about 1300 to 1600 that was characterized by a revival of the Classical influence, and vigorous aesthetic and intellectual activities; see ***periods.***

Reservist's stein, see ***regimental stein.***

Rib, a wooden scraper or forming die, used for smoothing sides and forming the bands and moldings of steins on a potter's wheel.

Rococo, the last, less colorful but more figurative, phase of the Baroque period, from aout 1735-1770; see ***periods.***

Rorken, or ***sampler,*** a shape of stein that has a pedestal base then becomes slightly wider with height.

Salt glaze, formed when salt is added to the kiln to form a glassy mist that coats all the wares; should not be confused with painted metal oxide glazes such as cobalt oxide blues and manganese oxide violets that are merely glazes that can withstand the intense stoneware firing temperatures; see ***glazes.***

Slip, a watered down clay or porcelain recipe that is sufficiently liquid for use in coating, gluing, or casting pieces of ceramic material; ***clay slip, colored slip,*** or ***engobe*** are terms used to describe slips that have been combined with coloring agents and used primarily as decorative coatings or paints, such as clay glazes; see ***glazes, clay.***

Slurry, a recipe of clays, water, and other additives which have been filtered, mixed, and poured into backs, or settling tanks.

Smoother, either a wooden paddle for smoothing the sides of wet, freshly turned pottery, or the person who smooths out turning marks with a wet cloth.

Stack marks, firing variations on the bottom of stoneware or pottery steins that show how they were stacked in the kiln, occasionally circles or parts of two or three circles are seen on some very old steins.

Stein, literally meaning *stone,* is a shortened form of *Steinzeugkrug* or *stoneware tankard;* generally expanded to mean any drinking vessel with a handle and an attached lid; a ***lidless stein*** did have, or was intended to have, a lid that is now missing; contrast with ***mug, beaker*** and ***pokal.***

Stein Collectors International, or ***S.C.I.,*** a club for the collectors of antique drinking vessels, concentrating mainly on steins; membership, which includes a subscription to the quarterly publication *Prosit,* can be gotten by sending the current annual dues of $20 to S.C.I., P.O. Box 463, Kingston, NJ 08528.

Stoneware, a vitrified ceramic material, usually a silicate clay, that is very hard, rather heavy, and impervious to liquids and most stains; achieved at temperatures between 1200°C (2200°F) and 1300°C (2350°F); ***early stoneware,*** or ***Fruhsteinzeug,*** does not quite reach those temperatures or was made from clays of higher vitrification temperatures, and was common from the 1300's to the early 1500's; see ***earthenware, pottery,*** and ***porcelain.***

Tankard, technically synonymous with *stein,* but since this was the British term, some reserve its use for the typically British silver or pewter steins.

Touchmark, a small stamp, usually found on pewter, that may indicate the name or symbol of the master pewterer, his city, or the pewter's purity.

Transfer decorated or ***transfer printed,*** see ***print under glaze.***

Waldglas, or ***forest glass,*** made from sand and wood ashes and generally having a grayish green color with small impurities and air bubbles.

Walzenkrug, cylindrical tankard, or ***straight-up tankard,*** a cylindrically shaped stein about twice as high as it is wide; the most common shape in the 1700's.

White gold, a name that was used for porcelain, porcelain clays, or for the valuable stoneware clays with the low vitrification temperatures and minimal warping and cracking potentials.

Wiremark, concentric whorls on the base of some older stoneware or faience steins that indicates the 'hump' was cut off the potter's wheel by pulling a wire across the base of the turning piece; as opposed to 'humps' cut off with smooth knives.

Zig-zag decor, or ***Knibistechnik,*** decorative ribbons of tight, wide, incised zig-zags made by wadding a wooden chisel across the surface of unfired clay.

Index